LIVING AT THE END OF THE WORLD

Marina Benjamin lives in London and works as a freelance journalist. A former Arts Editor of the *New Statesman*, she now writes for a variety of newspapers and magazines.

MARINA BENJAMIN

LIVING AT THE END OF THE WORLD

PICADOR

First published 1998 by Picador

This edition published 1999 by Picador
an imprint of Macmillan Publishers Ltd
25 Eccleston Place, London SW1W 9NF
and Basingstoke

Associated companies throughout the world

ISBN 0 330 34204 5

9 8 7 6 5 4 3 2 1

A CIP catalogue record for this book is available from
the British Library.

Typeset by SetSystems Ltd, Saffron Walden, Essex
Printed and bound in Great Britain by
Mackays of Chatham plc, Chatham, Kent

For Francis, Jessica and Anne

CONTENTS

ACKNOWLEDGEMENTS

Over the course of the past three years, I have benefited from the conversation, advice and encouragement of many friends and colleagues, in particular: Roy Porter, Jenni Calder, Abigail Morris, Jenny Uglow, David Martin, Julian Loose, Adrian Wilson, Boyd Tonkin, Kirsty Milne, Ian Hunt, Deborah Levy, Garry Kelly, David Gale, Patricia Fara, Ian Cotton and Emma Crichton-Miller. Regular top-ups of motivational fuel were supplied by my agent Clare Conville. Tony McCutcheon and Andri Solteri at INFORM let me spend long afternoons browsing through the centre's filing cabinets searching out strange and wonderful new religious movements. Judith Goddard and Marcelle Benjamin, amazingly, allowed me to subject them to the occasional test-run of random passages read out over the phone. Alain de Botton gave me useful feedback on chapter 1, and Alison Roberts at the *Evening Standard* regularly distracted me with commissions to write about the arts. I have been lucky enough to have had in Peter Straus and Jon Riley two incredibly talented editors; both offered tremendous support and incisive comment which I very much appreciate.

One of the great pleasures of writing this book has been meeting and corresponding with Norman Cohn, whom I would like to

Acknowledgements

thank both for his generosity in sharing his knowledge of millenarian history with me and for the time he gave so freely. I was not the ideal student; stubborn and dissenting, I surely tried his patience, but I believe our disagreements were of the fruitful kind.

In Utah, Don Lefevre, Coke Newell, Thomas Alexander and Jay Hammond helped give me my bearings, geographical and intellectual, while back in England Brian Grant dealt with some of the fallout from my trip. In Marilyn Warenski, I found an expert cultural guide; her quick wit and kind hospitality made my stay in Salt Lake more pleasurable than work-like. Steve Bridge of Alcor was similarly generous with time and information, and Mark Muhlestein and family drove me out to Biosphere 2 when I had no other means of getting into the desert. I am indebted too to the director, administrator and staff of Hawthornden Castle. There, on retreat, in idyllic conditions of beauty and quiet, a one-month fellowship allowed me to write chapters 4 and 5 with speed and concentration.

Throughout the long haul, Francis Spufford, who has a greater facility for playing with ideas than anyone I know, offered friendship and critical insight. Discussions with him broke the solitude of wrestling with persistent problems which I imagined no one else could possibly whip up an interest in solving and more than once served to shift a belligerent block. Anne Goldgar gave me sharp structural advice in the best rationalist spirit – 'anything to stop you becoming religious'. And Jessica Martin was ever willing to bring her extraordinarily clear thinking to bear on sticky issues and to share her knowledge of Christianity with me. I am much indebted to all three and dedicate this book to them.

LIST OF ILLUSTRATIONS

The Westinghouse time capsule awaiting burial in 1938 (reproduced by permission of The British Library).

The whore of Babylon, from a drawing by Francesco de Holanda (reproduced by permission of the Biblioteca Nacional, Madrid).

Joanna Southcott, engraved by William Sharp, 1812 (by courtesy of the National Portait Gallery, London).

The magnificent crib made for the messiah Shiloh, 1814 (by courtesy of the National Portrait Gallery, London).

Joseph Smith, from a portrait by Alvin Gittins (reproduced by permission of The Church of Jesus Christ of Latter-Day Saints).

The General Authorities of the Church of Jesus Christ of Latter-Day Saints (© Acey Harper).

Biosphere 2, Oracle, Arizona (© Martin Bond/Science Photo Library).

Steve Bridge in Alcor's cryotorium (© Laura Wilson).

PREFACE

Obvious as it may seem, the first thing to say about the end of the world is that it has not yet happened. It is an event that lies wholly in the future. Every expectation of its coming has been frustrated and every dated prediction thwarted. The fact that the end of the world continues to bait us with its non-occurrence is troublesome for all sorts of reasons, but not least because it means that those who write about it, like those who believe in its imminence, are for ever doomed to repeat themselves. Let me begin, therefore, with an afterthought. Let me loop round from the end back to the beginning, acknowledging that after all has been said there is always more to be done.

That afterthought is the idea of the leap – the leap of faith, the leap into the unknown, the leap on to a higher plane of existence. As I write, San Diego is recovering from one such leap. In the biggest mass suicide in American history, thirty-nine people, members of a religious sect called Heaven's Gate, fed themselves lethal doses of phenobarbital mixed with apple sauce and vodka in an attempt to reach for the stars. Almost no one had heard of the sect before this débâcle thrust it into the limelight, and there was an understandable hunger for any information that might explain its bewildering actions. From the first bits of news that reached us, we learned that sect members were quiet and polite, that they cropped their hair short and wore black. Then we discovered that they made a living by designing Web pages for commercial clients seeking a presence on the Internet. If we had scrutinised their own Website, we would have gleaned a good deal more, because it was there that Heaven's Gate began announcing that they were aliens who had been sent to Earth for a brief sojourn, and that a UFO concealed within the icy tail of the Hale-Bopp comet was coming to take them home. By day, group members got on with Earthlings as best they could, but every night they turned their telescopes heavenwards and gazed longingly at their home star in the north-east sky, impatient for the moment when they would leave this sinful world behind. When that moment came, Heaven's Gate went on-line with the good news: 'Our joy is that our Older Member has made it clear to us that Hale-Bopp's approach is the marker we've been waiting for. We are happily prepared to leave this world.' It turned out they were prepared in more ways than one, for when the bodies were found, neatly laid out on mattresses and bunks and draped in purple ceremonial cloaks, suitcases packed with personal belongings stood sentinel beside each one.

In a series of videotaped farewells, group members left various clues as to the nature of their final mission. They spoke of their desire to 'take off the virtual reality helmet' – the metaphor of perceptual readjustment hinting that the distorted vision of the external world needed correcting if inner vision was to triumph. And they talked, somewhat disconcertingly, about wanting to 'shed' their 'containers'. This was the ultimate goal of a spiritual quest that already exhibited anorexic traits, including the banning of drinking, smoking and sex. As evidenced by the fact that some of the men had been castrated to aid them in this latter duty, no measure was too extreme in the war that Heaven's Gate waged against human desire. At its limit, that war demanded the sacrifice of lives. By conflating human imperfection with physical appetite and reversing the commonsense understanding of illusion and reality (ours was the degenerate world of appearances, of shadows dancing in the void), Marshall Herff Applewhite and his followers came to regard suicide as emblematic not of a will to nothingness, but of a will to original purity and truth. Only by disincarnating, by sloughing off flesh and bone like buttlerflies shedding their chrysalises, could Heaven's Gate spring to a higher reality.

Such a rationale for suicide is strikingly similar to that expounded by the leaders of the Order of the Solar Temple. Before their own elaborately staged deaths in 1994, Joseph Di Mambro and Luc Jouret issued press statements in which they described using 'borrowed bodies to manifest in this world' and referred to their intended suicides as a 'transit' that would transform them into 'Christ-like' solar beings. 'Space is short,' they said, 'time is ending. It is with an unfathomable Love, ineffable joy, and without any regret that we leave this world. Men, cry not over our fate, but rather cry for your own. Ours is more enviable than yours.'[1]

Both of these kamikaze sects were millenarian. Beneath the fancy dress of extraterrestrial visions and techno-mysticism in the case of Heaven's Gate and the blending of theosophy with neo-Templar lore in that of the Solar Temple, they subscribed to an essentially Christian apocalyptic theology. In particular, they looked forward to the restoration of a primordial paradise – the Millennium that is described in the Book of Revelation. Due to commence at the world's spectacular end, the Millennium promises to offer a privileged few delicious refuge from global destruction and a thousand years of unmitigated peace. The idea of the leap, though only very rarely manifesting itself as suicidal, lies at the heart of millenarianism. In that apocalyptic prophecy insists on rupture, on there being a complete severance between the dying old world and the paradisiacal new, it is a means of bridging the chasm. And it is not just those sects whose leaders are wild of eye and whose beliefs lie on the outer side of extravagant that take salvation to be a matter of being catapulted directly into the lap of God. Within the millenarian enclaves of mainstream fundamentalist Christianity, the physical leap, the notion of being literally hurled into paradise, also has its place. For what else is the Dispensationalist doctrine of the Rapture but a form of supernatural transportation designed to carry the saved into the Millennium?

On the face of it, the millenarian leap appears to have little to recommend it. Hailing from the apocalyptic fringes of religious culture where madmen and extremists are wont to make their home, it makes no appeal to reason. Moreover, it is the perfect expression of a sublime arrogance that holds the world and all human life in it in gross contempt: come the end of the world, the millenarian will leap while the rest of us fry. It is even, paradoxically, self-hating. A desire to jump out of one's skin is, after all, a desire to cease being human – unless, that is, like the members of Heaven's Gate, you refuse to accept being human at all.

And yet, when we look more closely at millenarians we are in some ways also looking at ourselves. We too aspire to reach for the stars. In a series of essays written just before he died in 1985, Italo Calvino turned his attention to matters of transcendence in the face of the coming millennium – the lesser, non-capitalised, but nonetheless imminent millennium of numbers. No one else at the time seemed to be giving much thought to the year 2000, that arbitrary marker whose row of triple zeros speaks in its own way of rupture. Even the computer industry, now in a state of near-panic about the meltdown of commercial software systems expected to take place as 1999 clicks mechanically into 2000, was unfazed, never imagining that the systems designed in that decade would not soon be surpassed. But Calvino had early intimations of trouble, as well as the insight to see that in life, as in literature, one needed to master continuity and discontinuity in time. To this end, he devoted an essay each to those literary values he felt should be 'saved' for future generations: lightness, quickness, visibility, exactitude and multiplicity. 'Were I to choose an auspicious image for the new millennium', he wrote, in the first of these elliptical elegies, 'I would choose ... the sudden agile leap of the poet-philosopher who raises himself above the weight of the world, showing that with all his gravity he has the secret of lightness, and that what many consider to be the vitality of the times – noisy, aggressive, revving and roaring – belongs to the realm of death, like a cemetery for rusty old cars.'[2]

I cannot say whether this passage would have struck me with quite the same force had I not been reading Calvino at the time of the Heaven's Gate suicides. As it was, I was intrigued, as I had been many times before in writing this book, by the parallels that exist between millenarian thinking and forms of secular self-understanding which have iconic value even if they do not lend themselves to sectarianism. In this instance, there is the same impulse towards disincarnation, towards being able to levitate out of oneself on wings of hope, and the same longing to cast off the leaden mass of everyday existence – the unbearable weight of being, as it were. Equally, there is the insistence that what we take to be the nourishing qualities of life – those things which generate the pulse or beat against which we measure our progress – are in fact the very qualities that draw us ever closer to the grave. Calvino's views on transcendence match those of Heaven's Gate point for point. And yet how differently we treat the two kinds of leap. We frown upon the one as a symptom of social dysfunction, while cherishing the other as a symbol of human potential. And we shade them accordingly, driving a wedge of distinction between the blind leap into the dark and the veil-lifting leap into the light. The point I am making is twofold. First, when it comes to dealing with a sense of an ending, the millenarian world and the secular one resort to a shared repository of myths and imagery. And, second, this strange reciprocation or mirroring gives rise to an uneasy tension.

This book maps out both the common ground and the contested territories between millenarians and the rest of us. Its central premise is that, beyond being a matter of faith and physics, the end of the world is a moral issue: beneath the questions of whether and when the end will come lies the problem of how we reconcile the individual's conscience with that of society. Far from occupying the recondite reaches of abstract theory, the points at which we either meet or clash with millenarians engage some of the most fundamental means by which we strive to comprehend why we are here, where we are going and what lies in store for us. Everything, from how we apprehend the future and assimilate the past, to how we measure time, interpret history and fantasise about immortality, has a bearing on this quest to discover the nature of our own significance.

Such a project could of course have been undertaken at any time, since the shared patterns of thinking I explore reveal themselves as much in the twists and turns of millenarian history as in the way we deal with the world today. But because the approach of the year 2000 seems to have sensitised us to the multiple demands of an imagined end, there is a peculiar and sometimes uncomfortable poignancy in addressing such parities now. In particular, in our various attempts to circumvent the end, to get beyond it without passing through it, in the assorted ducks and manoeuvres, retreats and denials involved in wriggling out of finitude, there is evidence to suggest that the millenarian leap and the poetic leap are not so very different after all.

1. PROSPECTING THE FUTURE

Whatever happened to the future? Once it was a place where dreams would come true – empires would be built there, goals realised, ills cured, love rewarded. Everything that seemed, frustratingly, to exist just beyond our reach, the future promised to bring within our ken. The precise shape it would take, how it might feel to inhabit and what it would entail us leaving behind were details the imagination could savour. Hope made ignorance blissful. In this time of disenchantment, however, things look very different. The future has lost its lustre. It has degenerated into a land of foreboding, a place where, more likely than not, our nightmares will be realised and some form of payment exacted for our selfishness, greed and misdemeanours. We are suffering a drought of optimism. It is not just that we no longer dream of the future as bigger, better and brighter; we have ceased even to believe that it is inevitable.

In 1969, Herman Kahn, one of America's leading academic futurists, published *The Year 2000*. Twenty-one years later, John Naisbitt and Patricia Aburdene published *Megatrends 2000*. Two books with the same object in mind, to grasp where the world might be at the dawn of the new millennium, both are optimistic, identify similar trends and conclude on an upbeat note. Kahn, whose grip on the past was rather more tenuous than his hold on the future, wrote: 'I think there are good prospects for what the Europeans would call *la belle époque*, or, if you will, a good era, similar to that experienced between the turn of the century and World War I – a worldwide period of growth, trade, peace and prosperity on the whole, and a time, generally speaking, of optimism about the future.' Naisbitt and Aburdene write: 'On the threshold of the millennium, long the symbol of humanity's golden age, we possess the tools and the capacity to build utopia here and now.'[1] There, however, the similarities end.

In style, depth, tone, even in terms of self-regard, these books are quite distinct. Both directly and indirectly, massive institutional investment went into making Kahn's book. Kahn served his prophetic apprenticeship as a member of the futures forecasting team at the RAND Corporation, Santa Monica, leaving in 1961 to found the Hudson Institute in New York, whose staff of 150 researchers and consultants gave it the world's largest concentration of full-time futurists. And in 1965 he obtained funding to study the remaining third of the century from the American Academy of Arts and Sciences, which had just set up a 'Commission for the Year 2000' under the sociologist Daniel Bell. *The Year 2000* is an expert's handbook, dense with insider jargon such as 'basic, long-term, multifold trends', 'alternative futures scenarios', 'surprise free projections' and 'canonical variations'. Heuristic and paradigmatic in sketching out possible scenarios of a post-industrial world, it bulges with tables, graphs and statistical analyses and flags its high-mindedness with multiple references to the works of early pioneers of macrohistory. Though it requires perseverance, Kahn's book is even-handed and level-headed and its pages exude an air of scientific authority. Naisbitt and Aburdene's *Megatrends 2000* (1990), with its garish blue and silver cover, tabloid title and panting enthusiasm for cutting-edge technologies, looks and reads like airport-lounge pulp. Breezy, almost puckish in tone, and entirely lacking in an appreciation of the complexity of political and social tectonics, the authors see no real limits to economic growth, no prospect of an energy crisis and no long-term AIDS threat. Nor do they seem aware of there being a shadow side to the moral value of technological innovation.

One can't help wondering how optimism could have descended from the lofty heights of academic credibility to keep company with low-brow sensationalism in the space of a couple of decades – especially when it might be considered that, in real terms, little has actually changed since Kahn wrote up his study. And it is not as if Naisbitt lacks pedigree; a respected futurologist, he has held visiting fellowships at Harvard and Moscow State universities and conducted research at the Institute of Strategic and International Studies. Yet academics studying our social, political and technological frontiers are no longer willing to risk the kind of generalisations that only recently seemed plausible. They have retreated into particularity, where the tentative footsteps of futurism are promised surer ground. If the big picture, the world's large-scale dynamics, seems far more unwieldy and unpredictable these days, less amenable to analysis, however sophisticated, and less inspiring of confidence, it is largely because too many dreams, particularly those whose compass was global, have turned sour and too many good intentions have run to ground. Even less ambitious projections of optimism beggar belief: when Al Gore and Tony Blair wax futuristic on the unlimited potential of the coming Information Superhighway, for example, as though jumping on the electronics bandwagon might lend forward thrust to their political visions, they face not only a culture of disenchantment and a climate of instability, but a world in which certainty seems perpetually to elude us.

To the extent that doubt has come to characterise the tenor of our age, our senses seem peculiarly dulled to the light of our achievements but alive to the heat given off by our failures. Primed in this way for pessimism, all we seem capable of discerning on our horizons are signs of dreadful import. Our tendency to dismiss the vistas of possibility born of humanitarian or technocratic optimism with the ready cynicism usually reserved for the hare-brained schemes of renewal hatched by New Age fantasists belies a deep reluctance to embrace whatever might await us. Like Lot's wife, we would rather run the risk of backward-looking immobilisation than have to confront our mistrust of the future. Perhaps this explains our current mania for heritage, nostalgia and commemoration, for unearthing old gods and pastoral wisdoms, for every idealisation of the past. Such flight into retrospection may help us orient ourselves in a confusing world, but it seems to have less to do with recapturing what is gone than with grieving for what might have been. It is as though we have convinced ourselves that history has been our undoing. We wish that it had taken us elsewhere, but finding that it has deposited us in the precarious present, we begin to believe that it possesses its own forces and its own paths, and that it is carrying us with a momentum all of its own towards its final destination at the end of the world.

All this hand-wringing and doomsaying is excruciatingly familiar, part and parcel of the hysteria that greets the century's end and older cousin to the *petit mal* that afflicts us on the eve of each new year. It would seem that the limits of time, however arbitrary, however artificial, never fail to arouse anxiety. At new years, we have come to rely on well-worn rituals of transition to relieve this nebulous tension, we ring out the old and sing in the new and divert ourselves from our worries with thoughts of *rapprochements* and resolutions. Januaries make agenda-setters out of us all. But at the century's end, no such ritual comfort is to be had, save that of holding hands in empathy with Oscar Wilde, Huysmans, H. G. Wells or Max Nordau. Common sense also fails us, for however much we try to persuade ourselves that the century's turn is a materially negligible affair, a barely existing moment that passes almost as soon as it arrives, it recrudesces in our unconscious as symbolically momentous, a mystical portal to wave us into the brave unknown. It is little wonder that at its threshold we should not know which way to look, forwards with timorous anticipation or backwards with greedy nostalgia. We grow confused and indecisive, apprehensive and dismayed, and we ache to place the present moment in its proper perspective so that we may know where we stand in relation to the entire sweep of time. Why we tend at these critical chronological junctures to place ourselves near the mythical, biblical, apocalyptic End is a long and convoluted story, binding up hope and fear, history and time, myth and reality. In many ways it is the only story.

It is difficult to know what to make of successive centuries' ends. These tails of time that taper into nothingness are regenerated every hundred years; they thrash around creating havoc, then disappear with a reptilian slither. We ought to be wise to their antics by now, more especially since historians like Hillel Schwartz in *Century's End* (1990) and Asa Briggs in *Fin de Siècle* (1996) have lain them end to end for a comparative anatomisation aimed at diffusing their charge. Yet the fact of their almost organic recurrence as non-events does not somehow make for a reassuring thought. Although there is a certain relief to be had in identifying a 'Nineties mentality', relying on the usual cluster of hackneyed labels, decadence, terror, exhaustion, languor, restlessness, crisis, corruption and so on, it is profoundly uncongenial to our sense of occupying a unique historical moment to think that we are merely cogs in the wheel of a repetitious cycle, to look back upon a string of centuries' ends and recognise that they are notorious for tempting fate by conjuring up apocalyptic fantasies which never amount to any more than a whimper but which nonetheless succeed in plunging those who live through them into profound despair. Yet against having to conclude that the human psyche is a feeble thing, a humble and stupid slave to the Gregorian system of marking passing time, there is an arguable case for construing the late twentieth century as different, for believing that this is the century's end that will break the pattern of false alarm and for therefore defending the present sense of crisis as justified.

For one thing, this *siècle* has been blighted by an attenuated *fin*, beginning in 1914. The Great War seemed to realise the worst nightmares of the 1890s that had lain quiescent since the century's turn. It claimed hundreds of thousands of lives in the most gruesome trench battles known to mankind, devastated

6

the European landscape and toppled the pillars of national, political and economic stability whose steady construction had been the triumph of the nineteenth century. Widely seen as the end of *a* world if not of *the* world, the conflict occasioned a painful blistering of apocalyptic sensibilities; visions of final destruction, a sense of living in suspense, of existing on the brink of things. Feelings of hopelessness and helplessness abounded, as did desires for retreat, whether to a gloriously rewritten past, rose-tinted and sweet-smelling, or into rarefied dreams of peace and harmony. Reliving the heightened emotions of the era through its literature, the work of the war poets, the paintings of Nash or Dix, and the correspondence and diaries of politicians, foot-soldiers and novelists provides a contemporary *frisson* that is often as disquieting as it is unmistakable. In 1915, for example, D. H. Lawrence wrote to Lady Cynthia Asquith: 'I am so sad for my country, for this great wave of civilisation, 2000 years, which is now collapsing, that it is hard to live. So much beauty and pathos of old things passing away and no new things coming ... my God, it breaks my soul ... For the winter stretches ahead, where all vision is lost and all memory dies out.' Leafing through Lawrence's epistolary communications reveals that he was simultaneously penning letters to the likes of E. M. Forster, Bertrand Russell and Lady Ottoline Morrell, imploring them to sign themselves up as would-be members of an island utopia he called Rananim – a 'real community' forged by 'many fulfilled individuals seeking greater fulfilment', where 'the ultimate satisfaction and joy is in the completeness of us all as one'.[2] To each of his correspondents he complained, first with childish pique, then with increasing distress, that he could not find recruits, and like

7

Coleridge and Southey, drunk on Pantisocracy little more than a century before him, he was obliged, at length, to sober up.

The twentieth century has been an extraordinary one by any measure, its hapless inhabitants subject to one calamity after another. The foes of global economic depression, fascism, systematic genocide, warfare of unprecedented violence, the nightmare that was Hiroshima, the Cold War and devastating famines seem like the monstrous heads of a virulent hydra: cut one down and another rears up with a hiss. So frequently has humanity been threatened with the bitter promise of annihilation and so brow-beaten has it grown through having to endure extremes of brutality, insecurity and poverty, that signs of complacency have begun to show – even the word 'humanity' seems unnaturally strained nowadays, as though it were barely an appropriate collective noun for societies that have splintered into fractious individuality. Sir Isaiah Berlin called the present century 'the most terrible century in Western history' and in his intrepid, autobiographical history of the era, *The Age of Extremes* (1994), Eric Hobsbawm describes it as 'without doubt the most murderous century of which we have record'. These are harsh judgements, but as Hobsbawm points out, while the nineteenth century was a period of almost continuous moral, intellectual and material progress, there has, since 1914, been a marked decline in our aspirations towards those standards which in former days were both hard-won and fiercely defended. In view of the post-modernist agenda, it could be argued that we have systematically dismantled those standards.

From its inception, then, the twentieth century has been less a century to celebrate than one to survive. And as it draws to a close with threats to our continued existence multiplying both in scale and in number – so that to add to the evils of overpopulation, possible nuclear warfare and famine, we now face a catalogue of environmental hazards and a legion of new microbial foes – we appear to have become more circumspect in our dealings with the precious commodity of life. Less inclined blithely to throw away the term 'survival' in phrases like 'mere survival', which suggests that simply enduring has little to recommend it, or 'laws of survival', which implies there's some justice to the business of living, we are now more likely to talk of survivalism, the appended 'ism' serving to transform the will to live from a desire into an ideology. Yet as an ideology, survivalism is woefully limited. It is a blunt, one-track credo, overly enamoured of the unlikely blend of science fiction and primitivism that made such a monster of Allie Fox, the dubious hero of Paul Theroux's *The Mosquito Coast* (who in quitting civilisation for the jungle managed to leave behind him all that was good as well as bad), and undermined in its visionary aspect by an inability to look beyond the short term. Its association with the militaristic far-right in America, from whose ranks emerged Timothy McVeigh, the man responsible for the 1995 bombing of the Alfred P. Murrah building in Oklahoma City, further diminishes its appeal, as does the fact that survivalism finds its apotheosis in the nuclear fallout shelter. The imaginative poverty of salvation in a box hardly needs elaborating.

An altogether more resonant, if somewhat sentimental, monument to the will to live is the time capsule, a neglected byproduct of our industrial heritage, which came into being, appropriately enough, on the eve of the Second World War. In September 1938, the technical team of the Westinghouse

Electric and Manufacturing Company in Queens, New York, buried a seven-foot burnished-metal lozenge fifty feet under the earth in the grounds of the New York World's Fair in the hope that there it would remain for up to five thousand years (see plate 1). Months of painstaking construction, not to mention the combined expertise of engineers, chemists, geographers, metallurgists, philologists, historians and philosophers went into its making. Its outer shell was fashioned from cupaloy, a cunning blend of copper, silver and chromium designed to resist corrosion and pressure, while its 'inner crypt' contained everything that an anthropologist, or indeed a Martian, might need in order to reconstruct a full picture of life in the mid-twentieth century. There were detailed photographic records of the architectural and natural landscape, accounts of our scientific and technical achievements, our entertainment and culture, the variety of world religions and examples of newspapers all carefully preserved on microfilm. Copies of the Lord's Prayer in 300 languages were also included. The only books admitted into the Pyrex glass sanctum were a copy of the Holy Bible and a manual entitled *The Book of Record of the Time Capsule of Cupaloy*, which, among other things, provides tomorrow's heritage sleuths with geodesic coordinates for locating the capsule should all landmarks disappear, and a table of the heliocentric longitudes of the planets should our successors happen to abandon customary modes of time reckoning.

As a measure of the seriousness the Westinghouse men brought to their mission, *The Book of Record* opens with a quotation from the Book of Job: 'If a man die, shall he live again? All the days of my appointed time will I wait till my change come. Thou shalt call, and I will answer thee: thou wilt have a desire to the work of thine hands' (Job 14: 14–15). This concession to the inevitable is unusual among scientists, a group better known as over-reachers whose principal failing is to place too much faith in the world-shaping powers of their own innovations, and it is echoed elsewhere in their guidebook, notably when the authors acknowledge that 'history teaches us that every culture passes through definite cycles of development, climax and decay. And so, we must recognize, ultimately may ours.' These were men who, notwithstanding their position at the cutting edge of technological change, felt nervous about the future. In that the Second World War was, by this time, inevitable, it seems odd that they did not see fit to add the next two verses of Job to their epigraph: 'For now thou numberest my steps; dost thou not watch over my sin? My transgression is sealed up in a bag, and thou sewest up my iniquity.' Instead, they appended to the end of their manual a number of ambivalent messages from one age to another from some of the day's most celebrated thinkers, all of whom made implicit allusions to the coming war. From Thomas Mann: 'We know now that the idea of the future as a "better world" was a fallacy of the doctrine of progress'; from Albert Einstein: 'anyone who thinks about the future must live in fear and terror'; and from Robert Millikan, famed for isolating the electron. Millikan struck the only optimistic note. Describing the prevailing deadlock between the principles of ballot government and those of despotism, he wrote: 'if the rational, scientific, progressive principles win out in this struggle, there is a possibility of a warless, golden age ahead for mankind.'

On the evidence of *The Book of Record*, the Eloi and Morlocks of tomorrow would find twentieth-century man a rather perplexing creature, terrified by the prospect of the future yet unable to let go of a mythic idea that somewhere down the line paradise will be restored. The time capsule itself seems to contain this contradiction, even if its ostrich-like relationship to time amounts to a resignation from the need to resolve it. Still, it admits what the nuclear shelter cannot, that we are a species which requires posterity. We want to transmit the lessons we learn during our short lives to our children, our children's children and all who follow them. In lieu of immortality, we desire remembrance, a means of perpetuity by proxy.

If the twentieth century was swaddled in despair and dogged by evils throughout its adolescence and maturity, then, in its old age, it appears to have descended into chaos. Increasingly, the world appears to be inchoate, illogical. Causes blur with their effects, events are confused with their media representations and everything seems impossibly interrelated: it's like something Lewis Carroll might have invented. This hall-of-mirrors feel of late twentieth-century living has much to do with globalisation and mass communications, which appear to have shrunk the world only to multiply its contents, notably via a bewildering profusion of information. Moreover, for complex reasons having to do with forms of displacement, they have replaced the real with the virtual. Traditional institutional authorities, for example, have been supplanted by a global market whose power-base is both invisible and fluid and whose volatility consistently defies attempts to explain its workings. Because the contemporary world appears to lack definite points of anchorage, what scrutiny we bring to bear on our problems, rather than clarifying them, seems only to uncover problems of a greater order, deeper and more intractable than the first.

Benoit Mandelbrot's exasperating *fin de siècle* geometry, with its curdling contours, 'self-similar' Koch curves, and involuted Minkowski sausages and Peano trees, symbolises perfectly the irresolvable complexity of the present world. The all-pervasive fractal, twisted and inward-looking, is so utterly self-referential it replicates itself on resolution and, since it has no frame of reference outside itself, it is incapable of transformation. Mandelbrot rejects the 'monstrous' and 'pathological' tags that have been attached to his knotted squiggles, insisting instead that they are an accurate mathematics of a natural world ruled by 'turbulence'.[3] However, it is unlikely that even the visionary Mandelbrot, writing in 1977, could have foreseen quite how turbulent the world would become in the 1990s. At the mercy of forces it cannot understand, let alone control, it is for many people a truly frightening place.

So is the present *fin de siècle* really different from any other, inherently more unstable, more mordant, more portentous and more climactic than its predecessors? One could clearly go on for ever in the interests of demonstration scanning the century's decades, picking out examples of unprecedented ills, totting up fatal statistics and pointing to the doubts that have racked the minds of the great and good. Like bureaucrats, we could compile fat dossiers stuffed with all sorts of facts that weigh in on the side of doom. Ultimately, however, they would count for nothing, since our most strongly held beliefs, the ones in which we invest most, are those which in Pascalian fashion cannot in any way be demonstrated. What is important about them is not their credibility but their existential validity – their visceral rather than deductive appeal to truth. The sense that the present *fin de siècle* is more momentous than all the others owes less to any cumulative case we might bring against the twentieth century than to an overwhelming feeling that it must be significant because it heralds the year 2000, that mystical millennial moment which has become the focus for widespread apocalyptic belief. So intertwined in our minds are calendar and canon that it is almost impossible to think of the year 2000 without, at some level, also thinking of the world's spectacular end, or to contemplate moving forward without also imagining the fires, earthquakes and thunderbolts that will precede the stars falling from the sky, the rivers turning to blood, the sun being extinguished and the heavenly canopy rolling up like a scroll. Not even the most sophisticated among us are above experiencing this reflex apocalyptic. Thus if we want to understand the present *fin de siècle*, it is the future and not the past that we should be scanning.

Alternative Futurologies

Most of the time, the future isn't something we consciously contemplate. It would be more accurate to say that we unthinkingly absorb it. We take it in almost insensibly as time rolls silently on, moment by moment, second by second. In its temporal dimension alone, that is, in its primary, astronomical association with the calendar, the future is something which unfolds but which goes nowhere; it lacks sufficient distinction to shape our understanding of today. Only when we begin to survey the future in its spatial dimension, as another place, does the calendar take on a directional aspect. This future, The Future, the real tomorrow, is a foreign land, a vast, unconquered virgin territory that acts as a cypher for our wildest dreams of triumph and our darkest fears of defeat. Because it contains the unwritten chapters of the human story, we are unable to let it be, we are constantly prospecting and speculating, hoping to catch some glimmer of how the story ends, wanting to know whether God or mankind should be accredited as author and to discover, finally, if the idea of free will is nothing more than a human conceit. These are hoary questions, belonging properly to theology and philosophy, but they are engaged to varying degrees in all our attempts to fathom the future, be they prophetic, imaginary or predictive.

For much of this century, the balance of cognitive authority has been heavily weighted towards rational prediction. We have placed our trust in professional futurologists whose methods of accessing the future are accountable to reason. Dry extrapolations and mechanical projections have taken the place of the dreams, visions and transportations that served to disclose what is to come to the prophets of old. It was Kant, in the 1790s, who first inveighed the rational crusade for truth against latter-day seers and soothsayers, those 'mystagogues' whose shrill pronouncements of doom were inimical to his enlightened belief in the progress of civilisation. By what right, he asked, did they elevate themselves above philosophers, whose job it is to tell us what we can and cannot know, insisting that they had access to higher, intuitive, secret truths about the world's destiny?[4] But it was not until technology had supplied the religion of progress with graven idols that the future itself became a fit subject for rational enquiry.

In 1902, H. G. Wells published his *Anticipations of the Reaction of Mechanical and Scientific Progress Upon Human Life*

15

and Thought, which he conceived as a novel departure from the more usual fictive accounts of the future; it was a 'sincerely intended forecast of the way things will probably go in this new century', a 'prospectus' of sorts. It is difficult now not to marvel at the astonishing insight that brought Wells to some remarkably percipient conclusions. He predicted, for instance, that with the aid of developments in transport and communication, there would be a diffusion of the great cities, an urban sprawling that would expand apace with increasing social diversity and complexity. Politically, he envisaged the extension of democracy, the erosion of national borders and the potential formation of a 'world state' or 'New Republic', whilst, militarily, he rightly saw that the advantage between warring parties would be gained by commanding air conflict. In Wells's day the world was both bigger and smaller than it is today. It was more disparate, diffuse and far flung, but the principles that governed its operations were sufficiently limited in scale and scope to provide some basis for predicting the broad shape of things to come. This is not to overlook the fact that Wells tripped up a good deal. The book is full of charming anachronisms, a particularly amusing example being that with the advent of electric stoves, the temperature of which could be finely adjusted, cooking might 'be made a pleasant amusement for intelligent invalid ladies'. But his apparent slips only tell us that Wells found it harder to imagine a world without servants, say, than to leap with agility into the fresh pastures of technological possibility: the social consequences of change are always harder to apprehend than its causes. The crucial thing about Wells's predictions, regardless of whatever retrospective opinion might be formed of them, is that they were in tune with the times, and the overall message they transmitted to his twentieth-century heirs was that the future was a friendly place – there was no prospect of any ending in his sights – and negotiating it was simply a matter of the judicious exercise of choice.

In the wake of *Anticipations*, the future has been subject to a premonitory onslaught from a whole new class of professional futurologist, embracing scientific forecasters, trend-spotters, demographers, market researchers, policy planners, town planners, systems theorists and economists, each rushing to claim their stake in the ether. Buttressed by the solidity of mathematics, which conveniently translates plotting the course of lives into juggling with numbers, they draw curves, chart progressions and run statistics through hypothetical hoops and hurdles to make confident pronouncements, if not about where we are heading, then about what direction we're heading in. Their job is to manage the future and pin it down, empty it of its surprises and deprive it of the mystique of unknowability.

At the peak of its credibility, during the boom years of the Sixties, rational futurology emerged as a discipline in its own right, as rule-bound and hierarchical as any other, enjoying institutional prestige and government funding, and with theorists at its frontiers attaining guru status. One such was Bertrand de Jouvenel, journalist, economist, political scientist and author of *The Art of Conjecture*. In 1960, with support from the Ford Foundation, he founded the Futuribles group, whose purpose was to grasp a holistic picture of the future. Another French futurist who drew a following of tomorrow people around him was Gaston Berger, founder of the Prospectives group.[5] This was a time too when futurology went to the masses, thanks largely to Alvin and Heidi Toffler's bestselling *Future Shock* (1970).

Lately, however, the rational prognosticators have been spinning tales of woe, catapulting Malthusian scenarios on to our horizons, asking such pressing questions as: Can capitalism be sustained? Can the environment continue to sustain us? Can we sustain ourselves given the exponential swell in population and the depletion of natural resources? – and, from sober United Nations demographers to sensational populists like Robert Heilbronner and Rupert Sheldrake, answering in the negative.[6] Increasingly, they are acceding to the general view that our global problems are spinning out of control, whirling beyond the orbit of political remedy. Like us, they have lost faith in the religion of progress; like us, they have grown weary of programmatic solutions tried and failed; and, like us, they have become susceptible to the seductions of apocalypse. J. B. Bury, in his landmark polemic *The Idea of Progress* (1932), said that the illusion of finality was the great deceiver of mankind. Now we might argue that the illusion of command has been the great deceiver of futurology. It is as though we have tried free will and found that it leads only to self-destruction.

Over the course of the century, a parallel slide from optimism to pessimism has taken place in our literary imaginings of the future. In his sensitive and finely nuanced study of futuristic fiction, *The Pattern of Expectation, 1644–2001*, I. F. Clarke points out that the decades between the world wars saw the near total disappearance from literature of progressive ideal states such as Lawrence's Rananim, which had worthy origins in the utopias of Plato, Thomas More (who coined the word utopia) and Francis Bacon and, following the enormous impact of Yevgeny Zamyatin's *We* (1924), a remarkable proliferation of hostile, scientistic brave new worlds which allegorised an apocalyptic urge to destroy the industrial world. The great advantage that imaginative prognosis has over rational futurology is that it is free to reach for the post-apocalyptic, and the most enduring of the early literary dystopias are those which contain parables of sham salvation, with the redeemer – Orwell's Big Brother or Zamyatin's Benefactor, for instance – unmasked as despot and paradise sunk into robotic uniformity.

With each new technological breakthrough – nuclear power, space travel, the electronics revolution – the dystopic imagination has given expression to our collective fears and our collective conscience. In that electronic innovation is currently acclimatising us to rates of change so rapid that the present can actually taste the future, today's most resonant dystopias are set in the palpable tomorrow, in worlds that are much like ours only worse – faster, steelier and more violent. Writers like Philip K. Dick, William Gibson and Kim Stanley Robinson have given the theme of accelerated decline a powerful visual signature with landscapes that are simultaneously hi-tech and corroded. And on the back of Ridley Scott's film *Blade Runner* (1982) (based on Dick's cult novel *Do Androids Dream of Electric Sheep?* [1968]), where gleaming freeways soar and loop and glide over a rusting, noisy, congested pedestrian underworld, their aesthetic has become something of a cinematic cliché, potently reinforcing the narrative suggestion that if society moves forwards fast enough, it begins, in Einsteinian fashion, to go backwards. Progress becomes decline, development becomes degeneration. The very near future is thereby charged with a sense of evolutionary crisis, becoming the moment at which mankind, faced with the reality of being an endangered species, has, as a matter of urgency, to somehow transcend itself. Both *Blade Runner* and *Terminator* (1984) pervert this notion of transcendence by casting our successors as cyborgs or post-humans – beings at once electronically enhanced and dehumanised, echoing the contradictory qualities of the degraded landscapes they stalk. *Terminator* is particularly interesting from an apocalyptic point of view in that the plot is a salvation story complete with Messiah (new-born innocent) and Antichrist (cyborg). Using the conceit of time travel, it allows the final battle between them to be hauled back from the near future into the futuristic present, where the cybernetically empowered forces of darkness attempt to thwart the all too human forces of light by preventing the saviour figure from being born. The terminator of the film's title is quite literally trying to abort any hope for the future. The twist is that the future only appears to be at stake in the film, for the time-travelling cyborg is ultimately an interloper or foreigner; he doesn't belong in the present but is a sort of ghost from the future, a haunting emblem of the devastation that will inexorably come.

The catastrophe story is perhaps the most obviously apocalyptic of futuristic fantasies, and whether the calamity is natural, as in J. G. Ballard's *The Drought* (1965), or man-made and, more often than not, nuclear, as in Russell Hoban's *Riddley Walker* (1980) and Kim Stanley Robinson's *The Wild Shore* (1984), the common faith is in the new life that succeeds human or global obliteration. Lurking between the lines of the generic catastrophe tale is a semiotics of self-loathing, as though humanity itself were a global scourge whose annihilation would be somehow curative. Sometimes this theme is undisguised, as in Richard Preston's international bestseller *The Hot Zone* (1994), which inspired the film *Outbreak*, where the narrator, reflecting on the emergence of a new family of lethal airborne microbes, says: 'The earth is attempting to rid itself of an infection by the human parasite. Perhaps AIDS is the first step in a natural process of clearance.' As well as brokering a vision of a purified, renewed existence in which mankind can at last discover a way of living harmoniously and meaningfully, this sort of anti-humanism also functions to remind us that science has failed to take nature's measure. And not, it might be added, for lack of trying. Science has attempted to pin nature down with laws, probe its mechanisms, unravel its sub-atomic construction and harness its unruly forces for its own ends, but nature, as Preston fearfully cautions, can only be pushed so far. Push it further and it will revolt against us, unleashing its beautiful destructive power in an orgy of revenge.

The place of actual disasters in all this, of famines, the crashing of financial markets and environmental calamities like Bhopal, Chernobyl and the Exxon oil spill, is very interesting. On one level, they are simply the horrible evidence of our global mismanagement, of our inability to control the present, let alone the future. On another, their status is akin to that of the epidemics or inter-planetary explosions routinely invoked in catastrophe tales and now the latest subjects of non-fiction, what-if thrillers. Such mass-market works as Laurie Garrett's *The Coming Plague, Newly Emerging Diseases in a World Out of Balance* and Duncan Steele's *Rogue Asteroids and Doomsday Comets: The Search for the Million Megaton Menace that Threatens Life on Earth* (both 1995) trade, albeit simplistically, on the fact that we have learned to expect the unexpected, not in some ill-defined superstitious way, but within a cogent framework which views disaster, anomaly and error, natural or man-made, as inevitable. This rationale for explaining disasters is formally known as catastrophe theory.

Catastrophe theorists have developed topologies to account for the occurrence of singular, spectacular events within complex systems, a way of seeing earthquakes, revolutions, stockmarket crashes and so on as inherent within, rather than extraneous to, the order of things. According to catastrophists such as Warwick University's E. C. Zeeman, the world is both chaotic and particular. As a system it is liable to uncontrollable seizures from time to time, often as a circuitous result of tiny, seemingly insignificant changes, and these seizures, rather than bringing the entire system crashing down, act like pressure valves, operating as a form of self-regulation.[7] Through the distorting prism of popular culture, these ideas are often taken to imply that anything can happen or that anything can be true, but in the hands of futurologists they are incorporated into subtle predictive mechanisms. In that forecasters busy pouring over topological models of the way things work in the world repeatedly warn of the possibility, even the inevitability of financial or environmental disasters occurring, we might expect that after the event real-life calamities would be interpreted as fulfilments of secular prophecy. But the interesting thing about, say, Black Monday, the hole in the ozone layer or the Los Angeles earthquake is that overclouding any sense that the forecasters had been vindicated was a conviction that these disasters portended far worse.

Instead of being appeased by the dramatic twitches of a

system that is fundamentally self-ordering, our fears redoubled as we appealed to a higher order of existence, apocalypse. Within this overarching symbolic order, mini-endings – *fins de siècle* are one sort, disasters are another – hold enormous sway, manifesting themselves as ominous portents or foreshadowings, as though little bits of the future were visiting the present by way of presaging the end of the world. Sometimes the link between sign and symbol has been literal, with commentators identifying the explosion at Chernobyl, for instance, with the falling star of the Book of Revelation, 'burning as it were a lamp, and it fell upon the third part of the rivers ... And the name of the star is called Wormwood' (Rev. 8: 10–11). In Russian the name for a variety of wormwood called *Artemesia vulgaris* is 'Chernobyl'.[8] If apocalyptic arguments look appealing, it is largely because catastrophe theory cannot exhaust the meanings of the catastrophes it seeks to comprehend. Put another way, we might not find singularity and particularity an especially satisfying explanation of things, whatever its rational credentials. The allure of generality, of totalising visions of the world and the events unfolding within it, cannot be so easily set aside, even when, as in the case of apocalypse, it opens the door to allow irrationalism to reassert its grip on the future.

Conceivably, it is as a result of the same impulse towards generality that the trappings of unreason have so successfully nudged their way into our common culture of late. The popularity of horoscopes, psychic phone lines, homeopathic therapies, crystals, the whole New Age package, suggests that our tolerance threshold for cosmologies which resist easy explanations is shifting. The success of the national lottery, as well as the bestselling status of books on ancient Mayan mysteries, UFOs and the influence of the 'power planets', testifies to a tidal interest in the esoteric, archaic and para-normal, as if other worlds, older than or far distant from our own, possess the solutions to life's riddles. Even the miraculous has made a reappearance, to judge by the sharp growth in Britain and America of charismatic and Pentecostal Christianity, with their clutter of dramatically supernatural accoutrements, faith healing, ecstatic transports, automatic writing and speaking in tongues, not to mention the rash of Virgin sightings in Central and Eastern Europe.[9] What we are witnessing, culturally, is more than a passing attraction for forms of knowledge which are curtained off from the glare of reason and which therefore pique our curiosity. There is a genuine hunger for inspired truths, for alternative but nonetheless internally consistent schemes of comprehending the world, born of a gnawing need for ways of eliciting some sort of order from the jumbled appearances of contemporary life. And since science, politics and even, in its pastoral forms, religion are increasingly abdicating from making generalisations about the world, we are forced to seek them elsewhere.

It could be argued, indeed it is very fashionable to argue, that the grand narratives that have traditionally made all-embracing sense of our lives are outdated. According to this way of thinking, History, Ideology, Justice, Reason, Gender and Truth are spent forces, their once infinite reach curtailed by a new awareness that every culture has its own primal narratives and that our versions represent only one way among many of seeing things, not the only way or the right way. In the post-modern excitement about celebrating the freedoms and egalitarianism of relativism, little effort seems to have been expended on thinking through what we are leaving behind. It is easy to imagine that we can go on as before in the absence of the broad matrices that have served as the invisible underpinning of our thoughts and actions but, like an aerial artist required to perform a trick she has done many times before, only without a safety net, what ought to be routine is beset by anxiety. In the words of Canadian political scientist Arthur Kroker, we now live in a 'panic society' – everywhere unease wells up in the gaps of our fragmented lives.[10] Comfort and reassurance are in short supply and it is into this chink in our relativist idealism that apocalypse is able to insinuate itself. Apocalypse is a grand narrative unlike any other. It may be antiquated, arcane and crypted, having every appearance of redundancy, but it is able to account for the way things are in a manner that our other grand narratives cannot. It provides locations, a cast of players, a coherent script for the human story and it has an agenda. In all these regards it shares the specificity of, say, history or science, but – and this is the source of apocalypse's strength – its symbols are so rich, or else so vacant, that they lend themselves to endless reinterpretations and uses. Effectively, in apocalypse, we possess a grand narrative that refuses to die.

Not least among the advantages that apocalypse has over other grand narratives is its divine origin. It is the revealed truth of what is to come, a disclosure given directly by God and enshrined within texts that substantial numbers of people hold to be sacred. In this sense, there can be no fuller picture of human existence. What other narrative can compete with one whose sweep takes in the whole conception of things: creation, goodness, evil, death, resurrection, salvation, the separating of the streams of good and evil at the world's end and their return to the eternal source? It may not rank among our first-order explanations of the way things work in the world, but apocalypse is a grand narrative in waiting – when we have grown disillusioned with measuring things by the human standard, we can measure them by a higher one. Interestingly, people do not so much subscribe to its world view as surrender to it, falling into its net once persuaded that humanity has made a mess of controlling its own destiny. There they will be buoyed up by the romance of rupture, the idea that we can simply purge the world of its dross and start afresh.

So magnificently visual is apocalypse's telling of this moment of rupture that Ingmar Bergman could not resist filming part of it in *The Seventh Seal* (1957), while American televangelist Pat Robertson was at one time intent on being on hand with cameras to film the rest. Apocalypse possesses all the qualities of a spellbinding drama as it unfolds in grandiose cosmic splendour to mark the culmination of the age-old battle between good and evil, preordained to occur in the fullness of time. Just when it appears that evil has wrung every vestige of righteousness from the world, so that this beleaguered globe, demonic and demented, exists in a state of constant upheaval and chaos, subject to wars, natural disasters, rampant lawlessness and material greed, God intervenes to bring things to a sudden, violent and cataclysmic end. In the midst of this heavenly crusade against evil, Christ returns to earth in might and glory to do battle on behalf of goodness, battalions of angels descend from the skies, monsters rise up from bottomless pits to combat them, and their numerous clashes swing the balance of power first one way, then another, before goodness finally wins out and the wicked are hurled into the lake of fire. At this point comes a kind of interregnum, the Millennium, a golden thousand-year period during which Christ rules the saved in God's kingdom on earth. Once the Millennium has run its course, all who have ever dwelt on earth will be resurrected to face the Last Judgement. Everlasting torment and hellfire will be the lot of the wicked, while the righteous will be returned to a renewed paradise, one befitting a cleansed cosmos, to live in peace and harmony for evermore. Though apocalypse's terrible punishments and immutable judgements present the end of the world as a terrifying prospect, sweet salvation lies at its close. Beyond the nightmare, therefore, apocalypse is a purifier, gateway to a dazzling new era of abiding peace, the ultimate right of passage. Compared to the fiery conflagration it promises to ignite in time's doorway, the century's end is no more than the lighting of a memorial candle.

By way of bringing the real global situation into some sort of alignment with apocalyptic prophecy, it is extremely tempting to begin fleshing out comparisons between the various catastrophes or tribulations that are supposed to herald the Last Days and the turmoil of the present age, comparisons which seem to suggest themselves naturally. But like the idea of compiling a criminal dossier against the twentieth century, the listing of worldly woes, hidden evils and disasters waiting to happen would only add to the rhetoric of desperation about the future without revealing how that rhetoric works. Better to leave the task of casting about the contemporary landscape for evidence of the 'signs of the times' to millenarians and concentrate instead on examining apocalypse's undeniable allure.

Pulling back from the empirical, one might begin by looking at its promise of certainty. Arguably, this is where apocalypse finds its chief point of entry into our lives, its icy tendrils touching the very spot where darkness reigns.

The global resurgence of nationalism and religious fundamentalism already bears witness to the fact that post-modern societies, fractured and dangerously overcrowded with irreconcilable values, have strongly self-defining streaks running through them, perhaps by way of compensating for the loss of focus and identity, the 'de-centring' that is the sacrifice demanded by the twin idols of the late-twentieth century, difference and diversity. It is within this framework too that the peculiar blend of religion and identity politics preached by Louis Farrakhan finds favour with black Americans. Lamenting the rise of what he sees as totalitarianism in all but name and reflecting on humanity's legendary inability to live in communities which cohere and which work towards bettering the lot of all who dwell in them, George Steiner, in characteristically anarchic mood, has asked 'whether there may not be constants in our biological and communal make-up which do make it very difficult for us to live with others'.[11] This is his way of saying 'the unspeakable'. And the reason it is unspeakable, as Steiner knows very well, is because an oil-mixed-with-water image of humanity is implicitly apocalyptic and therefore just as uncompromising as the nationalism and religious reductivism he wants to indict on grounds of intolerance. All three fundamentalisms confer chosen people status on believers, which is to say that they legislate against tolerance; furthermore, they reinforce their own exclusivity by claiming a monopoly on distinguishing right from wrong.

Steiner wants to have things both ways, railing against intolerance while all along suspecting that intolerance is very much a part of the human condition. His critique of fundamentalism, therefore, adds up to an apocalyptic catch-22. Of course, there are good historical reasons for Steiner's mistrust of human nature. He belongs, after all, to that generation which experienced first hand many of the horrors of this century: Nazi occupation, the war, the camps – all the evil doings of a nationalist movement driven towards an apocalyptic Final Solution by a sense of its own special election. Younger generations are indeed fortunate to have escaped these horrors and, no doubt, the liberal humanisism of the postwar years *has* made the world a better, safer, freer place. But while Steiner is right to warn that we have much to fear from the strident certainties of religious fundamentalism and nationalism, his is a fear of the century's former evils repeating themselves and a fear, therefore, that younger generations cannot share in quite the same way. They have, besides, their own fears to contend with. And these, ironically, are almost of the opposite nature. In worrying about job security, environmental damage, the speed and direction of technological change, sexually transmitted diseases and poverty, they fear the dark side of the market economy – the products of freedom gone wild not of freedom constrained. Perhaps this goes some way towards explaining the collectivist yearnings that make nationalism and fundamentalism so prevalent among the young, and why contemporary cultural pessimism often entails a rejection of liberal compromises. In that the products of excessive freedom look very much like the signs of the times, moreover, there are grounds for explaining the current resurgence of apocalyptic fundamentalism or millenarianism.

Given the tendency for media interest in apocalypse to veer, without rhyme or reason, between scare-mongering and leg-pulling, it needs to be said that most of us, ultimately, are able to cope with feeling at sea in a world in which we have abandoned a biddable future without rushing to subscribe to the doctrine of the end of the world. As we stumble through the prevailing chaos, we seem determined to discover new opportunities and freedoms in disorder. Rather than concede failure in our attempts to live together harmoniously, as Steiner is tempted to do, we blame our endless conflicts not on ourselves but on others. We might mourn the discrediting of grand narratives, but if we need certainties we reinforce local ones, family ties or political commitments, for example. Leaving aside, for the time being, the issue of whether such coping strategies are merely the building blocks of an alternative fiction, we have become expert in confining our relationship to apocalypse to the self-consciously rhetorical. In the habit of invoking the potentiality of the world's end as a means of holding our worst excesses in check, or else as a means of lending polemical force to clean-slate political and social policy drives, we happily make use of apocalypse's narrative power. On a more nebulous level, we accede to its totemic function, letting it figure as a mighty emblem of death in order to grant us insight into the value of life. Pragmatically speaking, orthodox Christianity's acceptance of the world's end as immanent, as tied into the fabric of existence without being a matter of urgent expectation, serves much the same pedagogic purposes. It is only for those whose experience of destabilisation generates an insecurity so profound it can only be assuaged by cosmic certainty, that apocalypse is a tyrannical master. At this end of the narrative spectrum, apocalypse leaves no room for metaphor. And where it presides as a credo, millenarians are literally prepared to live or die by its word.

Unlike mainstream Christians, millenarians are clamouring for the resolution of all things. Though between them they generate dozens of competing versions of apocalypse, these are just so many means to justify an imminent End. The all-important thing is that soon, perhaps tomorrow, perhaps next week, this sinful world will be consumed in a fit of divine wrath, leaving the righteous (themselves, naturally) to proceed into the glorious hereafter unscathed. With so much to do and so little time in which to do it, millenarians are generally too busy fine-tuning their apocalyptic readings of global events and preparing for their own salvation to take much notice of the rest of us, or indeed to give us cause to notice them. But whenever they raise their heads above the parapets of their world-within-a-world to check the clock, sparks begin to fly. To borrow a metaphor from catastrophe theory, millenarianism as a whole might be seen as a complex system, ever-changing and protean, constantly adapting to the surrounding environment, but every now and then it produces spectacular seizures. These take the form of definite prognoses of the End, bare-faced confrontations with time itself that challenge the world to face up to its fate.

The seizures are of two kinds. One is less dramatic, a minor convulsion, if you like, and it arises when doomsday prophets take it upon themselves to set a date for the world's end. Instantly dispelled is the modern folk image of the harmless creature who wanders the streets wearing a sandwich board and mumbling jeremiads. Any gentle mockery of what we

31

invariably take to be delusion rapidly gives way to hostile denial when chronology enters the frame. And when time marches heedlessly through the appointed hour to no avail, the Kantian within us takes gloating satisfaction. The strength of this sort of seizure largely depends on how much media interest attends the countdown to destruction. Much entertainment was recently had at the expense of Sister Marie Gabriel, a London-based Belarussian nun from Poland, who nominated 16–23 July 1994 as the final hour. This was when an almighty collision between the comet Shoemaker-Levy 9 and the planet Jupiter was supposed to have signalled the 'COSMIC DAY OF JUDGE-MENT ordained by GOD'. In the months preceding, the good Sister took to gazing soulfully at us from newspaper ads, looking like a 1940s Hollywood starlet, with golden ringlets and Dietrich eyebrows, but with her hands clasped round a rosary and wearing what appeared to be a crown of thorns. She begged us to pray and to mend our wicked ways, suggesting that if we destroyed pornography, banned blood sports, closed down zoos and shared our food mountains there was a slim chance that disaster might be averted. The American press similarly had a field day in 1990 when Elizabeth Clare Prophet, a self-styled saviour who looks like a reject from a Seventies rock band and who goes by the name 'Guru Ma', galvanised members of her Church Universal and Triumphant by ear-marking 23 April for the world's end. Journalists feasted on the spectacle of some 2000 CUT faithful descending by air, bus and car on the group's 12,500-acre Royal Tetron Ranch in Paradise Valley, Montana, with the intention of taking up residence in its giant labyrinth of nuclear shelters. Millenarian history, past and present, teems with such outbursts of chronological hysteria.

The second sort of seizure is genuinely catastrophic, occurring when messianic sects, confident in the reflected glory of their own saviour-leader, attempt to hasten the end of the world through violent confrontation with their demonised foes or else try leap-frogging into the next world through self-destruction. The tragic results of betting on apocalypse in this way and losing are so well known that they have made international landmarks of the towns in which they occurred. Jonestown and Waco will for ever be remembered for their blood-baths. Nor are we likely to forget the mayhem caused by Shoko Asahara, the semi-blind herbalist from Osaka and founder of Aum Shinrikyo (Supreme Truth), whose militant army claimed 30,000 followers worldwide. In the spring of 1995, the group attempted to stage the battle of Armageddon on the Tokyo subway, using home-made bombs containing lethal sarin gas. Ten people died in the attacks and 5,000 were treated for injuries. In the face of such – admittedly rare – outbursts of millenarian activity, we can only look upon the carnage in horror and incredulity and wish that things had turned out differently. The double tragedy of Waco, where David Koresh and seventy-four of his Branch Davidian followers, many of them children, perished in an almighty conflagration, is that, in fact, things could have turned out differently.

The extraordinary siege at Mount Carmel, Waco, which held many of us spellbound for fifty-one long days, began on 28 February 1993 when eighty or so armed agents from the United States Bureau of Alcohol, Tobacco, and Firearms managed to bungle delivering a search warrant for illegal weapons to the Koreshan occupants of Ranch Apocalypse: six Branch Davidians and four agents were killed. The ensuing stand-off, during which an FBI Hostage Rescue Team joined the BATF in an attempt to secure Koresh's surrender, was finally brought to a close when the United States Justice Department approved plans to use tear gas in an attempt to ferret out the Davidians. In the words of Bob Ricks, the FBI's chief spokesperson, 'we had to up the ante'. In the early morning of 19 April, Abrams tanks amassed menacingly around the perimeter fence of the Mount Carmel compound, tightening the circle around their prey. Using battering rams, the first tanks pushed their snouts through the walls of the compound, fired off their gas canisters and withdrew. The Davidians did nothing. The process was repeated and again the Davidians stood firm. Before another tactic could be tried, the compound mysteriously caught fire.[12] As flames engulfed the building, flaring high into the sky, television audiences worldwide watched, impotent and bewildered, as a mini-Armageddon was enacted before their eyes – Apocalypse Lite; real-life disaster neutralised by the cathode ray. To this day no one knows exactly how the fire began and each side holds the other responsible. However, the FBI should have recognised the potential inflammability of the situation. What they failed to take seriously enough was that the perimeter fence of the compound was first and foremost an ideological boundary. Once beyond it, they were in a different world.

The most decisive events at Waco involved neither dramatic fireworks nor armed confrontation; they were simply not part of the theatrics that kept us glued to our screens. What determined both the outcome of the siege and its subsequent assimilation was the polarising and consolidation of two entirely opposed cosmologies. During the long and, apparently, uneventful stand-off, one set of interpretations of events took shape within the walls of Ranch Apocalypse, while another set of counter-interpretations was being manufactured in newsrooms and broadcasting houses across the globe. Both world views emphasised the absolute otherness of the Branch Davidians, but in starkly contrasting ways, and, strangely enough, both demanded the same resolution.[13]

Shielded from the prying eyes of government agents and reporters, David Koresh was busy putting his followers through intensive Bible classes punctuated by equally intense paramilitary training which included repeated video screenings of the Vietnam War movies *Platoon* and *Full Metal Jacket*. His rationale for mixing scriptural right with military might had been in place since the late Eighties, when he succeeded in persuading both himself and his followers that he was the seventh angel of Revelation come to announce the kingdom of God and promptly began preparing for Armageddon, stockpiling weapons for a ruthless confrontation with non-believers that would result in his resurrection and the salvation of his followers. By the time the authorities caught up with him, he had accumulated an estimated $200,000 worth of assault rifles, grenade launchers and machine guns. 'We're ready for war,' he announced when the FBI arrived. Koresh had been expecting the federal agents not, as one might have supposed, because he was sitting on a vast haul of illegal weapons, but because they fell directly into his prophetic remit. Antichrist, he taught his disciples, was at large in the world and his sole aim was to destroy the Davidians, God's Elect, using the American state apparatus as his unwitting instrument. The FBI were agents of Satan, destined to meet their doom at Armageddon.[14]

Throughout the siege the Davidians were spoiling for a fight, convinced that by dicing with death they would usher in new life. The showdown with the FBI was precisely the eventuality they had in mind, though they might have appreciated some angelic assistance. From start to finish, what propelled Koresh fatally onwards was the promise of the Millennium. It was the rest of us who were unable to square the vision of the burning compound with the thousand-year reign of milk and honey.

We might perhaps have been inclined to see, though not to sympathise with, the connection, but by the time the siege was drawing to its inexorable close, we had imbibed a demonology of our own – the one invented by the media. The hundreds of newspaper pages devoted to Koresh's theological idiosyncrasies, his polygamy, his suspected abuse of children, his love of sex, guns and rock'n'roll went into moulding an image of him as monster. Here, we were repeatedly told, was a criminal maniac, a deluded, probably psychotic and certainly dangerous man. Apostate Davidians were wheeled into television studios to point an accusing finger at their former idol, levelling against him charges of incest, brainwashing and unprovoked acts of violence as if they had never been willing acolytes. Thus the familiar machinery of denial went into full gear. The thorough pathologising of Koresh further served to underwrite the drastic measures taken to ensure his downfall; no one, it was presumed, would mourn the loss of a lunatic rebel. Had it been physically possible, Koresh would no doubt have been whisked off to the nearest asylum, but circumstances being as they were, we settled for the next best thing, a freak show. Like Victorians who marvelled at strong men, Siamese twins and Hottentots, we gazed in wonder and incredulity at this fanatical spiritual deviant, turning him into an object of derision and grotesque fascination. In this way, Koresh was uprooted from mainstream American culture and deposited at its table-rapping margins.

As far as matters of effective policing are concerned, the federal agents camped outside Ranch Apocalypse took, for the most part, a rather passive role. Uniformed, badge-wearing, gun-toting officialdom was reduced to playing a waiting game. A far greater zeal for maintaining law and order seemed to drive the media's tireless campaign to brand Koresh a criminal outcast. It was almost as if what needed, as a matter of priority, to be kept in line, was any sympathy we might feel for the Davidians' plight – in other words, our own vulnerabilities to apocalypse. This would suggest that the real social problem that surfaced during the siege was a widespread fear that the various categories of apocalyptic posturing are not as stable as they might be. It also suggests that what was being policed was not so much the Davidians themselves as the boundary separating them from the rest of us. If there is any substance to such an argument, then at its core lies the issue of dates. Were it not for our calendrical anxieties, every shade of apocalyptic thinking would have its place in society and the millenarian conviction that the world is going to end imminently would, in keeping with the exigencies of a secular age, be reassuringly located at the outer reaches of plausibility. But the approach of the year 2000 is muddling things, rounding up our horizons into an apocalyptic cul de sac, and forcing millenarianism and secular pessimism into some form of conference.

The Various Shades of Millenarianism

In the countdown to the end of the twentieth century, an essence of apocalypse has seeped past our rhetorical ease with endings and lodged in our collective unconscious. From these murky depths, dark end-time prophesyings of past and present seem to cast a shadow over our troubled negotiations with the future. Like phantoms, they play tricks with our perception of things, implanting visions of the terminal on our horizons and leading to suspicions, as threatening as they are indistinct, that at the point where the *fin de siècle* meets the new millennium, the history of man and the history of the world will collide, fatally. There is no more graphic embodiment of this creeping sensibility than the giant clock positioned outside Paris' Boubourg centre, which mesmerisingly ticks off the seconds remaining to point zero as you watch immobilised. It's a simple construct, but it harnesses the power of numbers to convey a sense of destination or limit, and in so doing it brings our mortality into sharp focus. At some dimly understood level, we transfer our fear of death on to the very numerals designating the century's turn, like children who thrill to the mordant game of Count to a hundred then I'm coming to get you. Similarly, the year 2000 squats ahead of us like a time-bomb, all those deadening zeros signifying finality, presenting us with a blank wall on which to project the potent fantasy that the present world order is doomed and reminding us that Cronos, the god of time, always carried a scythe. In spite of the past experience which tells us that after zero comes one – a small but sure step forward – then two, then three, it is as if our belief in the progression of things has been frozen. Instead of succession we imagine cessation. The merest hint of Biblical illumination, meanwhile, makes those same portentous zeros look fat with the promise of fulfilment, inviting a reading of the year 2000 as the fullness of time.

And so we return to the problem that so vexed Kant, the tug of war between reason and mystagoguey. Both want to lay claim to the trophy of the year 2000. The voice of reason, matured on the long backward vista of *fins de siècle* come and gone, argues that, as an ending of sorts, the all-important year ought to feel decisive, but that passing time will eventually unmask it as a year like all others. Leaning on psychology, it will indulge our need for a convenient linchpin on which to hang our existential sense of crisis, but at the same time it warns us not to be the dupes of our own desires. The mystagogues, meanwhile, rant and rave about the 'signs of the times', commune with angels and enter trances. They are consumed with a need to announce. What's more, they point confidently to the immense burden of historical expectation that devolves on to the year 2000 in the knowledge that, even if we refuse to believe them, we can do nothing to disprove them.

The millennial moment is the point at which numerous prophetic pointers, Biblical, astrological, ancient and mystical, converge. According to sacred Mosaic chronology, which dictates that the world will endure for 6000 years, the cosmos is nearing its expiry date, since a popular vein of Christian thinking contends that Christ was born around year 4000 of the world. My own copy of the King James Bible contains a chronological table giving the date of creation, *pace* Archbishop Ussher, as 4004 BC. The astrological mode of time-keeping, which reckons the various ages of man according to their zodiacal affiliations, alights on the year 2000 for the commencement of the Age of Aquarius (source of the New Age movement). This calculation is based on the idea that the Earth is supposed to wobble slightly as it spins through the solar system and that every two thousand-odd years this shift is sufficient to pull the vernal equinox into a different constellation. Currently we occupy the rotten and withered end of the Age of Pisces, which, the astrologers tell us, is known for sacrifice, struggle and Christian spirituality – hence the sign of the fish. The Age of Aquarius, meanwhile, is explicitly millennial in character, denoting a time of brotherhood, harmony and higher consciousness. Nostradamus, court astrologer to Henri II, and probably the most fêted mystic of all time, furiously scribbled cryptic quatrains when the Holy Spirit visited him, claiming that these verses encoded the rest of world history. His famous prophecy that 'The year 1999 . . . From the sky will come a great King of terror' has been widely taken to refer to the world's end. And, courtesy of Adrian Gilbert, Maurice Cotterell and Graham Hancock, there has been a timely rediscovery of the Mayan calendar, whose vast 5125-year cycle is due to end in 2012. This is just some of the freight loading the year 2000. There is much more; the point is that the present century's end is prophetically overdetermined.

Such is the commotion surrounding the year 2000 that the ecclesiastical establishment has sought to stake its own claim on the year. In an apostolic letter written in 1994, *Tertio Millennio Adveniente*, Pope John Paul II effectively cautioned Catholics against attaching too much significance to the auspicious date. He allowed for the two thousandth anniversary of

Christ's birth being a holy year, 'an extraordinarily great Jubilee', but clearly implied that it would not herald the final hour. Church of England officials take a similar view of the matter. Close inspection of the apostolic letter nonetheless gives the impression that the papacy wants to have it both ways in that it plans a three-year celebration of the Jubilee, a holy countdown aimed at rejuvenating Christian spirituality, effectively bypassing apocalypse to achieve renewal without an ending, a Millennium without Armageddon.[15] There have been rumblings from Catholic traditionalists who would like to have seen the Pope appear less excited about the year 2000. A greater degree of tactical pontifical denial would have suited them better. The Church, they feel, can afford to remain aloof from the chronological fray since it stands to gain from any eventuality. If the world ends, Christianity itself triumphs, and if it does not, then the Church is likely to be the principal benefactor of millenarian disappointment. This is what happened when the world famously failed to end in the year 1000, the close of the Augustinian Millennium. Although millenarian terror actually grew in the eleventh century, so too did Church membership, Church wealth and Church power, and there was a veritable renaissance in Church architecture.[16]

Oddly enough, it is the secular world and not the Christian one that most keenly feels the onus of denial and that insists, in spite of Jonestown and Waco, on looking upon the chronological obsessions of millenarians as the idle preoccupations of unworldly minds rather than as matters of life or death. When in 1995 the Jehovah's Witnesses publically announced that they would henceforth venture no more predictions of the world's end, we flattered ourselves that this self-restraint was an acknowledgement of the folly of date setting, that, having lost the numbers game several times before, they had finally come to see the error of their ways. The fact of the matter is that the Witnesses, having arrived at the absolute limit of their prophetic timetable in 1975 (*anno mundi* 6000 by their reckoning), were unable, not unwilling to speculate further. We are now living on borrowed time. This millenarian reality is understandably hard to swallow for those of us who for practical, sentimental and ideological reasons would, on the whole, prefer this world to endure a little longer. Decrepit and war-ravaged though it may be, this world is all there is if you have made no investment in the hereafter, or if you have banished God from the cosmos altogether. Given our fragile spiritual existence, it is little wonder we get into such a lather over millenarians. Yet however much we stamp and shout, pretending that millenarianism is a fringe affair, confined to the socially dysfunctional and the pathetically deluded, ultimately we are only deceiving ourselves. Difficult though it may be to digest, millenarianism is thriving the world over and, while most of its subscribers would share our rage at David Koresh's messianic arrogance, they are no less convinced than he was of the world's imminent end.

In America, millenarianism does not even need to compete with mainstream religion, since in terms of numbers and public profile it virtually is the mainstream religion and is currently spreading like wildfire across the fast growing Dispensationalist denominations. In Ronald Reagan, moreover, God's nation had a millenarian at its helm. Speaking to an Israeli lobbyist in 1983, the President confided: 'You know, I turn back to your ancient prophets in the Old Testament and the signs foretelling Armageddon, and I find myself wondering if we're the generation that's going to see that come about. I don't know if you've noted any of those prophecies lately, but, believe me, they certainly describe the times we're going through.' Wisely, he refrained from mentioning his parallel belief in America's special millennial destiny, a belief inherited from the seventeenth-century Puritan pilgrims who came to the New World in search of milk and honey and which has done so much to shape the American national identity. Here was a man David Koresh must have looked up to. He pumped up and preened America's war machine like no other modern President before him and his SDI initiative, aptly dubbed Star Wars, must have conjured up in the minds of millions of citizens that almighty battle Christ would wage in the sky against the hosts of Satan. Throughout Reagan's two terms in office, a cluster of high-profile millenarian preachers numbered among his closest advisors. Calling themselves the Moral Majority, they injected a potent brew of nationalism, millenarianism and conservative politics directly into the White House. There was Pat Robertson, himself a Presidential runner in 1988, who at the start of 1982 declared, 'I guarantee you by the fall of 1982 there is going to be a judgement on the world'; Jerry Falwell, who proffered a succession of prophecies of war with Russia in the eighties; and Billy Graham, the evangelical globe-trotter whose 1983 bestseller *Approaching Hoofbeats* read Revelation in light of contemporary world problems. In the background lurked Hal Lindsay, the father of modern American apocalyptic, who shot to fame in 1970 by turning the Bible into a manual for combat in the atomic age: to date more than 20 million copies of his *The Late Great Planet Earth* have been printed. Lindsay revamped his prophecies for the Reagan era with *Countdown to Armageddon,* which opens with the sentence: 'The decade of the 1980s could very well be the last decade of history as we know it.'[17]

Although America survived the Eighties, prophecy continues to be big business. Millenarians have their own publishing houses, their own star authors and boast books sales regularly running into the millions. However, as Paul Boyer points out in his extensive study of this literature, *When Time Shall Be No More* (1992), the industry tends to steer clear of setting dates for the end of the world, trading instead on its ability to diagnose the world's ills in light of apocalypse. Taking for granted that we have entered the Last Days, individual interpreters, caught up in a frenzy for eschatology – the theology of the last things – excitedly mix and match contemporary world trends and events with the ominous 'signs of the times'. Like the explosion at Chernobyl, wars, the making and breaking of political alliances, natural disasters, ecological threats, crime rates, promiscuity, viral epidemics, all take on deeper, darker meanings once slotted into the apocalyptic scheme of things. From one year to the next the focus of eschatological anxiety shifts from Russia to the Balkans to the Middle East, while Armageddonist fears switch from nuclear war to natural disasters to environmental catastrophes and back again. By constantly updating this end-time nosology, the eschatologists convincingly keep abreast of the rolling reality of the global situation. Outside of the newsrooms but very much within mainstream American culture, they provide an alternative running commentary on the state we are in. And in true grand narrative style, they posit a causal link between events so materially, geographically and temporally disparate, any self-respecting journalist would insist on their complete separateness. They weave a continuous story out of the random and episodic, seeing simple truths underpinning extraordinary complexity and supernatural intent behind what looks like chance occurrence. One could perhaps view apocalypse as the theological equivalent of chaos theory, but, in place of high-flown mathematics, the work of reductionism is done by Antichrist. Thus, while things may have the appearance of chaotic disarray, the rationale which accounts for the under-lying order of things is mind-bogglingly simple. From a secular perspective, the existence of Antichrist is extremely trouble-some because, like the prophesied significance of the year 2000, it cannot be disproved. While the signs of the times can be met with counter-interpretations, Antichrist can only be dis-avowed.

There are scant references to this diabolic figure in the Scriptures, so millenarians have to rely on a composite image drawn from various Gospels, from 2 Thessalonians, where he appears as the 'man of sin', Revelation, where he features as the 'false prophet' branded with the number 666 who pretends to be the returned Christ, Daniel, where he is symbolised by a horrific beast with ten horns, and the Johannine epistles, the only place to use the term 'antichrist'. The consensus among prophecy writers is that Antichrist will manifest his awesome power in the world immediately preceding Christ's return. He will exalt himself above God and deceive the world's population into thinking him a force of good by performing 'signs and wonders' in grim parody of Christ.[18] Beyond this, Antichrist slips into the shadows beneath a welter of incidental detail.

Traditionally, the Antichrist has been understood to be a man, a secular leader who claims divine honours or a religious leader who affects Christ-like powers. Nero, Pompey, Saladin, the Pope, Charles I, Napoleon, Hitler and Moshe Dyan have all at one time or another done service as Antichrist in Christian demonology. Although this kind of demonic personification still fixes on specific individuals, a recent candidate being Saddam Hussein, these days Antichrist is, more often than not, understood to be corporate or governmental, perhaps as a comment on the tendency of secular institutions to arrogate the divine right of kingship to themselves. Beneath the façade of democratically structured organisations, Antichrist's reach is international, his mode of operation insidiously invisible and his ability to produce mass disorder unlimited. In that he aims to achieve absolute world dominion, anything which purports to be contributing to a New World Order may be immediately suspected of demonic origins, be it the American Government, the UN, the World Bank, or the IMF, acting alone or in sinister concert. European evangelicals, meanwhile, detect a sulphurous whiff about the EC. From his base in Geneva, British-born Reverend Michael Wieteska runs NATION (No Antichrist Territory In Our Nation), an anti-EC Christian pressure group which identifies the emergence of a united European superstate with Daniel's ten-horned beast. The fact that the EC acquired its eleventh member state in 1981 when Greece joined the Community, or that its membership has subsequently fluctuated, does not stop eschatologists viewing the member states as the ten horns of the beast. These, the Reverend Wieteska anticipates, will emerge clearly in an imminent shake-out that will leave only ten single-currency nations in a central position within the Community. The leader of this infernal multinational-economic hybrid will of course eventually be unmasked as Antichrist.

Wherever there is evidence of increased centralisation coupled with a disenfranchising of ordinary people, millenarians see the invisible hand of Antichrist at work. Electronic technologies are obvious antichristian tools in this regard, since their mode of operation so well accords with the idea of producing maximum disarray from a single nerve centre and their implications for social control are already abundantly manifest. One prophecy writer, priding himself on his code-cracking skills, has discovered that if A=6, B=12, C=18 and so on, the word COMPUTER spells 666. VISA cards, the bank account numbers of multinational corporations, social security numbers, fax returns and fibre optics top the current hit list of components of the antichristian global economy. All are depersonalising, all are master-minded by a tiny elite of scientifically minded businessmen and most of them, somehow or other, implicate the demonic number 666. In 1981, Mary Stuart Relfe, a wealthy widow and real estate developer from Alabama, wrote a book about 'the cashless commerce of the end time' that sold over 600,000 copies. Its central thesis was that the asterix and hash keys on telephone buttons are antichristian surveillance devices. The following year, she produced a bestselling sequel, *The New Money System 666*, this time homing in on the Universal Product Code, which neatly fits eschatological requirements by virtue of representing both the hidden centralisation of the demonic global economy and the power of Antichrist to divert people from God's truth using the narcotic of mindless consumerism.

Surveying the range of demonic instruments cited in contemporary prophecy literature, Boyer observes that it includes 'social, economic and technological processes so broad as to be almost coterminous with modernity itself'. This extraordinary compass of evil, he suggests, reflects a general unease about the direction and pace of change within modern society, focusing otherwise diffuse suspicions that somewhere along the road society took a turn for the malevolent.[19] However, at a deeper level, the literature on Antichrist seems to play to the same undercurrents of self-loathing that catastrophe tales manipulate so well. And it does so with great subtlety. Instead of crass obliteration, the idiom used to articulate the idea that humanity is its own worst enemy is one of conspiracy. However competent a schemer and sinister a machinator Antichrist may be and however omnipotent he may seem, the orchestration of his plot to effect our downfall ultimately relies on our complicity, witting or unwitting.

Conspiracy theories are supremely useful in helping millenarians identify who is and who is not in league with Antichrist. The remarkable thing about them – and in this regard they echo the latent ambiguity of apocalypse itself – is that they are infinitely adaptable, expandable and updatable; moreover, they can accommodate the most glaring contradictions. In the mother of all conspiracy theories, *The Protocols of the Elders of Zion*, we have the perfect model. What began life as a nineteenth-century anti-semitic Russian forgery, only to enjoy enduring credibility across Europe and beyond, gives powerful voice to the myth of the Jewish world conspiracy to achieve global domination. As modernity's answer to medieval Christian paranoia about Antichrist's Jewish identity, it posits the existence of a secret Jewish government led by an autodidactic Grand Master, which organises international affairs behind a camouflage of political parties, government agencies, media empires and financial institutions. In pursuit of their megalomaniacal objective, the shady conspirators undermine and support governments, incite and put down revolutions, promote both democracy and repression, and scheme with Bolsheviks and bankers alike. They are the authors of both the capitalist plot and the communist plot; indeed, their invisible handicraft underlies any plot you care to mention.[20] As a consequence of its unlimited scope for explaining forms of skulduggery fomented on opposite sides of political, economic and ideological divides, the myth saw active service in revolutionary France, Tsarist Russia and Nazi Germany. Today, and with a worrying degree of zeal, former Hereford United footballer David Icke is breathing new life into the *Protocols*.

Over the last decade or so, Icke's career has managed to take in almost every conceivable apocalyptic posture, beginning with the secular-rhetorical, moving through the New Age messianic and culminating in conspiracy theorist *extraordinaire*. In the late Eighties, as the Green Party's most high-profile spokesperson, Icke flew the banner for ecological reform and, to his credit, helped generate such concern for the future welfare of the planet that no political party in Britain was able to sell itself to the public without at least donning a hint of verdure. Suddenly in 1991, as a result of a mystical conversion, he stepped down from his public-service platform, began dressing from head to toe in turquoise ('the colour of love') and hinted, somewhat indelicately, that it had been disclosed to him from on high that he was none other than the son of God. Declaring his special mission in *The Truth Vibrations*, he maintained, in the best messianic tradition, that the 'truths' set out in his book were not of his own devising but were given to him 'by some of the most evolved beings in this solar system' – some of them residents of Uranus. In his incarnation as 'an aspect of the solar logos', he believed his destiny to lie in bringing about a spiritual revolution that would crown him 'cosmic parent' to the planet and all humanity. His message, so admirably adapted to our eco-anxieties, was that our roads, buildings and electricity pylons, as well as a global surfeit of 'dark emotions', were blocking the earth's natural energies, causing a build-up of pressure which, unless relieved, would burst forth in a spate of cataclysmic earthquakes, causing the world to end in 1998.

Lately, however, Icke seems to have dropped his messianic guise, ceased talking about the end of the world and embarked instead on a witch-hunt for global conspirators. In two recent books, *The Robot's Rebellion* and *and the truth shall set you free*, he peddles a host of plot mechanisms, ranging from bar-codes to micro-chip brain implants, and chases the elusive conspirators through a labyrinth of secret societies. All the usual suspects are there, the illuminati, the Freemasons, the CIA, the FBI and the IMF, as well as a few new ones like the Trilateral Commission and the Bildeberg Group.[21] A couple of years back, I heard him address a gathering of 500 or so people in London and, on that occasion, the now doddering former Foreign Secretary Lord Carrington was, for some reason, allocated pride of place in his demonology. Given the rapt attention of his listeners, I doubted they would share my appreciation of Umberto Eco's conspiratorial *reductio ad absurdum*: 'There exists a secret society which branches throughout the world, and its plot is to spread a rumour that a universal plot exists.'[22]

Icke's cosmology, a crude amalgam of New Age folklore, apocalypse and conspiracy theory, is not in itself unusual. What makes Icke interesting is the way in which he abandoned a reformist approach to social change in favour of a revolutionary apocalyptic. Impatient with the clunking inefficiency of bureaucratic machinery, he simply flipped into millenarian gear, swapping meliorism for a clean slate, and after failing to win sufficient recruits to his cause for renewal by taking on a messianic mantle, he stood down from his self-made pedestal to join the humble ranks of the righteous oppressed. Icke, of course, is extreme in every way, yet the evolution (if one can call it that) of his thought clearly demonstrates the degree to which religious, secular and popular millenarianism are busy cross-pollinating each other. In today's contorted world, where our fears are no less plausible for being opaque to reason and our hopes no less tangible for resting on the belief that they will be mysteriously or supernaturally fulfilled, Icke and others like him are assured of finding sympathetic audiences.

Contrary to what one might expect, the twentieth century is remarkable not for its millenarian excesses but for its millenarian restraint. With the exception of the present century, apocalyptic thinking has been a more or less continually integral feature of mankind's self-understanding. Alight on any era, not just the centuries' ends, and you will find people succumbing to its seductions or else weighing the odds of the species' continued survival against those of its demise and concluding that time had run out for mankind. Kings and paupers, spiritualists and mathematicians, rich and poor, old and young;

all have at one time or other harboured the conviction that their own day would see the global dénouement foretold long ago. And if Albert Schweitzer is to be given credence, Jesus himself was first and foremost an apocalyptic prophet in the Jewish tradition, come to announce that the Last Days were upon us. Yet the roots of apocalypse stretch back further still, for before the Jews turned to apocalypse as a means of assuaging their cosmic loneliness, the ancient Persian prophet Zoroaster began to dream of an almighty battle between good and evil whose righteous victors would inherit a new world.[23] There cannot be many other ways of accounting for the purpose of human existence dating from 1400 BC that continue to have currency today.

Since we stand on the cusp of the *fin de siècle* and the new millennium, a time of transition that is both the centre of a web of end-determined myths and a hotbed of millennial expectation, the moment is opportune for exploring those elements of apocalypse reverberating within culture at large. But first those elements need characterising. We need to thread back through the spiritual ancestry of today's millenarians, putting aside our contempt for their occasional resort to violence – understanding does not lead inexorably to approval – and find some way of approaching millenarians that makes sense of their permanence. We may not share their conceit of election, their stubborn certainties or their tendency towards a myopic reductionism, but we can share their desire for a new world, despair of the future and fear of finitude. The end of the world is as much a feature of our common stock of imaginings as it is of the millenarian's. In the process of turning over the multiple significances of the End, we will see that apocalypse has its own internal logic, a mythic logic, attuned to our deepest concerns about our destiny and our unconscious assumptions about the course of history and the progress of time. Perhaps, too, we ought to be prepared to countenance the view that what we are appraising in millenarianism is a mirror-image of our own commitments to life itself, a negative impression without which we would lack self-definition.

2. THE ULTIMATE DESTINATION

Our apocalypse began with a broken promise, a retraction of
love. Some ten centuries before the birth of Christ, God blessed
his chosen people, vowing to King David through the mouth of
the court prophet Nathan, 'And thine house and thy kingdom
shall be established for ever before thee: thy throne shall be
established for ever' (2 Sam. 7: 16). Nothing could be more
certain than a prophetic utterance, or more literally understood,
for given to the office of the *nabi*, or 'the one called', was the
spiritual responsibility of discerning God's will and of translat-
ing his cosmic counsel into historical reality. In the Temple in
Jerusalem, the ancient Israelites sang Psalms in celebration of
the Lord's pledge:

> I will not lie unto David.
> His line shall endure for ever,
> his throne as the sun before me.
> Like the moon it shall be established for ever,
> it shall stand firm while the skies endure.
> (Psalm 89: 35–7)

Yet four hundred years later the spiritually exalted but geographically insignificant kingdom of Judah was no more. It had fallen to Nebuchadnezzar's mighty Babylonian armies who stormed Jerusalem in 587 BC, razing its walls, burning the Temple to the ground and deporting the Israelite elite to Babylon. The last Davidic king, after being forced to watch the execution of his sons, had been blinded and led out of Jerusalem in chains to die in captivity. For ever proved to be short lived.

With the monarchy abolished, the prophets inherited leadership of a dispossessed and desperate people driven from a homeland they had expected to inhabit as long as the cosmos endured. Against a vision of perpetuity, the Israelites faced a reality of humiliation. Looking at the situation dispassionately, one might reasonably expect them to have given up faith in a God who had patently failed to safeguard their interests, who had deserted them in their hour of need and who, it ought to have been conceded, must be weaker than the patron gods of rival cultures. But if the Israelites had opted for the obvious rationalisation of the exile, their faith would have been extinguished there and then. What saved it was prophetic ingenuity. The prophets steadfastly refused to let national disaster compromise the standing of their one and only God. With cunning resourcefulness they turned the situation inside out by insisting that God himself had caused the Babylonian invasion in order to punish his people for their disobedience and infidelity. The exile was part of his providential plan. Having rescued the covenant framework of promise and fulfilment from appearances by adopting a radical monotheism, they drew on the inspiration of the Exodus to suggest that, if God had delivered his people from bondage once before, he could surely do so again and this time for good. As a result, at the very moment when God seemed to have abandoned history, prophecy took to imagining his grand re-entry into history. He would deliver his people, punish their enemies and bring the world to an end.

Thus was prophetic eschatology, the precursor of apocalypse, born. It was a theology tailor-made for an abandoned diaspora, and in it the Jews found a means of accounting for the catastrophic disparity between their votive expectations of national glory and the harsh truth of their miserable history. Henceforth, whenever reality seemed to stray from the path of destiny, as it did with Selucid occupation, Hellenisation, Roman invasion and the destruction of the Second Temple, apocalypse brought the pressure of an end to bear on everyday experience. It allowed the Jews to make sense of a present which otherwise defied comprehension, to transcend its disappointments and to feel the nearness of their future vindication. Its effect was one of reassurance.

For a religious observer or critic, as opposed to a believer, it is impossible not to question the extent to which the recommendations, proscriptions, explanations and imaginings of religion may fairly be taken to be a response to human needs, both circumstantial and psychological. Do its grand schemes of the way things work in the world accord with our little schemes? Do religious formulations ring true because they claim special authority or because they satisfy some basic or primal longing in us? Such questions have been addressed many times before. In *Moses and Monotheism* (1939), Freud argued that religion is the eternal search for the ideal father, the punitive but loving masculine hero. Marx's notorious assertion that religion is the opiate of the masses is even more suggestive for implying an intoxication that is both nullifying and unhelpfully addictive. Then there is Durkheim's contention that religion is a kind of social connective tissue, binding us together in free-will submission to moral law, much as the invisible force of gravity maintains the solar system in dynamic tension. While speculations of this kind tend to be tangled up with projection – would Freud, for instance, have defined religion as a collective, obsessional neurosis were it not for his own oedipal struggles with his Yahwist inheritance? – they are extremely useful. They humanise the cosmic, attempting to discover the essence of what William James called 'the religious experience'. As such, their concern is not so much with religion *per se* as with the inner disposition of people, their peculiar conscience and impulses, and the feelings of incompleteness that characterise our relationship to whatever we happen to take as the divine. In terms of speculating in this manner with regard to apocalypse then, we might want to explore the sort of fit that exists between the theology of endings and the psychology of endings.

This is something Frank Kermode has studied, taking as a starting point the notion that a desire for closure is a basic feature of the human mind-set. In *The Sense of an Ending* (1966), he attributed our preoccupation with endings to a psychological need for consonance. The passage of time, whether it relates to life, history or the telling of a story, is imbued with meaning only if its structure, its journey from beginning to middle to end, is wholly concordant. Within this framework, the sense of an ending gives each moment its fullness. It follows that without the end lurking perpetually just around the corner, without it being somehow always on the edge of our consciousness, we are condemned to bewilderment and banality.

Kermode's masterstroke was to recognise that it is middles and not endings that require analytic attention. Endings, like beginnings, are cardinal points in time, significant markers. They are already replete with meaning. They can signify fulfilment or operate as figures for death. They are conclusions, destinations, limits and much more. In Aristotelian terms, they are final causes, capable of bestowing a purpose or *telos* on everything that has gone before. They also take shape in relation to beginnings. Indeed, the word 'end' is affiliated to the Greek 'anti', meaning opposite, which suggests that the end is more than a logical or poetic correlate to the beginning: its genealogy demands that it is actually prefigured in the beginning, that it is present or latent in the very act of creation. What we commonly refer to as a fitting end, therefore, is an ending that complements or mirrors the beginning and that satisfies the laws of harmony and aesthetics. The Biblical apocalypse is just such an ending, a repercussive reminder of the moment of creation. The stories modern astrophysics tells us about the universe are no less appreciative of the attractions of complementarity. If the universe cannot continue expanding, which it has apparently done since the Big Bang brought it into existence, it will contract into non-existence just as suddenly and violently. In the beginning the Big Bang, at the end the Big Crunch.

Middles, by contrast, lack form. They are indeterminate, meandering, unreliable. Because they are prone to drifting, we need to moor them in time by reference to beginnings and ends. Kermode makes this point with elegant simplicity by musing on the shortest possible middle that the psyche is able to grasp – the temporal beat contained in a *tick-tock*. Like all units of measuring time, *tick-tock* is a creation of the imagination, a fiction. So too is the perceived difference between the two sounds, between the upward lilt of *tick* and the bass tone of *tock*. It is this perception of difference that enables us to insert a pattern of expectation into the gap between them. The *tock* makes the interval between the two sounds a significant duration. For Kermode, *tick-tock* is a model of what we call a plot, though he is the first to admit that *tick* is a humble genesis and *tock* a feeble apocalypse, and that *tick-tock* does not allow much scope for story-telling. Nonetheless, even the most complex fictions we impose on passing time aim at conferring organisation, shape and rhythm on mere duration. Whether we are dealing with an elaborately constructed novel or with the various schemes of successive ages that we find in religious cosmology and secular historicism, our temporal fictions share with *tick-tock* a determination to give the middle concrete form. As Kermode puts it: 'They have to defeat the tendency of the interval between *tick* and *tock* to empty itself; to maintain within that interval following *tick* a lively expectation of *tock*, and a sense that however remote *tock* might be, all that happens happens as if *tock* were certainly following.' He concludes with a provocative announcement: 'time is not free, it is the slave of a mythical end.'[1]

As a literary critic, Kermode's primary concern was with writers and readers, with how individuals attempt to make sense of their own span on this earth. The duration that interested him most was the journey through life as it is refracted through literature and not the passage from this world to the next. Consequently, his most powerful example of his model in action is drawn from an extreme case of individualism – the life experience of Christopher Burney, a British agent who was imprisoned in occupied France during the Second World War. Alone in his cell and alternately preoccupied with hunger and the frustrations of being unable to escape self-encounter, Burney reinvented the world in order to preserve his humanity. With monastic self-discipline, he produced a metaphysics of his own adversity. He reinvented a theology of evil as privation, rediscovered a Neo-Platonic philosophy of light and, by wrestling with the day-to-day problems of survival (shall I eat my bread all at once, or space it out?), he formulated a theory of determinism and free will. On the emptiness of his reality, he imposed a fiction of plenitude. And, by improvising a clock using the shadow cast by a gable on a wall he could see through his tiny barred window, he gave that fiction a temporal bearing, a significance in relation to the hoped-for end of his plight. In *Solitary Confinement* (1952), which is a record of his experiences between the *tick* of his capture and the *tock* of his release, he wrote, 'One does not suffer the passing of empty time, but rather the slowness of the expected event which is to end it.'

The illustrative strength of this example lies in its suggestion that the more the middle has gone awry, the greater the need for an end which is imminent. Burney was living proof that, when deprived of meaning in life, the 'synthesising consciousness' does the work of replenishment. It restores directionality. There is clear correlation here between his experience of being torn out of the world and placed in captivity and the ancient Israelite experience of exile. Yet it was in solipsism that Burney reached for the myth of the end. If we are to throw greater light on the relationship between theology and contingency, the Jewish apocalypse and Jewish marginality, we need to ask whether what holds for individual psychology holds also for groups. And, if it does not, whether there are ways in which a parity can be manufactured, say, through the ritualisation of shared experience.

In talking about the phases of transition that occur in tribal rites of passage, anthropologists make use of the concept of liminality. Liminality, says Victor Turner, is like death. It denotes a period of invisibility and darkness, a spell in the wilderness. In a liminal period, society is unstructured: like the middle intervening between one significant moment in time and another, it lacks form. Its properties include transition, totality, anonymity, humility, sacredness, simplicity, the absence of property, status and rank, and the acceptance of pain and suffering. It is not unlike a controlled and temporary condition of exile. Tribal societies use liminal phases to make room for absolute submission to the authority of ritual elders who are charged with overseeing the passing of the group or society from one cultural state to another. Turner points out that, precarious as the liminal state is, being neither here nor there, betwixt and between, it possesses great potency because it reinforces a sense of *communitas*. (He uses the Latin *communitas* rather than community as a way of stressing the group ideal over group structure.)[2] We are all familiar with group-bonding, with the idea of the multitude acting in concert, moving with one heart and one soul towards a single goal, though we seldom trouble ourselves to analyse the passage quality in that movement. That passage, like the middle in Kermode's *tick-tock*, needs to be given ritual significance if the end is to signify the completion or consummation of a rite. And this is precisely what happened in prophetic eschatology, where prophets like Ezekiel and Isaiah stressed the unity of their people's plight as well as the uniqueness of their identity, and gave their common struggle symbolic depth by likening it to the Exodus.

But if prophetic eschatology gave the Jews a sense of *communitas* in the midst of their liminal confusion, making it possible for them to sing the Lord's song in a strange land, ultimately its vision of rescue was over-determined. That is to say, Ezekiel and Isaiah put *too much* organisation into the intolerable middle. It is important to understand exactly why prophetic eschatology failed if we are to grasp why apocalypse worked – and continues to work – and if we are to have a proper appreciation of the conditions under which there emerged a literature that has been relevant to the way we have explained history ever since, including the appearance of Christ.[3]

The Salvation Oracles of the book of Isaiah (chapters 40–55) represent prophetic eschatology at its most vivid and powerful. Some forty years into the Babylonian exile, when many Jews were displaying a worrying tendency to assimilate, the prophet known as Deutero-Isaiah insisted the community view itself as a disenfranchised people, as captives who, like the Israelites in ancient Egypt, would be delivered from bondage and restored to their homeland. His historicisation of Judaism allowed him to cite God's past intervention in history as a means of paving the way for a future integration of the cosmic vision into the lived reality of the people. The same hand that parted the Red Sea for Moses would dry up rivers and beat down mountains to clear a path for the exiles' passage out of Babylon. Isaiah presents God as an angry destroyer avenging his children: '*now I will cry like a travailing woman; I will destroy and devour at once. I will make waste mountains and hills, and dry up all their herbs; and I will make the rivers islands, and I will dry up the pools. And I will bring the blind by a way that they knew not; I will lead them in paths that they have not known: I will make darkness light before them, and crooked things straight*' (Isa. 42: 14–16). The cherished exiles could expect a radical transformation of the earth: 'For the Lord shall comfort Zion: he will comfort all her waste places; and he will make her wilderness like Eden, and her desert like the garden of the Lord; joy and gladness shall be found therein, thanksgiving and the voice of melody' (Isa. 51: 3). In an attempt to persuade his people that theirs was a God capable of imposing this kind of order on the present disarray, Isaiah stressed that this was the God who had created the world out of primordial chaos in the first place. The new Israel would be just as it was at the dawn of time. Her enemies, meanwhile, would be humiliated as they had formerly humiliated God's chosen. 'Kings shall be thy nursing fathers, and their queens thy nursing mothers; they shall bow down to thee, with their face toward the earth, and lick up the dust of thy feet ... And I will feed them that oppressed thee with their own flesh; and they shall be drunken with their own blood, as with sweet wine' (Isa. 49: 23–6).

As a means of shoring up his argument that the humiliation of exile was proof that God had given Israel to her spoilers because he was preparing her for a more glorious history, Deutero-Isaiah named a saviour. This sort of specificity was of a piece with prophetic tradition in that prophecy had always expressed itself in relation to history, that world of political machinations, social organisation and human welfare which had customarily served as the canvas on to which God's will might manifest itself as action. Accordingly, Cyrus, the king of Persia, was to have the honour of delivering the Jews. Isaiah claimed that God had especially groomed him for this role: 'I have raised him up in righteousness, and I will direct all his ways: he shall build my city, and he shall let go my captives, not for price nor reward' (Isa. 45: 13). This was one of those rare occasions when history obliged prophecy, because a few years later Cyrus overthrew the Babylonian empire and granted the Jews permission to return home. However, things did not proceed in quite the way that Isaiah imagined. To begin with, a considerable number of Jews elected to remain in Babylon – many were second-generation exiles who had carved out a comfortable existence for themselves and had never set foot in Judah. Those who did choose to return straggled back gradually, in dribs and drabs. There was no great in-gathering of the Tribes of Judah and nothing like the triumphant mass exodus that Isaiah had described. A divinely orchestrated drama simply did not materialise, the mountains stood firm and the desert remained as hostile a terrain as ever to cross. Moreover, while Judah was granted religious autonomy, it remained shackled to Cyrus as a Persian territory. National independence, never mind glory, was not to be.

The spiritual assimilation of this prophetic failure cut in two opposing directions. On the one hand, it gave rise to the religion of law and order, associated with the scribe Ezra, who was empowered by Cyrus to take pastoral charge of rehabilitating the exiles and of overseeing the rebuilding of the Temple. The 'Law of Ezra', whereby all Jews in Syria-Palestine were called to strict religious observance, was immediately implemented. Here was another means of increasing the sense of *communitas* among the Jews, but through solid ritual practice not the encouragement of a shared hope. On the other hand, the community's various prophets continued to cling to a future-oriented and utopian theology of escape. The followers of Deutero-Isaiah, responsible for writing chapters 55–66 of the Book of Isaiah – effectively an apologia for their leader – foretold of God creating 'new heavens and a new earth' (Isa. 65: 17), only 'soon' rather than 'now', while Haggai and Zechariah persisted in nuturing dreams of national independence, championing the Persian-appointed governor of Jerusalem, Zerubbabel ben Shealtiel, as heir to the Davidic throne. As the years wore on, most people submitted to Ezra's flat religion of expediency. In times of relative peace, the everyday care of cult and community took precedence, sometimes to an obsessive degree, over salvation theology. But the next time the Jews had cause to pray for their deliverance, during the Selucid occupation in the middle of the second century BC, prophetic eschatology gave way to apocalypse, whose relationship to history is far more complex: although the world of events retains religious significance, it loses every vestige of its power to affect Jewish destiny.

The Book of Isaiah contains all the central motifs of apocalypse in rudimentary form. It relates how the Jews will be vindicated, exalted and restored to a transformed Israel, a paradisiacal neo-Eden overflowing with milk and honey, in passages of lyrical beauty that lie cheek by jowl with terrifying

descriptions of how the wicked (everyone else) will be humiliated, enslaved and tortured. Where it differs from apocalypse
fundamentally is in communicating its message directly. Isaiah
employs a plain, guileless language that hints at the innocent
conviction, shared by the prophets responsible for writing it,
that history would be the instrument of the Jews' deliverance.
As they were later developed in the Book of Daniel and the
extra-canonical apocalypses of Enoch, Jubilees and Baruch, the
twin themes of vindication and vengeance are articulated within
a complex system of symbols and syntax coherent enough to
constitute what may be thought of as an alternative symbolic
universe. It may well be the case that such a cryptic form of
communication befits the revelation of secrets known previously only in heaven. Yet behind the visionaries' withdrawal
from realism and flight into mythopoeic fantasy lies a profound
disillusionment with history as the medium through which
salvation would be effected.

Time and again history had proved to be the enemy of
prophecy. On a practical level, it had abolished the political
institutions which gave the prophets a foothold in social affairs.
But, more importantly, it had persistently confounded their
prophecies. Cyrus had not turned out to be the eschatological
saviour that Deutero-Isaiah claimed him to be, and Zerubbabel
did not inherit the Davidic mantle as Zechariah and Haggai
had predicted. Everywhere, the realm of plain history, real
politics and human instrumentality had betrayed a reluctance
to serve as the context in which God's divine promises would
find fulfilment. The apocalyptic visionaries were not going to
be similarly outmanoeuvred by the world of events. They would
not err as the prophets had done by unwittingly attaching a

sell-by date to their predictions. Apocalyptic eschatology therefore shifted the entire drama of salvation on to the cosmic plain
and in so doing it respiritualised Judaism. By offering a timeless
vision of God's cosmic saving acts, it offered the Jewish people
a fail-safe escape from the perpetual difficulties of having to
square God's glorious promise of deliverance with an increasingly harsh reality.

In order to lend credence to a series of salvation scenarios so
far removed in shape and form from any known experience of
reality, the apocalyptists employed all manner of literary
tropes.[4] One such was the device of pseudonymity. We shall
never know the identities of the writers of apocalypse, because
they took the greatest care to cover their tracks. They wrote
under the names of wise men and ancient patriarchs, such as
Daniel, Enoch and Baruch, scrupulously reporting any event
that succeeded the time of their chosen persona in the future
tense. This technique had the desired effect of making the
turbulent events of recent history look like the mechanical
unfolding of some preordained plan that had been vouchsafed
to the ancient sages, but had subsequently been 'sealed up' until
that moment. The past was thus emptied of any salvific
potential. Neither history nor human instrumentality was
accorded any cosmic significance. No longer a chain of causes
and effects, history was demoted, becoming simply a chronicle
of how divine will had been opposed and frustrated by demonic
powers. The ultimate compensation for the obstructiveness of
history, however, was the assurance that some time soon it
would cease. At the same time, the present, or moment of
revelation, took on the strategic importance of being the point
of transition between past and future. And what a future it

would be. Divine will would reassert itself, obliterating evil for ever, stars would fall from the sky, cosmic warriors would do battle with the demon hosts who played havoc with the lives of mortals, wheels of fire would steer their course of destruction, rivers of blood would flow and cities would crumble. The faithful need have no fear for they would eventually luxuriate in a new paradisiacal order, but the wicked ought to tremble in the knowledge that, come Judgement Day, they would be condemned to everlasting torment and much gnashing of teeth in the fiery pit of Sheol, a precursor of hell.

Another device employed by apocalyptists was mediation. They learned of the shape of things to come as a result of dreams, visions, heavenly journeys or from the mouths of angels. And they communicated that knowledge in a descriptive and pictorial form – in a mediated language. Anyone familiar with classical prophecy will note the absence of reported speech in apocalypse; God did not speak to the visionaries directly, as he had once spoken to the prophets. In historical terms such a removal indicates how much the gap between heaven and earth had widened since Deutero-Isaiah's day.

The Book of Daniel, which is the only Jewish apocalypse to have won canonical status, employs all of these tropes. We know that it was written, probably by several authors, between 169 and 165 BC, around the time of the Maccabaean revolt against the oppressive regime of the Selucid Antiochus Epiphanes, yet it purports to be written by a single man who was supposed to have lived during the Babylonian exile of the sixth century. Its apocalyptic visions take the mediating form of allegorical dreams. And whereas Deutero-Isaiah named the people's saviour, Daniel introduces a saviour type, the mysterious 'Son of man' or 'Messiah the Prince', a quasi-human, quasi-divine instrument who is to appear at the end of time to rescue God's chosen people from a war-ravaged and corrupted world. The figure of the Messiah may be understood as an elaboration of the ideal Davidic king spoken of by the post-exilic prophets and the 'anointed one' of Isaiah, but also, somewhat more subtly, as a variation on the theme of mediation. Just as a noble delegation of angels mediated divine goodness, and a clutch of demon spirits and monsters powered the engine-house of evil, so, in a cosmos from which God had removed himself, the role of saviour is deputised to the Son of man.

Daniel contains several apocalypses, the first and best known being 'Nebuchadnezzar's dream' which Daniel is called to decipher. The great king dreams of a fabulous statue whose 'head was of fine gold, his breast and his arms of silver, his belly and thighs of brass, his legs of iron, his feet part of iron and part of clay'. This is smashed to pieces by a stone. The various metals and the clay become 'like the chaff of the summer threshing floors and the wind carried them away', while the stone 'became a great mountain, and filled the whole earth' (Dan. 2: 32–5). Daniel explains that the various body parts of the statue represent four kingdoms, the first and strongest being Nebuchadnezzar's. The last and weakest kingdom represents that of Alexander the Great, which will appear to be as strong as iron, though it is in fact riven by internal divisions, hence the mixing of iron with clay. Finally the stone is a signal from God that he will 'set up a kingdom, which shall never be destroyed: and the kingdom shall not be left to other people, but it shall break in pieces and consume all these kingdoms, and it shall stand for ever' (Dan. 2: 44). Nebuchadnezzar, duly humbled by learning of the great Jewish kingdom to come, offers the highest compliment a polytheist can muster and acknowledges Daniel's God as a 'God of Gods'.

The organisation of passing time into a succession of four declining ages symbolised by metals appears in the Zoroastrian apocalypse, the *Bahman Yasht*, where the image is a tree rather than statue, with metallic branches of gold, silver, steel and iron, each denoting a period of 3000 years. It entered ancient Greek thought in the eighth century via Hesiod, who in *Work and Days* spoke of races of gold, silver, bronze and iron.[5] Daniel transforms these ages into evil kingdoms that persecute the Jews, but he also introduces a fifth kingdom, a new golden age representing God's kingdom on earth. This was a more grandiose vision of restoration than that dreamed of by Deutero-Isaiah, in that instead of being limited to Israel, Daniel's everlasting kingdom covers the whole earth. Daniel's second apocalypse is a variation on this theme, featuring four terrible monsters, one more hideous than the next, rising out of the sea. The last and fiercest of these beasts has great iron teeth and ten horns, and as Daniel studies its fearful aspects there appears another 'little horn'. In the next vision of the ram and the goat, Daniel reports that the little horn 'magnified himself even to the prince of the host, and by him the daily sacrifice was taken away, and the place of his sanctuary was cast down' (Dan. 8: 11). This appears to be a reference to Antiochus Epiphane, who forbade the Jews the observance of the Sabbath and the offering of sacrifices, and forced them to pay homage to Syrian gods in the Jerusalem Temple. Daniel goes on to announce that it will be 2300 days before the sanctuary is cleansed. Other cryptic periods follow; there are to be seventy weeks for the reparation of sin and 1335 days to the end of time, when the Messiah will come. Daniel sees 'one like the Son of man came with the clouds of heaven ... and there was given him dominion, and glory, and a kingdom, that all people, nations, and languages, should serve him: his dominion is an everlasting dominion, which shall not pass away, and his kingdom that which shall not be destroyed' (Dan. 7: 13–14).

In mythologising eschatology, the Book of Daniel and the extra-canonical, or Pseudepigraphal, apocalypses offered Jews a more promising way than prophetic eschatology had done of keeping alive hope for an imminent and final vindication in that they resisted historical disconfirmation. Whereas prophetic eschatology was subjected to the trials of standing or falling with the unfolding of predicted events, apocalpyse's graphic transcendent types spoke of a higher reality that history could, at best, merely shadow. Put another way, apocalypse inserted a timeless quality into the interval between *tick* and *tock*. Thus, if one set of historical circumstances and identifications proved not to fit with its visionary scenarios, the Jews could always project their hopes on to the future and pray that their prophecies would soon be fulfilled. Yet for all this clever adaptability, and despite the continuing tragedy of their history, by the end of the first century of the common era the Jews had all but abandoned apocalypse. Why?

The centuries sandwiching the birth of Christ were troubled times for the internal development of the Jewish faith, times of schism and unprecedented sectarianism. Yet working against the fragmenting tendencies of factionism there were frequent moves to re-establish unity in the face of Hellenisation and Roman occupation. Such clarion calls were often apocalyptic, not least because of the literature's nationalistic slant. Most of the Pseudepigraphal apocalypses date from this period and, for the first time, they were used to sanction a messianic *praxis*. Indeed the period opened with many Jews hailing Judas Maccabaeus as the Messiah after he had successfully fought the armies of Antiochus Epiphanes and liberated the Temple. And it closed with the messianic ambitions of Shimeon Bar Kosiba, the military leader of the Second Revolt against the Romans (AD 132–5) who styled himself Bar Kokhba, meaning 'son of a star'. When not fighting battles, this larger-than-life character managed to find the time to re-strike a prodigious number of Roman coins, erasing the Emperor's head and replacing it with inscriptions like 'Year One of the Redemption of Israel' and 'Shimeon, Prince of Israel'. Fortunately for his detractors, his name lent itself to another pun – Bar Koziba, meaning 'son of a liar'.[6] Between the eschatological Maccabees and optimistic nationalism of Bar Kokhba, the messianic ferment of the period saw Judaea swarming with soothsayers and mystics, sibyls and itinerant preachers, seditious Galilaeans, Zealots and charismatic Nazarites like John the Baptist. A feverish time of discontent and insurrection, it spawned numerous local cults about whom nothing is known save the fact that the Romans crucified their leaders in an attempt to quell Jewish apocalyptic activism. Two sects to emerge from the general prophetic commotion were unusual for being almost as anti-Jewish as they were anti-Roman. This, however, was the only substantial thing that the Essenes, known to us from the Dead Sea Scrolls, and the Christians held in common. As for their destined ends, one sect met their fate in disappearance, while the other went on to change the course of history.

72

Every now and then, there emerges a scholar given to making the sensationalist claim that the Essenes were really Christians. To add to Australian theologian Barbara Thiering's flights of fancy, controversial scroll scholar Robert Eisenman has thrown two fat books into this particular ring. Both *The Dead Sea Scrolls Uncovered* (1992) and *James the Brother of Jesus* (1997) contend that James the Just was the sect's revered Teacher of Righteousness and that their arch-enemy, the Wicked Priest, was none other than Paul. Although there are undeniable similarities between the two sects, the fantasy of shared identity makes far too much of the small evidences of parity. It is true that both sects adopted celibacy, practised ritual baptism, pooled their wealth and taught penitence, poverty, humility and brotherly love. There is even a degree of textual correspondence between the Qumran Scrolls and the Gospels; both use such terms as 'sons of light' and 'the light of life' and refer to their own congregations as 'the many'. But their respective theologies, and in particular their apocalyptic, could not have been more different.[7]

In their self-imposed exile in the Judaean desert, the Essenes developed a militant apocalyptism. Their mental map drew a stark battle line between the righteous and the wicked, that is to say, between themselves and the rest of the world's inhabitants. They were to be the exclusive inheritors of the future Zion, Zephaniah's 'remnant of Israel'. On the other side of the eschatological fence were not only the Romans but the entire population of Judaea, who had acquiesced in the rule of the Wicked Priest (the consensus candidate is Jonathan Maccabaeus) and his Hasmonaean successors, whom the Essenes accused of defiling the Temple Cult. Indeed, they took the

Roman invasion to be an act of God designed to punish the wayward Jews of Judaea. Clearly, the Last Days had begun. Soon all non-Essene Jews would 'be handed over to the sword when the messiah of Aaron and Israel comes'. A catalogue of evil would then be visited upon the Romans before the true 'remnant' of Israel could claim Jerusalem for itself.

This apocalyptic, detailed in the *Damascus Document*, composed some time after Pompey's capture of Jerusalem in 63 BC, was augmented the following century by a more impatient eschatology. Under the oppressive prefects and procurators, the Essenes recovered a sense of nationalism, becoming less isolated, and began mobilising themselves for real-life battle against the Romans. Their campaign to repossess the promised land, outlined in the *War Scroll*, describes how the true Temple Cult would be restored within six years, then, how after a sabbatical seventh year, a forty-year war would defeat all the nations of the world, resulting in the 'everlasting dominion of Israel'. The Essenes' wildly unrealistic scheme to take on a sophisticated and well-rehearsed army that vastly outnumbered them exemplifies the dangers that lie in wait for those who subscribe heart and soul to an apocalyptic faith which demands belief in a higher order of reality and banishes the concrete world to the realm of shadows. Despite a dismal record of repeated back-firings, such self-aggrandising military ambitions have been regularly cherished by apocalyptic sects, most recently David Koresh's Branch Davidians. Yet this military bravado does make some kind of sense in view of the thorough-going mystic Persian dualism that the Essenes (and the later Christian apocalyptists) relied upon. In that a mighty squadron of angels was conjured into existence to weigh in on the side of the just, the Essenes' holy war was not to be a battle of man-to-man combat but cosmic conflict on the grandest scale between the righteous 'sons of light', aided by a battalion of heavenly warriors, and the wicked 'sons of darkness', behind whose every move the hand of Satan might be discerned. The two sides would be evenly matched, a victory for Satan's army being followed by a supra-Essene triumph until, in the seventh sparring round, 'the great hand of God is raised in an everlasting blow against Satan and all the hosts of his kingdom'. Needless to say, the Essenes' actual involvement in the Jewish war against the Romans in AD 66–71 proceeded very differently. It led to the sect's complete extinction.

The apocalyptic of Jesus, for all its gentleness and professed humility, was far more threatening to Jewish integrity. For one thing, not a trace of nationalism existed within it. Jesus rejected the messianic mantle of Daniel's Son of man. He was not to be the warrior-king or saviour hero who would defeat Israel's enemies, but rather the 'anointed one' of Isaiah, sent 'to preach good tidings unto the meek ... to bind up the broken-hearted, to proclaim liberty to the captives, and the opening of the prison to them that are bound; to proclaim the acceptable year of the Lord, and the day of vengeance of our God' (Isa. 61: 1–2). It is said that when Jesus read this passage as the lesson in the synagogue at Nazareth, he added: 'Today, in your very hearing this text has come true.' Like other charismatics and apocalyptic prophets, he encouraged the Jews to prepare for the imminent coming of the kingdom of God: repent and be saved, said the Nazarene. In this, his basic message accorded with traditional Judaism. But the mode of his preparation for the kingdom was hostile in the extreme. It called for a complete suspension of the law in the name of God's infinite love. The road to salvation lay not in obedience and ritual observance but in the practice of filial duty, the showing of boundless compassion to the poor, the renunciation of self and the courting of sinners and publicans. Satan would be conquered by love and by sacrifice rather than through armed struggle.

It was as a direct result of rejecting Jesus' messianship that the Jews ultimately rejected apocalypse. Enoch's 'Similitudes', thought to have been composed some time in the middle of the first century, attempted a riposte to Christianity, styling the still-expected messiah as the 'Elect One'. 'He is the light of the gentiles and he will become the hope of those who are sick in their hearts. All those who dwell upon the earth shall fall and worship before him.'[8] No Jewish messiah before this had appealed to gentiles or explicitly commanded worship. And none would do so again. The fact that the vast bulk of apocalyptic literature was relegated to the Pseudepigrapha when the Hebrew canon came to be established towards the end of the first century is a concrete reminder that this critical edit of God's book was geared towards granting no more than a nominal acceptance of apocalypse. In the aftermath of Titus' destruction of the Second Temple in AD 71, the need for a united Jewish faith was greater than ever. Messianic activism had always led to increased sectarianism, but with Christianity it had created a monster – an alternative faith. Christianity's precipitation out of Judaism, its rejection of the synagogue for the new *communitas* of the *ecclesia*, provided an example of messianism-in-action that made it difficult to regard messianic hope as anything other than the slippery slope that led inexorably to apostasy. As a result, no normative interpretation of messianism was formulated. In the Midrash Rabbah, there is a passage where Rabbi Akiba rushes excitedly to Rabbi Jonathan ben Tortha to tell him of Bar Kokhba. 'This is the King Messiah!' he cries. Ben Tortha's withering reply is, 'Akiba, grass will grow in your cheeks and he will still not have come.' Beneath the levity lies a warning not to expect too much and not to expect it too soon. As Amos Funkenstein has observed, the best messianic doctrine the Rabbinate could adopt was none at all. The vaguer the criteria, the less room there was for an actualising interpretation such as Christianity to emerge out of the Jewish tradition.[9] A new balance of priorities consistent with banishing the eschatological horizon to the never-never land of the distant future came into effect. Emphasis was placed on Judaism's this-worldly orientation in accordance with a perennial deferral of the messianic advent. The only hope permissible was literally hope eternal.

Though, in many ways, Jewish history is an exercise in the prolonged endurance of life without a messiah, the tiny chink of hope expectant that Daniel permits has always been kept open. It is even implicitly acknowledged in modern-day funerary practices, which veto cremation in view of the bodily resurrection that will accompany the final restoration. Nor has Jewish history been without its messianic moments; there was much casting about for suitable claimants when Palestine was invaded by the Persians in AD 614 and by the Mahometans in 637. And occasionally, as in the case of Sabbatai Zevi of Smyrna, or the Polish messiah Jacob Frank, for example, a fully-fledged messianism managed to get off the ground. But these were just distant echoes of turn-of-the-era sectarianism. In the wake of Christianity, Judaism essentially condemned itself to history even as it retained its utopian ideals. At times, this basic commitment to the possibility of creative dynamic change on this earth has itself taken messianic form – hence George Steiner's whimsical explanation of Marxism: Jews have often grown impatient, not of the Messiah being too long in coming but of being too long in not coming.[10]

One of the more intriguing modern outcrops of Jewish messianism is the Jews For Jesus movement, which currently claims between 20,000 and 50,000 members in the United States and several thousand more in Europe. The group's central belief that Jesus was the Messiah of Israel is underwritten by a complex theology which draws heavily on the Kabbalistic Zohar and involves reinterpreting the Hebrew Bible in light of a Jewish Christology. To take a simple example, the cardinal affirmation of Jewish monotheism as expressed in the first line of the Sh'ma reads, 'Hear, O, Israel, the Lord our God, the Lord is one.' An unambiguous statement, one would have thought. But the Jews For Jesus point out that in the Zohar the phrase 'YHVH Elohenu YHVH' substitutes for 'the Lord our God' – a clear indication of God's three-fold existence, of plurality in unity. Jews For Jesus are an odd bunch whose ecumenical reasoning is not dissimilar to that employed by the first-century sect of Jewish Christians. So they believe in the Trinity but celebrate Passover and if pressed for self-definition say that they are both Jews and Christians. Moreover, their messianism is unlike any other in that it is retrospective, at least in its overt claims. On a less obvious level, it does contain a certain futuristic element in that it seems to prepare the ground for arguing that the yet-to-be-manifest Jewish Messiah and the Christian Messiah of the Second Coming are one and the same. What are we to make of the Jews For Jesus? Are they merely the latest manifestation of Jewish self-hatred, of a bitter internal struggle that has its origins in Paul? Or are they just another example of the gradual drift from one faith to the other, another defection statistic to increase the alarm of the Jewish orthodox establishment? At the end of the day, however, whether their numbers rise or fall is by the by, because what makes them genuinely threatening to Judaism is that they mitigate one of the chief reasons the Jewish faith has remained intact for the past 2000 years – the rabbinical No to Jesus.

This original and definitive refusal had good foundation. The Jews could not overlook Jesus' lowly origins – his palpable non-Davidic descent – his confrontations with authority, rejection of the law and ultimately his ignoble death (nothing prepared them for a shamed Messiah). Yet even if they had found it within their capabilities to ignore all this, what precluded them from acknowledging the Nazarene as their messiah was that his coming changed nothing. And the Messiah must transfigure the earth. During his lifetime, Jesus had proclaimed far and wide that the kingdom of God was at hand and busied himself removing any obstacles in its way by wrestling with Satan, casting out demons, healing the blind and the lame, and by raising the dead. Even at the last supper, when he knew what his own fate was to be, he remained convinced that he had begun ushering in the new paradisiacal age. Mark, for instance, reports him as having announced to his disciples, 'Verily I say unto you, I will drink no more of the fruit of the vine, until that day that I drink it new in the Kingdom of God' (Mark 14: 25). Yet nothing had changed. Neither Roman rule, nor the persecution of Jews, nor the persecution of early

Christians. This brings us to the theological ingenuity of the Apostles. And to the serendipity of the resurrection, without which they, too, in all likelihood would not have been able to withstand Jesus' death. Not only did the resurrection offer proof of Jesus' divinity, but the necessity of rationalising it created an opportunity for a complete rewriting of the messianic function, one that spiritualised the concept of salvation, made of it an inward thing. Once Jesus was viewed as having delivered mankind from its bondage to sin and restored it to communion with God through his sacrificial death, it became possible to argue that the kingdom of God had indeed arrived, despite appearances.

If the Jewish rejection of Christ led to an insistence on the indefinite extensibility of passing time, early Christians effectively imported the end into the now. Anyone who accepted the Good News could enter the kingdom without delay. In their initial euphoria, early Christians became model citizens of God's kingdom, adopting celibacy, sharing their goods in common and spreading the teachings of Christ. The Holy Spirit seemed to be everywhere, filling disciples with the power to heal and preach, and aiding them to live virtuously. But Jesus had promised his followers eternal life and what they faced was a reality of persecution in which immortality could not even be metaphorised. If the faithful perceived themselves to be under threat, it was because it became increasingly difficult for them to sustain belief in an already redeemed world. Jesus' prophecies concerning the kingdom of God soon began to look very much like Deutero-Isaiah's prophecies of a triumphant return from exile: they were fulfilled, but not in the way that prophecy predicted. History had undermined fulfilment and so the problematic middle of passing time needed to be extended and reorganised. As a means of shutting out reality and keeping the kingdom alive, apocalypse beckoned. This is why the Gospels are full of references to Jesus' Second Coming, spine-chilling descriptions of the end-time tribulations and Pauline assurances that the faithful would be raptured, or carried up to heaven, beforehand. All are attempts to reassure Christians that Jesus' promises will not be broken. In other words, the Apostles recognised that if the new religion was going to survive its oppressors and hold its own against Jewish disavowal it needed a forceful eschatology of its own.

3. REVELATION REVISITED

The Revelation of St John the Divine is the best known, most
influential and most energetically disputed of apocalypses.
Though it is neither the first nor the last, it stands in a class of
its own. It is the by-word for apocalypse, not just in the context
of religion, but within literature, art and popular culture. In
officially providing the divinely ordained 'happily ever after' to
Genesis' 'once upon a time', Revelation has been a touchstone
for millenarians past and present, throughout Christendom and
beyond, while it has supplied the rest of us, the uninitiated as it
were, with what the late Northrop Frye called 'our grammar of
apocalyptic imagery'.[1] Few people are unfamiliar with the basic
syntax, the thousand-year reign of earthly bliss, the wicked
Antichrist and the heroic Faithful and True. Babylon, Armageddon and New Jerusalem have come to occupy as significant a
place on the conceptual atlas as heaven and hell, and the
diabolical digits 666 seem to crop up everywhere, lurking
cryptically in the names of tyrannical world leaders and, more
insidiously, according to certain paranoid elements within the
American fundamentalist movement, in the universal bar-code
or the insignia, names and bank account numbers of multi-

national corporations. In the popular imagination, the entire Jewish apocalyptic tradition in all its richness has been eclipsed by the succinct twenty-two chapters that constitute the Book of Revelation.

Whatever else may be said for the book, it invariably provokes an extreme response. For every millenarian prepared to stake their life on the belief, recently expressed by the sleuth-like monk in Umberto Eco's *Name of the Rose*, that 'the book of John offers the key to everything!', hundreds of others would close ranks with George Bernard Shaw, who confidently dismissed it as 'the curious record of the visions of a drug addict'. Outside of learned circles, the fundamental debate around Revelation is not about what sort of sense it makes, but about whether it makes sense at all. Despite taking its name from the Greek *apocalypsis*, meaning to 'unveil' or 'uncover', which implies that its essential promise is enlightenment, its complex character – its confusing recapitulative form and its colourful language, thick with obscure metaphors and arcane symbolic imagery – seems to suggest that it was contrived solely for the purposes of mystification. Such an exaggeratedly Biblical disparity between promise and fulfilment qualifies Revelation as one of those rare pieces of literature that manages to remain almost as much of an enigma to those who have read and reread it as to those whose knowledge of the book comes second-hand from hearsay alone. But therein lies its peculiar and paradoxical charm. If anything, its stubborn impenetrability has enhanced its reputation, lending the book an air of mystery and profundity, a unique aura, which ensures that whether regarded as a pearl of the wisdom tradition or as a stream of hallucinatory clap-trap it emerges with its mystique intact.

That such intrigue has attached itself to a book so readily and widely available is in one sense remarkable. Pick up any Bible and Revelation is open to inspection. It's not as if you skip through the Gospels and Acts, persevere stoically with Paul, gathering pace with the Catholic Epistles, only to come up sharp against lock and key or an ingenious variety of hermetic seal. The problem is not a matter of being able to read it, but of knowing *how* to read it. In promising to disclose cosmic secrets while at the same time erecting multiple barriers to any commonsense understanding of them, Revelation issues a challenge, it baits the reader. This, coupled with the fact that the book makes near enough the same claims for itself as Eco's monk makes on its behalf, is irresistible enticement to countless would-be initiates, from believers to the casually curious, who religiously (in all senses of the word) comb its every line in the hope of perceiving some light through its obfuscating mists. Yet its very attractions present another problem, for the book of John has been over-read, exhausted by the strain of non-stop excavation. Competing interpretations, theological, academic, sectarian and plain wild, many extending to multi-volume editions, have accumulated around it like so many layers of intractable, solidified dust: the detritus of two millennia, for Revelation has been the object of obsessive study since the day its ink dried.

For a book whose posterity has been so superlative, its origins are more than a little obscure – even the date of its composition is something of a moveable feast, though the majority of accounts fix on AD 96. Most of the early Church fathers believed, wrongly as it turned out, that Revelation was the work of the apostle John, son of Zebedee, which might explain why the book managed, amid much controversy, to scrape into the canon. Its real author is the rather shadowy and altogether more volatile John of Patmos, about whom only the barest biographical details survive, and these relate principally to his comings and goings. Legends about him abound, however, including a story of how he miraculously survived being plunged into a cauldron of boiling oil on the orders of the Emperor Domitian. This so angered the Roman that he apparently exiled John to the Island of Patmos. John is also said on his return to Ephesus to have raised a woman called Drusiana from the dead and, with gender politics worthy of Paul, promptly instructed her to prepare him a home-coming meal. These and other wondrous acts are preserved in Jacobus de Voragine's *The Golden Legend* – the hugely popular medieval collection of the lives of the saints.[2]

What we know with certainty is that John was a native of Ephesus, home to one of the largest Christian communities in the Roman province of Asia, and that he penned Revelation on Patmos, to which he had either been banished for some offence against the authorities or which he visited on a preaching tour. Whatever the reason for his stay on Patmos, being there seemed to encourage his faith and assure him of the enemy's imminent demise. Even today, the ruins at Patmos are strangely suggestive of the bizarre amalgam of piety and megalomania that suffuses John's testament and makes his message all the more vivid.

Even the most cursory read of the book, one that serves simply to gauge its mood and tempo, throws light on its enduring appeal. There is an immediacy and urgency about it that speaks to the modern reader as eloquently as it spoke to urban Christians in Asia during the reign of Domitian. In driving its message home, it relies heavily on that well-known rhetorical ruse beloved of speechifiers, namely repetition. But beyond the impression that John is insistently trying to communicate something extremely important, things start to get complicated. What begins as an epistle dictated by the risen Christ to the seven churches in Asia rapidly flowers into a story of mythic proportions. One minute John is urging the churches to be steadfast in their faith so as to withstand the terrible tribulations soon to come – for 'the time is at hand' – the next he is moving in a world populated by demons, dragons, brides and whores, blazing angels and man-eating beasts, Christ and Antichrist. As if this were not taxing enough for newcomers to the book, John is at the same time being transported ecstatically back and forth between the present world and the world to come, and up and down between heaven and earth. Somehow, though, all these disparate elements are expertly interwoven into a seamless whole, a rapturous, visionary outpouring whose undifferentiated totality is perhaps best captured in musical terms. With its contrapuntal harmonies and fast and furious rhythm, the action most nearly resembles a fugue; the story, meanwhile, rather than being carried by a single-strain melody, is effectively sung in rounds, each element in John's complex orchestration making a contribution to the unfolding of the narrative.[3]

The first of these rounds is denoted by seven seals and begins when John, in the higher state of consciousness symbolised by being 'in the spirit', is beckoned up to heaven to witness a resplendent scene of heavenly worship in which white-robed elders and marvellous beasts with innumerable eyes offer praise to God. In his right hand, God holds a 'book sealed with seven

seals', each of which discloses either earthly destruction or a
heavenly scene, but since no one is found worthy to open the
book, the worship is interrupted and John collapses, weeping.
One of the elders comforts him, saying, 'weep not: behold, the
Lion of the tribe of Judah, the Root of David, hath prevailed to
open the book' (Rev. 5: 5). But when John looks up he sees not
a lion but 'a lamb as it had been slain'. This symbolic reversal
is the first of many affirmations that suffering and death lead
to conquest: the lamb *is* the lion; Christ's testimony lies as
much in his death as in his word. This, of course, is the vision
of the martyrs, for whom true life could only be bought by
dying. Indeed, when the lamb opens the fifth seal, John sees
'the souls of them that were slain for the word of God, and for
the testimony which they held ... and white robes were given
unto every one of them; and it was said unto them that they
should rest yet for a little season, until their fellow-servants also
and their brethren, that should be killed as they were, should
be fulfilled' (Rev. 6: 9–11).

With the breaking of the first four seals, the four horses of
the apocalypse are set loose on the earth to inflict war, famine,
death and plague. And with the breaking of the sixth, a string
of catastrophes representing the 'wrath of the Lamb' succeed
them. The sun is extinguished, the moon turns to blood, stars
fall from the sky and the whole of heaven rolls up like a scroll.
At this point John sees a vision of the 'hundred and forty and
four thousand of all the tribes of the children of Israel' (Rev. 7:
4), who receive 'the seal of the living God'. This seal is a sort of
quality-control stamp, prominently displayed on the foreheads
of the righteous as a sign to the heavenly host that they should
eventually join the martyrs in heaven. Shooting forward to this

glorious day, John sees a 'great multitude' standing before God's throne and is told that 'these are they which came out of great tribulation, and have washed their robes, and made them white in the blood of the lamb'. These specially favoured children of God receive the gift of immortality and assurances that they 'shall hunger no more, neither thirst any more; neither shall the sun light on them, nor any heat. For the Lamb which is in the midst of the throne shall feed them, and shall lead them unto living fountains of waters: and God shall wipe away all tears from their eyes' (Rev. 7: 14, 16–17).

The opening of the seventh seal discloses a throne scene, which initiates another round of seven events, this time symbolised by trumpets, at the end of which the heavenly service of before is resumed. The sounding of the first six trumpets heralds another spate of earthly tribulations and introduces us to a number of John's *dramatis personae*. In particular, there's the fallen angel who holds 'the key of the bottomless pit' (Rev. 9: 1) where Satan will eventually be bound, and the two witnesses who shall 'prophesy a thousand two hundred and three score days, clothed in sackcloth' (Rev. 11: 3), before being killed by Satan for preaching God's truth. Being people of God, however, the witnesses are resurrected and ascend to heaven on a cloud. Then an angel appears to John and reads him secrets concerning the end of time from an open scroll, which John is instructed to eat. He also informs his charge that when the seventh trumpet is sounded 'the mystery of God should be finished' (Rev. 10: 7). A good deal of suspense thus precedes the last trumpet blast, which announces the arrival of God's kingdom on earth and the opening of the heavenly temple.

With the close of the trumpet cycle, a sequence of action

that runs from tribulation through to salvation and judgement is completed, only to be immediately repeated, this time as a colourful potted version of the ancient Near Eastern combat myth. The sequence begins when the pregnant 'woman clothed with the sun' fights the great red dragon, later revealed to be the Devil, and ends when the archangel Michael takes up her cause, casting the dragon and his demonic host out of heaven. At this point an angel declares, 'now is come salvation, and strength, and the kingdom of our God', and we learn that the dragon had been overcome not by might but by 'the blood of the Lamb, and by the word of their testimony' (Rev. 12: 10–11). All may be well in heaven, but on earth the exiled dragon persecutes the mortal counterpart of the heavenly woman and inaugurates a reign of terror during which time he amasses great power. He champions two beasts, one a sea-monster with seven heads who gains sway over 'all kindreds, and tongues, and nations' (Rev. 13: 8), and another whose number is 666 (Rev. 13: 18). This is the Antichrist or false prophet, who 'doeth great wonders ... and deceiveth them that dwell on the earth by the means of those miracles' (Rev. 13: 13–14). Besides being the source of the New World Order that millenarians everywhere are intent on exposing and opposing, Satan's earthly sojourn demonstrates the parity that exists between events in heaven and events on earth. It is a parity that is echoed in the Lord's Prayer. Many Christians may not know it, but when they recite 'Thy kingdom come. Thy will be done, on earth as it is in heaven', they are effectively calling for not only the overthrow of the Devil but also the end of the world.

Somewhat confusingly, the final terrestrial battle to defeat the forces of darkness now ruling the world is described three times and in three different ways. But the effect on the reader is cumulative, so that by time Christ appears in the clouds flanked by his heavenly host expectation is at its peak. In the first account, there is the pouring of the 'seven golden vials full of the wrath of God', which culminates in the battle of Armageddon. With tremendous gusto, John relates how devil worshippers are plagued with festering sores and scorched by fire before all the seas and rivers turn to blood and the entire world is plunged into darkness. Armageddon, the subject of so much millenarian mythologising, is in fact skirted over quite perfunctorily:

> For they are the spirits of devils, working miracles, which go forth unto the kings of the earth and of the whole world, to gather them to the battle of that great day of God Almighty. Behold, I come as a thief. Blessed is he that watcheth, and keepeth his garments, lest he walk naked, and they see his shame. And he gathered them together into a place called in the Hebrew tongue Armageddon (Rev. 16: 14–16).

That is all. The next verse has God's voice booming out from the temple in heaven announcing, 'It is done'. It is hard to imagine a more economical description of an almighty battle, especially one claiming as many casualties as the world has to offer. Yet nothing has preoccupied millenarians so much as the finer details of this military assault on Satan. And nothing has earned them more reproach than their longing for its commencement.

The second description of the last battle is allegorical and highly imagistic. It introduces one of John's most famous characters, the whore of Babylon, who is 'arrayed in purple and scarlet colour, and decked with gold and precious stones and pearls, having a golden cup in her hand full of abominations and filthiness of her fornication' (Rev. 17: 4) (see plate 2). This gaudy strumpet inebriates herself on the blood of the martyrs and rides a scarlet beast, which may be identified as Rome by its seven heads, which represent the seven hills of the city. In historical terms, Rome's fate as Babylon was sealed when her armies destroyed Jerusalem in AD 70 and subsequently ratified by her persecution of early Christians. Later generations of millenarians at odds with the Church, meanwhile, were able to retain the identification by virtue of the fact that the Imperial colours of purple and scarlet were adopted by Church cardinals. But this is to run ahead of matters. In Revelation, the beast has ten horns, which represent ten wicked kings who make war with the Lamb. When it becomes clear to them that they are fighting a losing battle, they turn against the whore, strip her naked, eat her flesh and set her alight. As she smoulders in raging fires, the whole of heaven rejoices, crying, 'Babylon the great is fallen, fallen' (Rev. 18: 2).

The final account of the last battle is the only one to detail actual events. It begins when the heavens open to reveal Christ, clad in blood-drenched robes, sitting on a white horse. On his thigh is inscribed the name 'King of Kings and Lord of Lords'. This is the cosmic warrior-Christ of the Second Coming, who leads the heavenly cavalry to victory against the beast and his mortal minions, flinging the Antichrist into a lake of brimstone and slaying the wicked remnant by the 'sword which proceeded out of his mouth'. Once again there is a symbolic reversal at play here: just as the lamb *is* the lion, so the word *is* the sword. In the interchangeability of word and sword, the Crusaders (and many a millenarian cult since) found a solid basis for rationalising the pursuit of holy war. If Christian martyrs could take inspiration from 'Faithful and True', who 'in righteousness ... doth judge and make war', then violence, brutality and bloodshed become compatible with the true spirit of the faith, as well as a legitimate means of ushering in the Millennium. As with Armageddon, John rather brushes over the Millennium, or 'first resurrection'. After claiming that it begins when an angel swoops down from heaven to seize the beast and chain him in the bottomless pit for a thousand years, he immediately jumps to its close, when Satan is released from the pit to attempt a final flurry of evil-doing, marshalling the armies of Gog and Magog against the Saints. The Millennium, however, is a foreshadowing of the eternal bliss to come after the Devil's final defeat, when he is hurled into the sulphurous lake to join the Antichrist and is 'tormented day and night for ever and ever' (Rev. 20: 10).

Once evil has been banished once and for all, first from heaven, then from earth, God is able to execute the Last Judgement. John sees the enthroned deity reading the deeds of men from the 'book of life' as hoards of resurrected dead file past him. Anyone found to be in moral debit in the holy ledgers is sentenced to eternal suffering in the lake of fire, while the Saints, or survivors of the 'second resurrection', are rewarded with eternal life in 'a new heaven and a new earth' (Rev. 21: 1). Now a new age may begin, a bountiful, everlasting era in which 'there shall be no more death, neither sorrow, nor crying, neither shall there be any more pain' (Rev. 21: 4). This beautiful sigh of a verse signals the calm after the storm, the glorious stillness that follows the frantic strife-ridden action. Speaking directly, God assures believers that 'he that overcometh shall inherit all things' (Rev. 21: 7).

In the last of the visions granted him, John is carried off by an angel to survey 'the Holy city, new Jerusalem, coming down from God out of heaven, prepared as a bride adorned for her husband' (Rev. 21: 2). Jewel-encrusted and iridescent, New Jerusalem boasts twelve pearly gates inscribed with the names of the tribes of Israel; the foundations of its walls bear the names of the twelve Apostles; its streets are paved with gold, and along the main street the waters of life flow directly from God's throne to nourish the tree of life. Specific mention is made of the fact that there is no temple in the city, 'for the Lord God Almighty and the Lamb are the temple of it' (Rev. 21: 22). At this point John snaps out of his visionary trance, falling to the ground to worship the angel who revealed all this to him and who tells him 'seal not the sayings of the prophecy of this book: for the time is at hand' (Rev. 22: 10). Revelation then closes with a quasi-liturgical passage which ends with the plea 'even so, come, Lord Jesus' (Rev. 22: 20).

One of the most striking and, in narrative terms, captivating features of Revelation is that it contains such an emotive depiction of a world at war, blood-drenched, devoid of mercy, full of unspeakable horrors and defenceless victims. More than any other *mise en scène*, the theatre of war befits the kind of drama in which heroes and villains are clearly identified, unprepared to negotiate and ready to die rather than surrender to the enemy. In other words, it is particularly suited to the operation of binarisms or dualisms, to the strict opposition between good and evil, present and future, above and below, that makes for the tension in John's world. In this regard,

Revelation resembles what you might get if you rolled 1 Enoch together with the Qumran War Scroll and sealed it with the blood of Christ. Although the book is profoundly Jewish, drawing freely from 1 Enoch, but also quoting extensively from Hebrew prophecy, with which it assumes continuity, and exalting the Twelve Tribes of Israel, every divine promise of old is reinterpreted with reference to Christ. Only Christians, especially those prepared to die for their testimony in Jesus, stand a chance of being saved; only those who wash their garments in the Lamb's blood will be made white and clean; and only the Christian faithful receive the seal of eternal life. Jews who persist in rejecting Christ in favour of the 'synagogue of Satan' are doomed to share the fate of the bulk of John's extensive cast of eschatological players. In sum, the visions born on the island of Patmos are a distinctly Christian conclusion to the prophetic tradition of Israel, an elaborate cosmic vision of rescue that has its original in the Exodus.

As it happened, Christians soon ceased to need a rescue fantasy. Since a community cannot survive long term in an urgent state of expectation, pinning the integrity of its entire belief system on a mere five words, 'even so, come, Lord Jesus', this was perhaps just as well. As time went on, and John's prophecies continued to show no signs of being fulfilled, the early Church began asking itself why the end of the world and the Second Coming, or Parousia, had been postponed. When such a rationale was offered the Church occupied a very different position in the world. With Constantine the Great's conversion on his deathbed in 337, and the subsequent adoption of Christianity as the religion of the Roman Empire, Christians lost their apocalyptic sense of utter alienation, they became urbane and integrated themselves into civic life. Once allied to the present world order, the Church grew increasingly reluctant to condone a theology that demanded it be swept away. Christ's return had obviously been postponed because there was work still to be done on earth, the Good News had to be spread, everyone was entitled to the chance to be saved. Eschatology became an individual rather than collective prospect. As the revolutionary expectation of a sudden end gave way to an evolutionary expectation of gradual perfection under the Church's stewardship, increasing emphasis was placed on history as already consummated.[4] Such an argument went hand in hand with attempts to discredit a Millennium of earthly abundance as unspiritual and Judaistic, and a stream of allegorical readings of Revelation followed. Of these, St Augustine's *City of God* (413–26) is by far the most important, since in managing to square the perfectionism of Christ with the necessity of having to make do with an imperfect world, it steered the Christian faith on a comfortable course into the future.

Augustine transformed Revelation's warring factions, the righteous and the wicked, into two metaphorical cities, the city of God and the city of man. He explained: 'By two cities I mean two societies of human beings, one which is pre-destined to reign with God for all eternity, the other doomed to undergo eternal punishment with the devil.' These communities were of fundamentally different character: 'the two cities were created by two kinds of love: the earthly city was created by self-love reaching the point of contempt for God, the Heavenly City by the love of God carried as far as contempt of self'.[5] The populace of the city of man lived (often literally) as if there were no tomorrow, indulging in all manner of luxury and vice, and pandering to the wealthy and powerful, as Augustine was in a position to know, having led a roguish life before he came to see the light. The Bishop of Hippo was an original born-again Christian and his monumental work is stamped with the hallmark of the convert's zeal. He heaped abundant praise on the members of the heavenly community who spent their lives in devotion, acknowledging no other wisdom than that of God. They would collect their reward in the extended tomorrow of the hereafter. Augustine was particularly clear about there being only one hereafter, and that would succeed Judgement Day when the co-existing invisible communities would finally be sifted apart so that one might be exalted and the other damned. The Millennium did not qualify as a hereafter in Augustine's opinion, for it was already underway, having been ushered in in the form of a spiritual paradise with the foundation of the Church.

The supposedly allegorical intent of Revelation elucidated by St Augustine became an official article of faith in 431 when a meeting of the Council of Ephesus condemned belief in a free-for-all millennial banquet as a superstitious aberration. However, while the new Augustinian orthodoxy effected a clever compromise between affirmation and caution, it erred on the side of affirmation. By identifying the Millennium with the history of the Church, it unwittingly created a millenarian time-bomb which exploded once the year 1000 passed without event. But as Damian Thompson has shown in *The End of Time* (1996), even before the Augustinian Millennium expired, there was substantial millenarian activity on the fringes of the Church, which strongly suggests that the Council ruling only succeeded in driving literal belief in an earthly Millennium underground. There, in the shady world of heresy, amid the enthusiasms of Christian extremists, assorted Church reformers and the outreaches of popular religion, the Christianity of St John has been kept alive. In fact, it has thrived, for Revelation has offered a permanent refuge for those suffering from a deep-seated despair of the future, the marginalised, persecuted, oppressed and disillusioned – people who in the complete absence of rational political hope have turned to its pages for steel-clad justification that their sense of alienation is proof of their election. By imagining themselves to be a disinherited élite, millenarians down the ages have stoked their indignation at a world that pays them little or no heed, taking comfort in the assurance that its obliteration and their vindication will come soon.

Although the secondary literature on millenarianism is vast, its range extending beyond Christianity to embrace Islamic Mahdist movements, Melanesian Cargo Cults, native American cosmology and, less literally, political theory, the influence of two historians, Norman Cohn and Christopher Hill, dominates its approaches, its spirit and, for the main part, its conclusions. Cohn's *The Pursuit of the Millennium*, first published in 1957, remains the deepest and most engaging study of European millenarianism in the Middle Ages. It pages are saturated with accounts of the most chilling acts of violence enacted in the name of God by various groups purporting to be the Elect. The Crusaders, for example, driven by a mission to purge Europe of anti-Christian influence, massacred thousands of Jews and Muslims *en route* to the Holy Land. In the process, they were joined by marauding hoards of peasants, such as the barbaric

Pastoureaux, motivated more by blood-lust than by any desire to liberate Jerusalem. Equally convinced of their duty to kill in order to combat irreligion were the flagellant movements of the thirteenth and fourteenth centuries, whose fanatical members would whip themselves into a frenzy using leather scourges stuck with iron spikes before conducting murderous rampages on unsuspecting townsfolk. Cohn's study culminates with the revolutionary millenarian movements of fifteenth-century Bohemia and sixteenth-century Germany, whose militant armies were determined to fight the people of Gog and Magog hand to hand. Entirely lacking among these groups is any sentiment we would normally understand as Christian. Embarking on a holy war aimed at realising the Millennium, the Bohemian Taborites, for example, dreamed not of peace and harmony, but of a world in which taxes, dues, rents, tithes and private property would be abolished. And German Anabaptist Thomas Müntzer, who spent years drilling his revolutionary army in preparation for Armageddon, finally put his 'League of the Elect' to battle during the peasant revolt of 1525.

Of particular interest in the history of Anabaptism is Jan Bockelson's messianic reign of Münster during 1534–5, which in so many respects foreshadows David Koresh's tyrannous lordship over the Branch Davidians. Better known as John of Leyden, Bockelson barricaded the Westphalian town against the forces of Antichrist, declared it to be New Jerusalem and crowned himself king of the world. Subjects of the Anabaptist king were coerced into accepting a communist regime, whereby all wealth, accommodation and food supplies were pronounced common property. In truth this was but a charade: the wayward messiah and his pampered entourage hoarded anything of value for themselves. Yet no one protested or they would have had Bockelson's army to answer to. As was David Koresh's wont, Bockelson practised polygamy, taking five wives for himself. But the most striking parallel between Münster and Waco is the siege that finally starved out the town's 10,000 Anabaptists. All the while that Bockelson indulged his megalomania, executing anyone who disobeyed his laws, the local Bishop's army of mercenaries camped outside the town walls. For almost a year, a war of attrition was waged. Anabaptists who were weak with starvation were surrendered to Antichrist, while those who died as famine and disease raged through the town suffered the worse fate of being eaten. When the Bishop's army could be certain of victory, they brought the reign of terror at New Jerusalem to an abrupt end in a gruesome massacre. Bockelson was captured and publicly tortured to death with hot irons. To this day, three cages hang from the spire of St Lambert's Church, Münster. Once they held the mortal remains of Bockelson and his two closest collaborators.

Although Cohn acknowledges that a sense of disorientation whose sources might be both vague and internal is a critical precondition of millenarianism, he nonetheless locates the millenarian constituency squarely in the world of 'peasant revolts and urban insurrections'. More interested in violent millenarians, the angry and impatient rank and file who periodically tried to establish the Millennium by force, he allows quietists and reformers who opted to wait for God's miraculous intervention in earthly affairs to slip by with barely a mention. His treatment of world-withdrawn, neo-apostolic sects, such as Waldensians, Albigensians, Benedictines and Franciscan Spirituals, is fairly scant, and he omits to consider the twelfth century's most famous heretics, the self-immolating Cathars, whose quest to find New Jerusalem was bizarrely mapped on to the human body. The *imitatio Christi* that fascinates Cohn took its model from Revelation's raging warrior-Christ rather than from Jesus' exemplary life. And the recurrent theme in his book is the insecurity of the *plebs pauperum*, the desperately underprivileged who had nothing to lose in seeking to better their lot by overturning the status quo.

If, for Cohn, apocalypse is the religion of the poor and disenfranchised, for Hill it is the religion of the political radical. In terms of breadth and understanding, Hill's books have done for seventeenth-century England what Cohn has done for the Middle Ages. Stuffed with material from hard-won sources, parish records, prison ledgers, village diaries, rare pamphlets, rarer manuscripts and juicy gossip (Hill's scholarship is unimpeachable), they nonetheless paint a picture of Stuart England which leads one to imagine that a millenarian radical hid under every bed. Like Cohn, he is more concerned with militants than with sober exegetes. While he is intimate with Puritans, extremists, separatists, Ranters, Levellers and Fifth Monarchy Men, who saw the Civil War as the herald of a millennial rule of Saints, he has little time for conservative or apolitical academics, such as Joseph Mede or Henry More, whose commentaries on Revelation supplied his religious and political radicals with their credo. Like the Taborites, the Fifth Monarchy Men acquired a taste for bloodshed, relishing the taking up of arms in the millenarian cause: 'they had tongues like angels, but cloven feet', warned Oliver Cromwell, who until 1653 had regarded them as allies. With the failure of Cromwell's New Model Army to inaugurate the Millennium, millenarians began to look back to God to effect the miracle of democracy. In the hands of Ranter apologist Abiezer Cope, God's promise to treat all men equally was provocatively extended as God became 'the Almighty Leveller'.[6]

Perhaps it is only to be expected that a Marxist historian should place such stress on the revolutionary aspects of millenarianism, on the desire – to paraphrase the title of Hill's best known book – to turn the world upside down. Indeed, we owe the introduction to English readers of popular millenarian uprisings in nineteenth-century Italy to another Marxist historian, Eric Hobsbawm. The most colourful (and dangerous) of his characters is David Lazzaretti, the 'messiah of Monte Amiata', who believed himself to be Christ reincarnate. He amassed a personal army, the 1000-strong 'militia of the Holy Ghost', whose stated purpose was to regenerate the moral and civil order, and in 1878 – a year he had prophesied would witness the dawn of his new age of love and peace – he took on the mantle of Faithful and True, and moved to succeed both monarch and pope, only to be killed in the skirmish.[7] The problem with the Cohn–Hill consensus is that it boxes millenarians rather too neatly into the category of Christian materialists, stirred above all else by the prospect of worldly gain. Their leaders, meanwhile, come out of the wash as power-hungry manipulators eager to exploit the grievances of the needy and destitute in pursuit of their own political goals.

Generally speaking, historians are uneasy about straying from the concrete world of social circumstance in order to delve into the millenarian mind. Psychology is not really their province. Yet their scholarly respect for disciplinary boundaries makes it difficult for them to admit any more than in principle that experiences of alienation, oppression and disillusionment are not confined to the materially disadvantaged or the socially and politically marginalised. Such historically indeterminate facts of life are better illuminated by psychological tacks of inquiry. According to sociologist Leon Festinger, for example, what separates the millenarian from the rest of the disenchanted is their greater sensitivity to the inevitability of the end and their greater need for consonance.[8] According to D. H. Lawrence, the point of divergence comes when a socially acceptable fear of the end is replaced by an uncouth longing. In both cases, the implication is that millenarianism is not entirely Other, that it sits at one end of a continuum of self-understanding along which it is possible to slide back and forth. It would be disingenuous to talk of Festinger and Lawrence in the same breath without pointing to the very substantial differences that exist between them. Festinger arrived at his conclusions through a detached investigation of an American apocalyptic cult active in the 1950s; Lawrence came to his through an emotional tussle with the Book of Revelation. Festinger presented his findings as an academic case study (regarded in the literature on millenarianism as a classic), while Lawrence delivered his as an impassioned lament (frequently passed over in silence by his biographers). While Festinger's interest was rooted in curiosity, Lawrence's took flight from reluctant empathy.

Lawrence is an interesting figure. A self-styled champion of true 'aristocratic' Christianity, he branded millenarianism the religion of feeble-minded, mealy-mouthed Christian 'democrats'. Yet he was himself vulnerable to its temptations. He had regarded the Great War as the great pause of Revelation, and at the height of his apocalyptic fervour cast himself as messiah

– 'I shall change the world for the next 1000 years'. The Last Days haunted him down to his own last days, the result being *Apocalypse* (1931). The complex product of a lifetime's wrestling with the End, it was completed just two months before he died. In this extraordinary little book, which is a sustained attempt to demystify – and therefore disempower – Revelation, erudite historical passages exploring the pagan roots of apocalypse are intercut with denunciations of millenarianism so bitter they make sense only in the context of self-reproach. Essentially, Lawrence had come to believe that the meek did not deserve to be exalted in heaven and he railed against Revelation's sanctification of their undying will to power: 'If you have to suffer martyrdom, and if all the universe has to be destroyed in the process, still, still, still, O Christian, you shall reign as a king and set your foot on the necks of the old bosses.' This was not religion but vengeance. Pointing the finger of accusation at St John the Divine, Lawrence pronounced him guilty of dealing 'the death-kiss to the gospels', of forsaking the noble religion of Jesus and Paul and of harbouring a 'lust' for the end of the world. Not least, he was responsible for spawning an endless stream of 'Patmossers' – smug devotees of his 'religion of the self-glorification of the weak' with its 'millennium of pseudo-humble saints'. So wild was Lawrence's fury that it is impossible to tell whether scorn or pity led him to conclude that 'John of Patmos felt himself weak, in his very soul'.[9]

Since it is in the nature of things that causes are harder to pin down than effects, however we choose to account for the millenarian impulse, whether we bow to the forces of history or the insights of psychology, we are stranded in the realm of speculation. The products of millenarianism, on the other hand, readily offer themselves up for scrutiny. Chief among these is credulity. Millenarianism is a wonderful primer for credulity, which is why history's motley cast of prophets and would-be messiahs, having convinced themselves that they were any one of a number of players in Revelation, found it incredibly easy to convince others of the same. That said, a hospitable religious milieu such as existed in what Roy Porter has called 'the Miltonic spirit-drenched world' of Restoration England, where a cocktail of enthusiasm, superstition and fanaticism was a boon to any prophet following Bunyan's trail to the inner light, is undoubtedly advantageous. In such a climate, apocalypse works like a narcotic, conjuring up a world filled with signs and signifiers that gets superimposed on reality: to the intoxicated, history rapidly begins to look millenarian. Natural catastrophes like the Lisbon earthquake of 1755, cosmic spectacles like comets or novae, or political calamities like the English Civil War or French Revolution, for example, all float into higher significance before the dilated pupils of millenarians. If we were to plot a graph of the intensity of millenarian activity against the passage of time and then plot instances of natural catastrophes, celestial anomalies and social upheavals on the same graph, we would find that the peaks pretty much coincide.

Commonwealth England is one such double peak. The nation was awash with prophets as the spirit of inspiration entered the likes of Christopher Love, Mary Gadbury, Anna Trapuel, Eleanor Davies (otherwise known by the anagrammatic appellation 'Reveale O Daniel'), as well as numerous Quakers, Fifth Monarchists, Ranters and Seekers. Several would-be messiahs declared their missions into the bargain. In 1649 a London goldsmith called Thomas Tany experienced a vision that revealed to him that he was 'a Jew of the tribe of Reuben'. He immediately began scheming to return the Jews to the Holy Land to rebuild the temple, in which he would minister as 'high priest'; he even circumcised himself. A spell of detention at Newgate failed to sober him and in 1652 he retired to Eltham, where he began constructing tents for his expedition, decorated with the figures of the twelve tribes. Little more is known of him, except that he claimed the throne of France in 1654, and, according to Lodowick Muggleton, the most successful of the decade's prophets, he drowned on his way to Holland, where he had hoped to gather some Jews.

Small-time farmer turned Ranter God, John Robins was similarly preoccupied with the restoration of the Jews. He taught himself Hebrew and energetically began recruiting an army of 144,000 Saints to liberate the Holy Land, insisting that his volunteers subsist on bread and water alone. Imprisoned for ten months in 1651, he reduced his personal claim to inspiration and eventually obtained his liberty by writing to Cromwell recanting his former claims to divinity. Quaker preacher James Nayler was imprisoned in 1653 for alleging that Christ was in him – though in Quaker parlance that may well not have meant what his predominantly Ranter following took it to mean. Still, Nayler did nothing to stop his followers kneeling before him and kissing his feet in divine homage, even after George Fox as good as excommunicated him. John Stranger, a combmaker from London, wrote to Nayler in 1656, 'Thy name is no more to be called James, but Jesus', while the printer Thomas Simmons styled him 'the lamb of God'. His presence in Exeter that year caused such a stir among the common folk that he was jailed. This served only to add to his mystique and when he made his way into Bristol on his release he was greeted by a concourse of believers crying 'holy, holy holy, Lord God of Israel'. By this time Nayler was persuaded of his own supreme status and his refusal to recant his claims before a House of Commons Committee led to a sentence of horrific punishments, which included being pilloried, publicly whipped, having his tongue bored with a hot iron and his forehead branded with the letter B for blasphemer. In 1659 he came out of prison a penitent.[10]

Lodowick Muggleton and John Reeve embarked on their prophetic careers as the two witnesses of Revelation after receiving their 'commissions' from Jesus in 1651 – Reeve as the messenger of the new dispensation and Muggleton as his 'mouth'. Muggleton was Lord Macaulay's 'mad tailor', who 'denounced eternal torments against all who refused to believe, on his testimony, that the Supreme Being was only six feet high, and that the sun was just four miles from the earth'. It is true that Muggleton and Reeve commandeered the power to pass such judgements on whomsoever they pleased. Muggleton wrote, 'God has chosen us two his last messengers unto this bloody unbelieving world, and hath put the two edged sword of his Spirit into our mouths, to pronounce blessing and cursing to eternity.' But their wrath fell less on unbelievers than on their rivals. The witnesses personally visited both Robins and Tany in jail in order to commit them to eternal misery and, of the 103 people named in their works as belonging to the party of the damned, more than half are Quakers, a sect particularly vociferous in their opposition to the witnesses. Unlike Robins and Tany, however, Muggleton and Reeve did at least use their 'knowledge in the heavenly mysteries' to attempt a theology. Reeve made the spiritual contribution with the doctrine of the 'two seeds', the divine seed of Faith and the diabolic seed of Reason. Although this gave rise to two distinct races of beings descended, respectively, from the demonic Cain and the saintly Abel, the witnesses believed that everyone was a hybrid and that the relative proportion of seeds within any one individual was what would swing the balance between their salvation and damnation. This was consistent with their view that Antichrist was 'the spirit or seed of reason in man'. Reeve was of the opinion that there was no Devil except those persons suffering an imbalance of seeds and that God was a man, hence Macaulay's quip about the dwarfish divinity. For his part, Muggleton abolished prayer and denied the sanctity of the Sabbath. Muggleton's following never exceeded a few hundred, but the faith survived in a local way in London, Kent and Cambridgeshire, handed down in families of believers from generation to generation. Alexander Gordon, a Victorian historian of the movement, estimated that in 1863 there remained a total of nearly 400 Muggletonians.[11]

Spiritually ambitious men did not have a monopoly on salvation, and over the years a number of women have come forward to claim their part in the cosmic drama. The late eighteenth-century double peak on the millenarian graph alone throws up a cluster of colourful characters; there's the Cornish Trumpeter who believed she was to sound one of the seven trumpets that proclaimed the Second Coming, and a Mrs. S. Eyre who was commanded to announce the pouring out of the vials of wrath. In 1782, Luckie Buchan, an innkeeper's daughter from Banff, affirmed that she was the woman clothed with the sun, and when Robert White, Relief Minister at Irvine, declared his faith in her, she responded in kind by designating him the 'man-child' of Revelation 12: 5 who would rule the world with a rod of iron. After Buchan suffered a severe beating at the hands of an angry mob, she, White and a bunch of their faithful escaped further persecution by fleeing into the wilderness, first to Dumfriesshire, then to the moorlands of Kirkcudbrightshire. Their community home, known locally as Buchan Ha', operated on communistic lines and, although sect members sometimes hired themselves out as farmhands, the community generated most of its bare living from weaving: indeed, its members could be distinguished by their light green homespun apparel.

The group's central belief was in the divinity of the 'Friend Mother', who claimed that she was the Holy Ghost and sister of Christ, whose return they expected almost daily. At the peak of their anticipation, Buchan bid her followers fast for forty days, after which time they staggered up to the top of a nearby hill to await their rapture. According to an eye-witness report:

> platforms were erected for them to wait on till the wonderful hour arrived, and Mrs Buchan's platform was exalted above all the others. The hair of each head was cut short, all but a tuft on the top, for the angels to catch by when drawing them up. The momentous hour came; every station for ascension was occupied; thus they expected every moment to be wafted into the land of bliss. A gust of wind came, but, instead of wafting them upwards, it capsized Mrs Buchan, platform and all!

Brimming with barely suppressed hilarity, this report is hardly valuable for its on-the-scene reliability. Instead, its worth lies in its being a testimony to the speed at which cultish life gets incorporated into folklore, making it all the more easy for lines to be drawn between 'them' and 'us'. Although this sad non-event was the cause of a mass defection, the prophetess managed to hang on to a core following who accepted her argument that their faith had not been strong enough to be rewarded with Christ's appearance. However, Buchan exerted little pull from beyond the grave and her cult did not long survive her death in 1791.[12]

While the Buchanites were celebrating their election in the wilds of Scotland, across the Atlantic a similar cult had developed around the personage of Jemima Wilkinson.[13] Daughter of a Quaker farmer from Rhode Island, Wilkinson announced that the spirit of Christ had entered her and that she was to reign on earth for a thousand years. Renaming herself the 'Universal Friend of Mankind', she set about recruiting followers by taking up as a travelling preacher and within a few years had drummed up sufficient support for the lot of them to decamp to the fertile plains of west New York State, where she founded 'New Jerusalem'. More a village than a commune, its residents bought their own homes and made good livings off the land, but all submitted to Jemima's autocratic rule. A feature of the sect that provoked much ribaldry was its female hierarchy. Jemima's deputy was a consummate businesswoman who deftly handled all temporal affairs, and female independence was encouraged in every way. At one meeting, the Universal Friend told her posse of female intimates that they 'ought not by intermarrying with men, to give them a pretext according to the fashion and custom of a wicked world, for exacting obedience from us'. Although she did not forbid members of her flock from marrying, Wilkinson frowned upon the contract, clearly believing her feminist Millennium could do without it. Buchan too was no fan of matrimony, which she termed 'that accursed yoke', but wriggling out of this particular convention was not nearly so critical a matter for either her or Wilkinson as it was for Ann Lee, founder of the Shakers.

Lee's spiritual aspirations, all of which flowed from a resolution to become celibate, had their origin in an 'open vision' of Adam and Eve in carnal intercourse that left its recipient in no doubt that sex rather than disobedience was the essence of original sin. Lee experienced the vision in 1770 while serving a prison sentence for disrupting the Sabbath and it qualified her on her release to assume leadership of the small band of mystical Quakers to whom she belonged. A further vision which led her to claim 'it is Christ who dwells in me' sealed her messianic status in the eyes of her followers, who, once convinced that the second advent had been fulfilled in Mother Ann, could joyously proceed into the Millennium. Since the North of England – all satanic mills and mines on the eve of the industrial revolution – was so palpably lacking in milk and honey, 'Ann the Word' and a number of her celibate devotees emigrated to the promised land of America and established the first community of Shakers (or shaking Quakers) in New York State. At first the Millennium refused to run smoothly. Hounded by the Puritan faithful for their sensual love of dance (which in fact so successfully dissipated their carnal desires), the Shakers' early years were marked by persecution. But their renouncing of all sacramental forms of worship, their adoption of a communitarian way of life and the imposition of strict sexual segregation appealed to the revivalist spirit of the time, and gradually hostility was converted into respect. Shaker communities multiplied across New England, the ban on natural means of expansion notwithstanding, and, compared to the dozens of experimental religious communities that sprang up on the East Coast in the early nineteenth century only to disappear almost as quickly, the Shakers fared quite well.[14]

With just a few examples of the messianically inspired in sight, it is clear that the best biblical credentials usually failed to impress the terrestrial authorities and spells of detention at the earthly monarch's pleasure have been a common feature of the prophetic life. By the same token of disbelief, the inspired words of numerous visionaries and enthusiasts met with their destiny in the demonologist's furnace or else the physician's case notes. With the dawn of the age of reason, 'divine madness' was transformed into 'religious mania' and Bethlam became home to a stream of prophets. As if a portent of medicinal things to come, Lady Eleanor Davies became an early inmate, having given vent in the 1630s to her anti-Catholic feelings by daubing pitch and tar on to the altar furnishings at Lichfield Cathedral. The political spin on her prophetic gift made a verdict of derangement all the more imperative in the eyes of the establishment, for in the guise of 'Reveale O Daniel' she had pronounced Oliver Cromwell to be the one with the 'Flaming Sword' who would 'execute judgement of all'. Accordingly she had assigned him the flattering, if inaccurate, anagram Howl Rome. Margaret Nicolson, who attempted to kill King George III after an angel told her to prophesy, and James Hadfield, discharged from the army in 1793 for claiming he was Jesus Christ and God, were also sometime residents of

Bethlam. Jonathan Martin was confined after attempting on divine instruction to burn down York Minster in 1829, while Beatrice Webb's grandmother, Mary Seddon, who to Webb's childhood eyes had been 'a Hebrew prophetess to look at', spent years in an asylum on account of her divine calling. Webb recalled that 'she became sane on all but one subject – her special mission to lead the Jews back to Jerusalem'.[15]

Richard Brothers was not so fortunate: his affliction proved incurable. In the 1790s this one-time naval officer produced numerous prophetic tracts in which he unmasked himself as 'Prince of the Hebrews', chosen to restore the Jews to Palestine. Not the 'visible Jews' who professed the faith, but the 'invisible Jews', descendants of the Lost Tribes, who had somehow managed to end up in England. Convinced that London was the great whore of Babylon, he began preaching an Armageddonist philosophy to anyone who cared to listen. In 1795 *The Times*, adopting a playful air of factuality, reported: 'his daily and nightly apparitions amount to about 600, and in all and every one of them, God reveals to him, that within a fixed time, which is to begin the 1st of June 1795, and to end in 1798, all sovereigns shall be struck down and destroyed forever'. Later that year, Brothers was examined before the Privy Council, declared insane, and confined in Fisher House, Islington, a private asylum, where he was to remain for eleven years.

In Fisher House Brothers flourished, the ultimate product of his sublime madness being *A Description of Jerusalem* (1801). Subtitled 'its houses and streets, squares, colleges, markets, and cathedrals, the Royal and private palaces, with the garden of Eden in the centre, as laid down in the last chapters of Ezekiel . . .', this slim volume marked Brothers' evolution from

Hebrew prince into holy town planner. In the grip of a frenzy for measuring, Brothers listed the dimensions of the aforementioned buildings in obsessive detail for page upon page; the height of the storeys, the number of windows, the length and breadth of their gardens. Yet hidden away in this soporific production are gem-like clauses which hint that what actuated Brothers' messianic ambition was a passion for social reform. His design for your run-of-the-mill Hebrew household, for instance, was arrived at after 'carefully consulting the health and convenience of the inhabitants'. And he apportioned a garden to every house so that 'the poorest families may walk and enjoy themselves – where their children may play in safety, to acquire daily fresh health and strength'. Incorporating the latest developments in sanitary reform, he was adamant that Jerusalem's sewers should not run beneath the houses since in Palestine's hot climate this 'would be productive of foul and unwholesome air' and consequently of 'bad health to the people'. Had Brothers managed to capitalise on his instinctive reformism in his attacks on the Babylonish metropolis, he might have retained his freedom as well as his disciples. But many of these defected to the camp of rival prophet Joanna Southcott after successive attempts to obtain Brothers' release, led by MP Nathaniel Brassey Halhed, failed.

While there is no formula for messianic success – the line between prophetic prosperity and incarceration being a fine one – claiming one of the apostolic gifts invariably served as useful showmanship for a would-be prophet in search of disciples. The eighteenth-century prophet John Lacy was renowned for being able to speak in tongues, John Robins claimed the power of raising the dead (his boasts included the resurrection and redemption of Cain and Judas), Richard Brothers attempted to heal the blind, and both Joanna South-cott and Joseph Smith, founder of the Mormons, claimed the gift of inspired writing. It is said that, goaded on by a crowd of raucous sceptics, Jemima Wilkinson was almost persuaded to attempt walking on water but changed her mind at the last minute and preached her way out of having to perform.

Antinomianism, the idea that ecclesiastic and moral law ceases to apply to those filled with the spirit of God, was additionally seen as an apostolic trait. It is most commonly associated with the Ranters' penchant for nakedness and the Free Spirit movement's advocacy of free love, but, in the case of messiahs, variations on the antinomian theme had little to do with a theology of libertinism. Rather, they allowed them to place their individual stamp on religious history. Jan Bockelson, for example, distinguished his tribe by the practice of polygamy; Ann Lee put her mark on hers by institutionalising celibacy; Jewish messiah Sabbatai Zevi of Smyrna abolished various sacred feasts, replacing them with ones of his own invention; while nineteenth-century messiah Zion Ward targeted his assault against established authority on the calendar, instructing his followers to begin reckoning their years from the date of his illumination, 1826 being 'First year, new date'. Antinomianism had the added advantage of binding believers together in a common identity. The business of adopting new creeds and rituals while spurning the entire gamut of established ones reinforces the cosy exclusivity characteristic of millenarian groups from the Qumran sect to the Jehovah's Witnesses – an exclusivity that compounds the belief that only they, the Elect, the remnant of Revelation, will be saved.

Individual and intricate as are the histories of messianic movements past and present, it is their sameness rather than their particularity that raises the more interesting questions about the human predicament. At the centre of them all, we can see a repetitive core, an archetypal career trajectory that comes straight from St John the Divine. Revelation has been mined by generations of messiahs with their own social, political and personal agendas, and has provided what was needed in each instance. It is the bedrock of apocalypse precisely because it allows for such adaptability. Its elasticity, profound ambiguity, and its play with signs and mystical numbers admit of an interpretive largesse that has guaranteed its survival. Every messiah has his or her own ideas as to when the world will end, where Babylon and New Jerusalem are located, who might be branded Antichrist or Faithful and True, and what part of humanity is destined to accompany Christ into God's kingdom leaving the rest to be eternally damned, yet all of them can cite Revelation as their ultimate authority. The book is a perfect model of convenience functionality. Like a pilot light it radiates the permanent warm glow of reassurance, but it is ever-capable of flaring on the oxygen of urgent expectation. Yet even an everlasting flame is perhaps too limiting, too vertical a metaphor for the book's endurance, because, as well as remaining viable for successive generations of millenarians, Revelation possesses horizontal currency, a liquidity that allows its influence to continually seep out of the world of religious sectarianism into mainstream secular culture. It is not unlike the theological equivalent of gold. And its exchange value lies in the fact that it promises to lift anyone, anywhere, at any time, whatever their ideological complexion, out of a quotidian reality replete with disappointments and deposit them bang in the centre of the cosmic stage. In this sense Revelation functions like myth.

The book is tugged some way into this literary category by its fabulous cast of beasts, wicked kings, distressed damsels and knights in shining armour, and also by its furnishing earthly affairs with cosmic dimensions – it is a story of heroes and gods if ever there was one. Nevertheless, its claims to universality are the real source of its mythic power. Because myths trade so successfully on being perpetually and universally relevant, we imagine them to be timeless entities capable of somehow bypassing our conscious understanding in order to commune directly with our true, inner selves, as if they had special access to the deepest, darkest levels of our psyche. It is little wonder that Freud expressed such interest in them. Roland Barthes has done more than anyone else to dispel this illusion, his ground-breaking *Mythologies* (1957) being a thorough exposé of the duplicity of myths. I use the term duplicity advisedly, since, in implying deception but also the idea of a double layering of meaning, it conveys the spirit of Barthes' central argument, which is that myths dupe us into thinking that they constitute a primary language which somehow nestles closer to truth than other forms of representation, whereas in reality they utilise a second-order language, one remove further from meaning than, say, writing or pictorial representation. In other words, they retreat from meaning into form. Myths deploy what we commonly take to be 'referents', or things signified, as 'signifiers' (that is, terms still in need of a referent) and in so doing they empty language of its content, of meaning. Barthes was fascinated by the insidious way myths are able conceal all kinds of particularity – political, religious and ideological – beneath the surface of ubiquitous form. But he was also suspicious of it, as though there were something underhand in the way that myths masqueraded as innocent simpletons while promulgating very pointed concerns, and these suspicions drew him into using demystification more as a weapon of combat than as a tool of understanding.

Latterday analyser of myths Marina Warner agrees with Barthes that myths are 'historical compounds, which successfully conceal their own contingency', thereby appearing timeless, but, at the same time, she takes a far more charitable view of their accommodating nature. Her 1994 Reith lectures, published as *Managing Monsters*, offer keen insight into how as a culture we actively mystify and mythologise our experiences as a means of making contact and communicating with others. Myths become a vehicle for talking about contemporary debates concerning gender, childhood, history and national identity, a means of articulating in general terms the particularity of our own anxieties about belonging. It seems to me that this is precisely where Revelation comes into its own in the mythic realm. It is an open resource for the insular. On top of its binary constructions of hope and despair, vengeance and vindication, there is the fundamental opposition between good and evil. The whole book embroiders the tension between righteous and wicked, saved and damned, insider and outsider: them and us. It plays to our insecurities about identity and belonging, but also to our desire for self-preservation, material and spiritual. Nobody (well, with the exception of nineteenth-century occultist Aleister Crowley, who boasted that he was the Beast) reads Revelation and identifies with the dispensable crew. Since only those who belong are assured of a glorious destiny, we project our desire for posterity on to its narrative, making Revelation as much a lesson in the salvific potential of stories as it is a story about salvation.

It is no accident that the most successful messiah in modern history was first and foremost a story-teller. Instead of identifying himself with one of Revelation's actors and playing out a pre-scripted role, Joseph Smith afforded himself greater flexibility by grafting its plot on to a salvation myth of his own. The *Book of Mormon* (1831), Smith's American Bible, is essentially an expanded apocalypse. A few decades earlier, in England, Joanna Southcott also used the written word to further the millenarian cause. But she had not the talent to graduate from propaganda to myth. Her imagination was too literal for such invention. Nonetheless, her writings acquired a certain mystique and have been preserved to the present day. In Smith and Southcott we have two author-messiahs, one English, the other American – near contemporaries with a claim to divine inspiration in common. Yet one movement flowered in its own day only to wither as time went on, while the other survived protracted bouts of persecution to emerge as an established faith with worldwide appeal. The next two chapters tell their stories.

4. JOANNA SOUTHCOTT'S BOX

Legend has it that Joanna Southcott, England's greatest prophe-tess, finally came to her senses on her deathbed. Ravaged by illness and radically disillusioned with her own prophetic 'Voice', she is supposed to have gasped, 'Oh England, how I have deceived thee.' True or not, in accordance with these infamous last words of 1814, Joanna has gone down in national memory as a charlatan and a fraud or, failing that, an hysteric. The first word of her *Dictionary of National Biography* entry is similarly pejorative – 'fanatic'. For many years a tablet bearing the epithet 'Imposter' hung beside her portrait at the National Gallery, so incensing one of her Edwardian followers that he threatened the gallery with divine retribution: 'I am com-manded by the Lord,' he intoned, 'to say that He will strike the National Gallery *thrice* with his lightnings, destroying the valuable collection of the Nation.'[1] The gallery did in fact remove the offending tablet, in 1918, replacing it with one that read 'Prophetess', but only after receiving remonstrances of a more civil nature from Alice Seymour, Southcottian propa-gandist and founder of the still-active Panacea Society.

The indignity of posthumous vilification was the final twist in Joanna's crown of thorns, for over the course of a brief prophetic career she endured a lifetime's worth of abuse; she was scorned, derided, mobbed, lampooned, caricatured and burned in effigy. It is a credit to her strength of character that she persisted under attack in her conviction that the world was fast coming to an end. She even pulled the abuse into her web of self-justification:

> Tho' some have laughed thee to scorn,
> And others did thee blame,
> Thy steadfast heart doth still obey,
> And thou art still the same.
> Therefore I'll own thee for the bride,
> Thou art the ev'ning star,
> By thy appearance all shall know
> That night is coming near.
> The morning star is gone and past,
> The sun his course hath run,
> The ev'ning star doth now appear,
> And night is coming on.[2]

Joanna was born in 1750, the daughter of a Devon farmer who had experienced 'reverses', and as a young woman she earned her keep in Exeter working as a domestic servant and upholsterer's assistant. On account of her hearing 'voices', she joined a Wesleyan congregation, thinking perhaps that there she would find, if not her calling, then at least acceptance and belonging. But the Methodists rejected her in 1792 when she announced that providence was working through her. It was then, at the mature age of forty-two (which, incidentally, is the same age at which Hildegard of Bingen, the twelfth-century

'Sibyl of the Rhine', went public about the existence of her inner voice), that Joanna began penning prophecies in a mixture of rambling prose and verse. She only acquired a following, however, after William Sharp, the engraver, friend of Blake and follower of Richard Brothers, launched her upon the world by bringing her to London. Sharp decided once and for all to abandon Brothers for Joanna on reading her *Strange Effects of Faith* (1801), and thereafter he financed the publication of many of her sixty-five prophetic books and pamphlets.

The Southcottian movement had two phases, the first lasting from 1801–05, during which time Joanna was preoccupied with her mission to overthrow Satan and establish Christ's kingdom. It then flagged for some years, but burst forth in a second frenzy in 1814 when Joanna announced that, at the grand old age of sixty-four, she was to be the vessel for a second virgin birth. At this time she was able to claim over 20,000 followers – a remarkable achievement considering the stigma that, under the consistent fire of abuse, must have attached to anyone who came out in her support. Even Sharp, her most passionate champion, succumbed to the exigencies of self-explanation: 'I am not ashamed to take her part,' he announced to the public in 1802.[3]

Thanks largely to the efforts of E. P. Thompson, the Southcottian movement has earned a place in social history even if it continues not to figure much in religious history. Because the vast bulk of Joanna's support came from working people living in London and the industrial west and north – Bristol, West Riding, Leeds, Stockport and Stockton-on-Tees – Thompson could usefully work the Southcottian movement into his symptomology of the 'emotional disequilibrium of the times'. In a decade in which war-weariness, a string of failed harvests and grinding poverty (circumstances to which the prophetess cannily directed her ill-augurings) took a heavy toll on the nation's morale, stoking an apocalyptic despair that spread far and wide in the aftermath of the French Revolution, Joanna promised ordinary working people sweet salvation and a bricks-and-mortar Millennium:

> When I my people do redeem
> From every power of hell and sin,
> Your houses I shall build anew,
> And palaces bring to your view;
> For golden mines I have in store:
> The foaming seas shall send on shore ...
> To build Jerusalem up again,
> And those that are the first redeem'd
> May say, these promises we claim.[4]

However, her concrete paradise was not the exalted utopian goal of a programmatic and revolutionary millenarianism. It originated in something far less grand, her innocent literalism. This Thompson acknowledged, even as he continued to classify the movement as a 'cult of the poor'. Yet if Joanna's appeal was most keenly felt among the nation's working population, accident rather than design was the principal cause. She never set out to lead a cult of the poor, even if her limited imagination was ultimately able to offer her followers only what the charwoman rather than the prophet most yearned for – stability, security, respect and material well-being. In that her nut-and-bolts Millennium soon found its secular apotheosis under the radical wing of Owenism, a strange irony seems to suggest itself, for it is just possible that Southcottianism drew the largest part of the breath that sustained it from a pre-existing constituency, as if Regency England somehow contained a ready-made movement in search of a leader to bring it to life. If that is the case, the Exeter prophetess simply pushed the right buttons and triggered the right nerve endings.

In common with the most vainglorious of would-be saviours, Joanna believed her appeal to be universal. It was simply her misfortune that the rhyming doggerel that was her all-purpose vehicle for conveying dreams, visions, prophecies, biblical exegeses, warnings, threats, diatribes – and, not least, a record of her own inner struggles with 'the Spirit' that dictated all this to her – was just the kind of crude pabulum that nourished the common man while causing the educated to gag. 'To suppose that the Holy Spirit is the Author of such trash,' railed one member of the latter party, 'betrays a weakness of mind bordering on insanity.'[5]

Joanna's greatest innovation as a messiah was 'sealing', a business that manifested itself in two ways. First, in 1790, she adopted the practice of sealing up her writings so that they could be opened and, hopefully, marvelled at once the predictions contained in them had come to pass. Then, in 1802, she began 'sealing' her followers. She invited them to sign a petition calling for the overthrow of Satan and the commencement of the Millennium, in exchange for which she gave them a promissory note, or seal, certificating the recipient as one of the saved. It read:

The
Sealed of the Lord, the Elect precious,

Man's Redemption to Inherit the
Tree of Life
To be made Heirs of God and Joint Heirs
with
Jesus Christ

The practice of thus sealing her followers proved so successful that Joanna sent the Reverend Thomas Foley, one of her inner circle of believers, a copy of her petition, along with a bunch of seals, so that he could meet the demand for these precious commodities among his Worcestershire parishioners and beyond. If she was going to seal the 144,000 Saints to be redeemed from the earth in the Book of Revelation, then time was of the utmost essence. Foley noted in his dairy that people 'will doubtless be desirous to sign his, or her, name, to such a paper [the petition] ... especially when they are told that every person so signing it, will be entitled to a paper from Joanna ... which will be a protection to that house, where Faith and Fear are in, when the destroying Angel passes thro' this land, as He did thro' the land of Egypt in the time of Moses and Aaron'.[6]

Sealing brought a stampede of new members into the Southcottian fold and before long there existed a market in seals comparable to the late medieval market in relics of the cross. This commerce infuriated Joanna, who supplemented her strenuous denial of ever accepting money for her seals with venomous threats against any of her followers who dared to sell theirs. She was no less put out by reports that people were using the seals as magic charms or talismans, but since she herself had turned them into a shibboleth, habitually referring to them as 'THE SEAL of CHRIST's protection', she was hardly

124

in a position to complain. By 1804, 8144 people had been sealed. By 1807, and despite Joanna having made passing an examination on her writings prerequisite to obtaining a seal, this figure had risen to nearly 14,000, while Southcottian records for 1814 list 20,505 people as sealed.[7] As might be expected, Joanna's critics pounced on the seals with relish. As well as accusing her of plying a profitable trade, they exercised their wit on the credulity of those who asked for them to be placed in their coffins when they died, or who thought that in obtaining this 'hieroglyphical letter' they had gained 'a passport, or admission-ticket, at the Gate of Heaven'.[8]

Exactly when Joanna hit on the idea of bonding her followers together as a 'Sealed People' is not clear, but it may have taken root in 1790 when she discovered, 'as if by accident', a commonplace seal bearing the initials 'I C', with a star above and below, while sweeping out a shop after a sale. This providential find convinced Joanna that the 'I' stood for Jesus and Joanna and that the 'C' stood for Christ. Moreover, if the upper star was the Morning Star, symbolising Jesus, then she herself must be the lower star, or Evening Star, whose appearance was to signal the Midnight Hour. Joanna regularly used this seal in her personal correspondence as well as to bind up her prophetic writings, but 'sealing' only acquired apocalyptic significance once she had contrived the plan of thwarting Satan by getting up a petition that would effect his final doom.

Satan and Joanna were long-time foes. The Prince of Darkness often haunted her dreams, appearing in one as a cup which proceeded to be transmogrified into his hideous form and in another as a pig with his mouth tied. Once she claimed to have succeeded in skinning his face with her nails during a fierce battle. Jane Townley, who served as Joanna's scribe and protectress, housing the prophetess during her London years, reported that Joanna would often rise from her bed at night, pacing and exclaiming against her sulphurous tormentor. Steeling herself to courage, she finally set to wrestling with the Devil in person. For seven days and seven nights the two of them were locked in mortal combat, or at least in an exhausting bout of fast-flung verbal abuse. At first the Devil has the upper hand. 'Damn thy Redeemer, and thee too; is my power to be overthrown by the desire of a cursed woman?' runs his haughty taunt. He then threatens to tear her to pieces unless she destroys her seals, but, fortified by faith, Joanna stands her ground and Satan is soon worn down by her tirade of self-righteous ramblings. 'A woman's tongue can no man tame,' he concedes. 'God hath done something to chuse a bitch of a woman, that will down-argue the Devil, and scarce give him room to speak – for the sands of a glass do not run faster than thy tongue. It is better to dispute with a thousand men than with one woman.' Finally, the Devil capitulates and in a surprising *volte-face* reveals that beneath his fiendish horns and scaly skin there beats the heart of a democrat. 'If Christ can gain the Kingdom by most votes, I will own it is just for me to lose my footing here,' he says, further stipulating that his destruction 'must be by a fair election'.[9]

In spite of its unintentional humour, *A Dispute Between the Woman and the Powers of Darkness* (1802) is a most harrowing book. Nowhere else does one receive so strong an impression of Joanna's tragic plight. Its angst-ridden dialogue brings into sharp focus the pathetic image of a hounded woman, incessantly persecuted by mysterious voices and caught in a tug-of-war between the Holy Spirit and the Devil, as though her mind and body had been forcibly recruited into serving as the physical battleground on which the forces of good and evil were compelled to sling it out in the Last Days. At times it seems as if Joanna manifested at once every textbook case of religious mania. She thought she was possessed by demons, she thought she was holy, she whirled and raved in paroxysms of fear and ecstasy, she took to her bed with raging fevers, she rambled incoherently and she convulsed in her sleep, the victim of unknown and unspared tortures. What is extraordinary is not that she experienced self-doubt, or on occasion felt herself to be on the verge of losing her senses, but that she somehow managed to hold on to the belief that all this suffering was for a good cause, even if much of the time she did not seem to know precisely who she was, what her role in life was supposed to be, or where destiny was guiding her.

Joanna's self-image vacillated continually. One day she would confidently announce herself to be the Evening Star, the next she would exalt herself as the bride of God. Scanning her writings, we learn that she also claimed at various times to be the Lamb's wife and the woman clothed with the sun. And while she quoted 'The seed of the woman shall bruise Satan's head' (Gen. 3: 15) often enough for it to become almost an incantation, her true purpose and identity remained shrouded in mystery until her Spirit finally put her out of her misery with the following revelation:

This year, in the sixty-fifth year of thy age, though shalt have a SON, by the power of the MOST HIGH, which if they receive as their Prophet, Priest and King, then I will restore them to their own land ... it is by the power of my Spirit, the power of my strength, that a SECOND SON must be born, like the first; that is, of God and not of man.[10]

In other words, Joanna was to be the mother of the Messiah, the long-awaited 'Son of man' who would restore the Jews (for which, read the Sealed) to the promised land. The baby's name was vouchsafed to Joanna as Shiloh, and he was to reign on earth as a king and defeat the powers of darkness, relieving his mother of the sword with which she had so tirelessly fought her old adversary.

Although no one was more shocked by this apparently miraculous turn of events than Joanna herself – 'I never had knowledge of man in my life...' – she took to playing the part of the expectant mother with astonishing ease, going so far as to develop an otherwise inexplicable craving for asparagus. Complaining of pain, sickness, vomiting and loss of appetite, the swollen-bellied prophetess took to her bed in October 1813 and there remained to await her fate. For once in her life, she succeeded in convincing those in authority that what she was experiencing was real, for seventeen of the twenty-one doctors who examined her, including the eminent London surgeon Richard Reece, confirmed that she was indeed pregnant. Experiencing a surge of vindication, Joanna brazenly wrote to the Archbishop of Canterbury requesting him to furnish her with rooms for her accouchement, which request was perfunctorily denied.

Her followers were beside themselves with excitement. For some years now, their movement had been stagnating; the war with France was looking less like Armageddon and, rather more worryingly, Joanna seemed to be losing her prophetic prowess. In 1802 she had boasted: 'there never were prophecies more clearly fulfilled in the Bible, than mine have been from 1792 to this present day. The War with France, Spain and other nations, came, as foretold by me, in 1792. The dearth followed, as foretold by me at that time. Every distress on the nation came to pass as I then wrote. Every harvest hath come as I said.' But by 1810 she would not have been so bold. One critic, who had evidently kept a close monitor on Joanna's career, published a record of her mounting prophetic failures; in 1803 England was threatened with instant ruin if the government did not release Richard Brothers from his incarceration; in 1807 Joanna was supposed to have conducted the Sealed to a safe haven outside London; in 1809 she claimed that Mary Bateman, a prisoner condemned to the gallows, would be miraculously rescued; and in 1810 the Beast Napoleon was to have landed in England and met his death at the hands of her faithful.[11] With such astute critics at large, Joanna's virgin birth was just the tonic the movement needed, and amid the commotion attending it people began clamouring for seals by the thousand.

Gifts from believers and well-wishers came flooding in to Joanna's London abode. There were 'laced caps, embroidered bibs, worked robes, a mohair mantle, silver pap-spoons & caudle-cups'. But the tribute that surpassed all these was a magnificent crib, hand-made by a Mr Seddon of Aldergate according to the designs of a benevolent and wealthy believer (see plate 4). It was constructed from an oblong square of satinwood, richly ornamented with gold, and its sides and ends were lattice-worked and gilded. The inside of the crib was lined with blue satin and its head-cloth bore a celestial crown of gold beneath which the word Shiloh was embroidered in Hebrew letters. Above the crib was suspended a canopy of white muslin decorated with a gold dove holding an olive branch in its beak, and its rim was inscribed with the words 'A Free will offering by Faith to the promised Seed'. A cool observer of this madness commented dryly that this 'manger', costing £200, was fitted with swivels so that a small cot could be hung within it 'for whenever the Young Prince may require rocking'.[12] Imitations of the crib draped in pink calico crowded the shelves of the city's toy-shops, so that now there was a trade in the virgin birth to rival that in seals.

Throughout 1814 the press undertook a running commentary on the physical condition of the nation's most talked-about mother-to-be, turning Joanna into a freakish *cause célèbre*. The finer points of her diet, the shape and condition of her breasts, the precise degree to which her belly button protruded, not to mention the furious exchanges between believers and sceptics, proved so engrossing that the summer came and went without anyone paying much attention to the fact that Joanna ought by this time to have been delivered. By September, when the first whiffs of imposture began to dampen the party atmosphere, an angry mob attacked Joanna's house, breaking windows and throwing brickbats, and causing the prophetess, whose condition was now deteriorating, to go into hiding.[13] It was while she resided at Blockley, in Gloucestershire, that Joanna secretly married; having never let a suitor anywhere near her, she now decided on this drastic step out of a nagging concern that an illegitimate child might be stigmatised and, more importantly, denied inheritance of her now-substantial wealth. As things turned out, this painful compromise was entirely unnecessary, for within six weeks of her November marriage Joanna died without Shiloh ever materialising.

For three days William Sharp, Jane Townley and Thomas Foley kept vigil by the body, believing that at any moment their leader would return to them from the dead. On the fourth day, in accordance with Joanna's last wishes, Richard Reece conducted an autopsy of her now putrid corpse. In a public statement published the next year, he recalled that as he set about his unenviable task 'the believers were all on tip toe to see Shiloh appear', and that upon discovering her womb to be the size of 'a small pear' they turned away 'abashed and dismayed'. In fact, they rallied themselves with astonishing speed, announcing to the Southcottian masses that Joanna had had a *spiritual* birth and that Shiloh had been caught up to heaven. Soon he would return in power and glory.

One cannot help but feel for Reece as he struggled to rescue his reputation after having been so thoroughly duped, especially since all the arguments he marshalled in his own defence caved in under the weight of self-reproach. Still, his injured professional pride made him unable to resist taking the odd swipe at Joanna. Concluding his blow-by-blow account of the autopsy, he wrote, 'it was thought unnecessary to examine the brain, where it was probable all the mischief lay'. In the end, he chose to exculpate himself by incriminating Joanna directly. Calling her a 'miserable woman', he declared, 'her apparently artless behaviour, I now consider the chief engine of her deception'.[14] Reece stopped short of writing his own medical obituary, but others took up where he left off, linking his name to those celebrated seventeenth-century physicians who had been made a laughing stock by Mary Toft, the notorious rabbit-breeder of Godalming, whose elaborate hoax exploited their obsession with monstrous births.

Joanna's death devastated her followers, but it did not destroy them. Rising phoenix-like from the ashes, the invisible Shiloh provided the gel which allowed the movement to cohere until new leaders emerged to lay claim to Joanna's mantle. Under John Wroe, the Bradford woolcomber whose strange career was recently novelised by Jane Rogers, George Turner and Zion Ward, Southcottianism went through a succession of reincarnations, finding new messiahs, new hopes and New Jerusalems down to the end of the nineteenth century.[15] One strand of the movement, however, which owed its existence entirely to Joanna's own ingenuity, outlived all the others. Indeed it survives today. At its centre sits 'Joanna's Southcott's Box', or 'The Ark of the New Covenant'. A hallowed vessel made of sturdy oak, nailed shut with copper nails, bolted, roped and weighing 156 lbs, it contains the sealed prophecies of the late prophetess. If Joanna could have known that her box would bob untroubled across the passage of time, buoyed by the hopes and fears of her latter-day followers, she would in all likelihood have been amazed, since, rather than being the product of her triumphant conviction in herself and her mission, the box is the very embodiment of her self-doubt.

Most of the time Joanna hid her insecurities well, usually behind extravagant tributes to herself such as abound in her writings:

> Since the earth's foundation plac'd I tell you here,
> Such wondrous woman never was below . . .

Westinghouse scientists and engineers admire the time capsule
of cupaloy minutes before it is lowered into the ground at the
New York World's Fair, there to remain for 5,000 years.

CONCVPISCENTIA

OBEDIENTIA

BABYLON

AEGYPTVS

CXXXIIj

Omne quod est in Mundo Concu
piscentia Carnis est, & Concupiscē
tia oculorū, & Superbia Vitæ ·&·

William Sharp's 1812 engraving of Joanna Southcott shows her holding the Bible open at Isiah 65, which promises 'new heavens and a new earth'. In 1806, a less demure Joanna vandalised 1000 prints of an engraving Sharp had made of Richard Brothers, daubing them with red paint.

Facing page The whore of Babylon astride the scarlet beast, drawn by sixteenth-century Portuguese engraver Francisco de Holanda for his *De aetatibus mundi imagines*, fol 67.

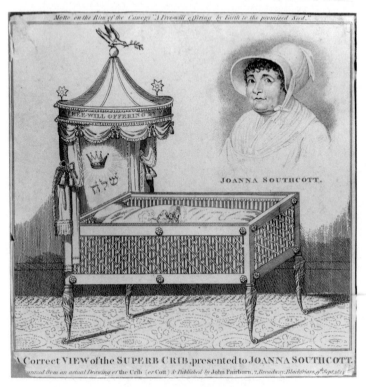

The customised crib commissioned by a Southcottian
enthusiast in anticipation of the birth of Shiloh.

Facing page **Alvin Gittin's portrait of Joseph Smith is one
of the more idealised images of the prophet available.**

Facing page The First Presidency of the Church of Jesus Christ of Latter-Day Saints (seated) and the Quorum of the Twelve Apostles in front of the Christus statue in Temple Square. This uniquely informal portrait radiates a sense of ease mixed with 'Masters of the Universe' self-assurance.

Left Part of the Biosphere 2 complex showing interconnecting biomes.

Steve Bridge in the Alcor cryotorium with three of the dewars containing the frozen corpses of Alcor's cryonauts.

She displayed a keen awareness of the need to establish her authority as a woman as much as a prophet. 'Is it a new thing for a woman to deliver her people? Did not Deborah do it? Did not Judith do it?' she asked. More simply put, the question might read: Can a woman be a saviour? In that Joanna developed a crude sort of feminist theology in which she figured as the saintly alter ego of Eve, the answer was yes: 'As she at first plucked the fruit, and brought the knowledge of the evil fruit; so at last she must bring the knowledge of the good fruit.' This argument crops up with such frequency in her writings, it is as if Joanna thought that by mere repetition it would acquire the savour of truth. But at root, no matter how hard she tried to align herself with her biblical predecessors, she had neither the regality of an Esther nor the guile of a Judith; she was just, as she would every now and then admit, 'a simple woman, dust and ashes, having no more knowledge of her own, but all that is given her from the Lord'.[16]

No doubt a convenience value attached to Joanna's duality, for it allowed her to go forth boldly in the world, a wondrous woman, prophesying to her heart's content, while at the same time giving her the final disclaimer against accusations that she was nothing but a jumped-up and vicious charwoman: if she uttered expletives against those who crossed her and damned scoffers to hell, ultimately it was the Spirit who spoke and not she. Yet it was precisely because the Spirit was her sovereign ruler that Joanna desperately felt the need to be certain it was the Lord and not the Devil whose commands she was compelled to obey. Hence in *The Strange Effects of Faith* she wrote of her Spirit: 'though I was strongly influenced to write by it, as a Spirit invisible, and convinced in my own mind that it was from God; yet knowing Satan might come as an angel of light, made me earnest in prayer, that the Lord would be my director, my Guide, and my Keeper.' Such genuine misgivings led Joanna to a preoccupation with external validation. This first manifested itself in her sealing her prophecies so that they might be objectively proved. Later, however, she devised a means of obtaining the coveted credentials of being declared authentic so extreme, it borders on the masochistic. Perhaps the practice of sealing her prophecies had not given her sufficient confidence? Or perhaps she had simply divined that a woman's belief in herself counted for little in a man's world? Whatever the reason, Joanna began to demand that she be put on public trial.

In 1794 the Spirit had commanded her to seal up her writings each year and place them in a box to be opened at an hour 'that neither men nor devils can frustrate'. Seven men, including Sharp and Foley, had examined the contents of the box at the Guildhall in Exeter in 1801, after which it was 'nailed up, never to be opened till brought into the presence of the twelve who will meet as judges of them'. This was effectively Joanna's first trial and with it her prophetic career was launched. Her second and third trials were more elaborate affairs, advertised in the press and open to all comers – though her critics insisted that no non-believers ever attended them. In January 1803 twelve judges and twelve jurymen (representing the four and twenty elders of Revelation) were selected from a company of fifty-eight people at High House, Paddington, to spend seven days adjudicating Joanna's writings. Depositions were read out, cross-examined and transcribed, and once again Joanna was vindicated by her Sanhedrin. The third and final trial took place at Neckinger House, Bermondsey, in December 1804 with forty-eight people in attendance. On the second day of this trial, resolutions to censure the clergy for their disbelief were unanimously passed; on the third day Joanna is supposed to have entered into a mystical trance; and on the seventh day a verdict was given that her visitations were 'by the Spirit of the Living God'.[17] After this trial, the box was resealed with express stipulations that it should not be opened for 120 years and then only in the presence of twenty-four Bishops, who were obliged to spend seven days in sombre conference before the act.

In 1974 a straggling Southcottian (who knows how many are left?) called Emma Grayson wrote an impassioned defence of Joanna called *Had They Had Knowledge*. Aside from the usual biographical history overladen with the misty-eyed flattery of an idolater, there is a curious and surprisingly detailed history of Joanna's box. After Joanna's death it seems that charge of the box, which Grayson believes to contain the 'Leaves of the Tree of Life for the Healing of the Nations', moved from Sharp to Townley to Foley and thence to Foley's son. While it resided with the Reverend Richard Foley at the Rectory in North Cadbury, Somerset, one Lavinia Jones from Bradford attempted to steal it. Disguising herself as a man, she forced entry into the rectory, slipped quietly upstairs and seized an old deal box, only to be captured by Foley junior. On Foley's death in 1869, Samuel Jowett of Leeds was elected custodian and thereafter the box has been passed from father to son. Its current whereabouts are a closely guarded secret, but the present secretary of the Panacea Society assures me that it remains in safe keeping.

When the 120-year embargo expired in 1924, the intrepid

Alice Seymour, fresh from her success with the National Portrait Gallery, tried her hand with the Archbishop of Canterbury. She got up a petition supported by 10,000 signatures demanding that the Bishops convene to open Joanna's box. Undeterred by rejection, she tried again in 1929, this time presenting the Primate with 28,757 signatures. Again, she did not succeed. Grayson recounts how at around this time the press got wind of the Panacea Society's activities and began championing its cause. In 1923 the *Daily News* contacted forty-nine Bishops about opening the box. Only twenty-one thought the matter merited a statement and not one of them offered to attempt gathering twenty-four of their peers. Six refused under any conditions to take part in a ceremonial opening; five expressed no opinion; two criticised the conditions attaching to the opening; and the remaining eight placed themselves in the hands of the Archbishop. This flurry on the fringes of the Church of England yielded unexpected fruit. In 1925 a 'Southcott box' came to light in Hammersmith; it was a small, black, coffin-shaped receptacle found to contain a copy of the New Testament, a wisp of silvery hair and piece of torn parchment purporting to be a Sibylline leaf. A genuine Southcott box, although not *the* box, also surfaced that year, containing the memorabilia of an early believer. And two years later the *Daily News* carried a report about a box being X-rayed at the National Laboratory of Psychical Research in the presence of the Bishop of Grantham. This vessel was found to carry a horse pistol, some eighteenth-century prophecy books, some coins, a dice box and a novel called *The Surprise of Love, or an Adventure in Greenwich Park* – hardly the sorts of thing to alleviate the sorrows of a nation in distress.

These days the Panacea Society has ceased bothering with petitions and taken instead to advertising. Every year the British public, or at least readers of the *Daily Mail* and the *Daily Telegraph*, are thus reminded of the 'Divinely appointed treasure' in their midst and warned that 'Crime, Banditry, Distress of Nations & Perplexity will continue to increase until the Bishops or their representatives open Joanna Southcott's Box of Sealed Writings'. Panacea activists firmly believe that only when the box is opened will Israel (that is, England) 'learn the things that belong unto their peace and may know how to prepare for the Coming of Messiah'. But although they keep announcing that 'this Coming is very near', the Bishops remain intransigent. And so the deadlock continues.

Of course, the Bishops' reluctance to open the box only perpetuates Joanna's mystique. And in this there is poetic justice, for Joanna was no more an imposter than she was a saviour, she was merely the innocent victim of her own credulity. That something of her essence should remain inviolate is only her due. In an odd sort of way, a virgin box is the best epithet for the virgin bride who sired it.

5. JOSEPH SMITH'S KINGDOM

Towards the end of 1829 Martin Harris, a wealthy farmer from Palmyra, near Rochester, New York, decided to mortgage his farm. It was not for agricultural purposes that he needed to raise funds, but to finance the publication of an edition of 5000 copies of a mysterious new bible. As scribe to the unlettered man who claimed to have found the bible on a set of golden plates buried in a stone chest, Harris had painstakingly taken down part of its 'translation'. He never saw the golden plates, save with the 'eye of faith', but an angel assured him that the bible was 'Another Testament of Jesus Christ' and along with ten other believers he bore official witness to its authenticity. The printer's bill cost him $3000 and his marriage. Lucy Harris had a mind of her own. Convinced that the new bible was an elaborate forgery, she had already taken action to prevent it coming to light, stealing the first 116 pages of the manuscript and destroying them. Now she tried every trick in the book to stop her husband mortgaging their farm, but to no avail. Had she succeeded, the world might never have heard of Joseph Smith and his *Book of Mormon*, and there would be no jokes about the Osmonds, tithing or the oddities of a stimulant-free diet.

Not everyone, however, was as suspicious as Lucy Harris. Palmyra, after all, lay in the heart of the 'burned over district', so called because of the strength and frequency with which the fires of religious revivalism tore through its towns and villages. And as news of the strange new bible spread through the region, the simple desire to believe was speedily rekindled. On 12 February 1830 Lucius Fenn of Covert wrote to an old neighbour in Connecticut, reporting excitedly that the bible 'speaks of the Milleniam day and tells when it is going to take place'. With such glorious promises trailed before him, Fenn could not but 'hope that there will be a greater out-pouring of the spirit than ever'.[1] Yet for all the speculation it roused, when the *Book of Mormon* finally appeared in March it met for the most part with jeering cynicism. Leading the critical onslaught were newspapers which only a few months earlier had advertised the book's publication and which now gleefully took to mocking 'Holy Joe' and his 'Golden Bible'. Somewhat more chagrined, the *Rochester Daily Advertiser* opined, 'A viler imposition was never practised. It is an evidence of fraud, blasphemy and credulity, shocking both to Christians and moralists.'

It was not so much that the book itself, arriving amid a storm of rumour and anticipation, proved a disappointment, but that the story of its discovery, which strained public credulity to breaking point, was irresistible material to sport with. If Joseph had been a more respectable character the journalists might have been kinder. As it was he hardly merited serious consideration. A poorly educated farmhand, he had so far distinguished himself in and around Palmyra only as a layabout, womaniser and inventor of tall stories. In his adolescence he regularly got himself into trouble for roping people into mad schemes to unearth chests of buried treasure which he claimed to have located using either a seer stone or by dowsing with a mineral rod. Neither the treasure chests nor the money Joseph collected as an advance from gullible prospectors ever saw the light of day. Now he was claiming that a heavenly messenger called Moroni led him to a nearby hill under which was buried a set of gold plates engraved with ancient hieroglyphics and supplied him with two transparent seer stones, the Urim and Thummim (Joseph's 'stone spectacles', according to the press), which, once fastened to a silver breastplate, enabled him to 'read' the bible. The tale seemed preposterous, both at face value and because there seemed no logical explanation as to why a twenty-four-year-old youth who had so far shown no respect either for truth or moral probity should suddenly want to portray himself as a paragon of religious virtue; more, as a millenarian prophet.

Joseph rode out the controversy with élan. True, he could not produce the golden plates to silence critics and sceptics – he would always maintain that he delivered them directly back to God once the work of translation was completed. But their material absence actually worked to his advantage. It allowed his supporters to crow about the miracle of divine inspiration, while forcing his detractors to trip and stumble in perplexity over the curiosity of how a virtually illiterate youth could have dictated several hundred pages of turgid scriptural prose with unhesitating rapidity and fluency if he had *not* received supernatural assistance. Joseph, comforted perhaps by imagining that the 'great desolations by famine, sword and pestilence' that would 'come on the earth in this generation' might do him the favour of consuming his enemies, played this take-it-or-leave-it

140

situation to maximum effect.[2] With a touching show of sincerity mingled with extraordinary confidence, he asked only that people read the *Book of Mormon* and appeal to the Holy Ghost as to whether or not it was truly from God. This they did, and promptly joined his Church of Jesus Christ of Latter-day Saints by the thousand.

Though the book clearly possessed a magnetic attraction for Joseph's readers, we can immediately discount the idea that this owed anything to its literary qualities. It is a hopelessly disjointed affair, leaden, plodding, convoluted and repetitive to the point of tedium. Moreover, large chunks of it are unintelligible, partly because of the difficulty of navigating its alien geography (where are Bountiful, Manti, Cumeni, Zarahelma, Sidon, Antionum and Jashon, for instance?), and partly because of the tangled web of genealogical ties binding together its multitudinous cast of cardboard kings, military leaders, holy men and villainous apostates. The best that can be said for it in relation to the Christian scriptures it purports to be an addition to or extension of is that it too comprises a series of books named after prophets or chroniclers, like Enos, Jarom, Mormon, Mosiah, Alma, Helaman, Nephi and Ether, and that these divide into chapters and verses complete with annotated cross-references. Beyond this, its attempt at scriptural parity only confirms it as second-rate pastiche. Although Joseph sought to give his sentences an authentic King Jamesian ring, he consistently fell short of the mark: witness, 'For behold, they had hardened their hearts against him, that they had become like unto a flint'. Famously lulled into a stupor by the book, Mark Twain branded it 'chloroform in print'.

But if the *Book of Mormon* is a miserable effort by literary standards, as a work of myth it is a masterpiece. Pared down to its core, it relates the religious history of two peoples of Hebrew extraction who migrated to the American continent in separate waves. First came the Jaredites, who fled Judea when God destroyed the Tower of Babel and confounded the languages of the people. They built a great civilisation in the New World, committing their records to a set of brass plates to be discovered by the second group of Israelite immigrants, the Nephites, who arrived by ship around 589 BC. This group were led to the promised land by Lehi, an ancient patriarch cast in the mould of Abraham. Like Abraham, Lehi had a number of sons among whom jealousies raged, leaving open wounds that made bitter enemies of the 'white and delightsome' descendants of Nephi, Lehi's most righteous son, and the tawny-skinned descendants of Laman, the family rebel. The bulk of the *Book of Mormon* details the many conflicts and apostasies between the Nephites and Lamanites, as chronicled by a succession of Nephite prophets, which culminated in the destruction of the Nephites in about AD 420. The Lamanites continued, but without the Nephites to guide them they eventually abandoned the God of Israel. This explained the sorry spiritual state of their American Indian descendants. The Nephites, meanwhile, were gone but not forgotten; God promised Moroni, the last of their prophets, that before the end of time he would deliver up their records to an unlearned man who would be charged with restoring the faith of the people.

It is easy to see how this epic story of two great rival cultures that posits a direct biblical link between the Old World and the New appealed to nineteenth-century Americans searching for historical roots and a uniquely American identity. It possessed the added fascination of identifying the American Indians as a Lost Tribe, the 'remnant of the house of Israel', an idea which, though not original to Joseph Smith, functioned to make his tales about ancient Hebrew immigrants somehow more palpable and proximate. It also enabled the Mormons to make an analogical leap, for if the American Indians were direct descendants of the Lamanites, then they themselves were heirs to the Nephite legacy. As a chosen people bound into a covenant with God, they believed that the promised land was theirs to inherit. In one stroke, Joseph thus gave his followers a sacred origin myth with which to dignify their past, as well as a quest to redeem America and rebuild Zion that set them on a future path of conversion and colonisation.

Joseph's binding up of the spiritual past and future pivoted on yet one more essential component, Christianity – or at least a version of it. Recall that the *Book of Mormon* is subtitled 'Another Testament of Jesus Christ', and if you turn to the third book of Nephi you learn, startlingly, that Christ visited America before his ascension and ministered to the Children of Lehi. Establishing his church among the people (Lamanites included), he chose twelve apostles from the Nephites and conferred upon Nephi himself 'power that ye shall baptise this people when I am again ascended into heaven' (3 Nephi 11: 21). It was on this testament that Joseph based his claims to have restored genuine apostolic Christianity. It is a remarkable piece of theological construction work. Recognising that a new faith cannot succeed by occupying itself with structural niceties – erecting decorative turrets and spires on the prayer-houses of its spiritual forbears when it ought to be knocking down walls – Joseph had the baton of Christianity pass directly from Christ to Nephi to himself, thus voiding 1800 years of Christian history. Without the religion of Paul, Augustine, Aquinas, Luther, Calvin and the rest muddying the waters of true faith, the Mormons could get down to acquainting themselves personally with Christ and to steadily deepening their understanding of his message. This intimate godly knowledge became the condition of entry into the Kingdom of God. In other words, dispersed Israel would only be regathered under the banner of Christianity.

Were it not for the fact that Mormonism has endured, it would be tempting to side with the journalists of 1830 and leave matters there. We could then have treated the religious sensibilities of men such as Harris and Fenn with a cool historical detachment, which, however much it respects the cosmological peculiarities of its subjects, allows us to wrap them up in the specificities of time and place. And we could have dealt summarily with Joseph, branded him a charismatic, muttered a few words about his aura and his creative inscrutability and then forgotten him. But history, in this instance, has not obliged the sceptics. While the majority of millenarian sects have perished almost without trace, their impatient calls for salvation discarded like unwanted silt by the flow of time, the Church of Jesus Christ of Latter-day Saints which Joseph founded on the basis of the *Book of Mormon* has more than managed to survive. It has been victorious. Mormonism is currently the fastest-growing new religion in the modern world. Its subscribers number 10 million and rising, and it continues to attract converts from across the globe at an astonishing rate of 900 per day. The *Book of Mormon* can be read in dozens of languages, Japanese, Samoan and English braille included; Zion has been built in Salt Lake City, Utah; and the angel Moroni, immortalised in effigy, blows his golden trumpet from atop the spires of forty-eight temples stretching from Seattle to New Zealand. Not since Mohammed founded Islam has a new faith been so successfully launched upon the world.

Those who do not share the Mormon belief that Joseph Smith was divinely inspired surely have to wonder at this achievement. In view of the current extent of Mormon political and economic power, perhaps there is good reason to fear it. Then again, when one considers the odds against which the faith has survived, the temptation is to simply admire it.

In *The American Religion* (1991), Harold Bloom does all three, more or less simultaneously, as if unable to decide quite how to absorb Mormonism's triumph. Bloom is in no doubt that Joseph Smith was an 'authentic religious genius', and by that he means someone who had an innate, almost intuitive, grasp of what was needful in order for a religion to work. The apostle Paul would be another example; both men understood how certain beliefs could be made to fit with their own aims. To put it in contemporary terms, they had agenda. Specifically, according to Bloom, Joseph 'had the genius to see that only by becoming a people could the Mormons survive'. This, of course, is the Jewish model, reliably tried and tested through three millennia shot through with conquests, inquisitions and holo-causts. Like a latter-day Moses, Joseph infused his followers with an incredible sense of identity and purpose, the former consisting not just of Lost Tribe status but of his very own version of The Law. By fashioning an entire set of commandments (unfolded over the years through a series of revelations) he confirmed the Mormons as a people apart. Everyone else was a Gentile. Of the distinct set of credal strictures and practices that Joseph imposed on his followers, the best known is probably polygamy, which, without going into the whys and wherefores, he viewed as a route to god-hood. The most absurd, meanwhile (because it had no theological basis), is the Word of Wisdom, the official title for the Mormons' strictly stimulant-free diet that places a total ban on the consumption of caffeine and alcohol, and the smoking of tobacco. Although the Mormon leadership banned polygamy over a century ago in deference to federal law and as a *quid pro quo* for Utah's admission into the Union, it is still practised by Mormon fundamentalists living isolated lives in the rural wilds of Utah, Colorado and Nevada. In their view, the Utah church has abandoned the religion of Joseph Smith. But I will come back to the modern church, whose position *vis-à-vis* Joseph is less diluted than first impressions might suggest.

Bloom acknowledges that history had a hand in further ratifying Mormon group identity. From 1831 to 1847, with a few stop-overs during which Joseph put his empire-building skills to use, the Mormons were more or less nomadic, and not by choice. Continually hounded by violent mobs and state militia, they wound their way from New York to Ohio to Missouri to Illinois, spurred by dreams of Zion and future Nephite glory. Already they were adept missionaries and their number was multiplied in this first decade by the arrival of thousands of immigrants from Britain and Scandinavia who crossed the seas to reach the promised land. Joseph intended to settle his people at Independence, Missouri, which he revealed was the 'centre place', a holy spot mid-way between the Atlantic and Pacific that was the original site of the Garden of Eden.

But state Governor Lilburn Boggs would not have any of it. Boggs developed a murderous hatred of the Mormons and, at one point, actually issued an extermination order against them. After the prophet's martyrdom in Carthage gaol in 1844, the Mormons fled civilisation altogether, embarking, under the leadership of the Church's second President, Brigham Young, on a pilgrimage to Zion that took them right across the American wilderness. By the time they finally came to rest in Utah, they had endured all kinds of biblical-style hardships.

Malise Ruthven, who in the 1980s spent over six months carefully retracing every leg of this difficult journey to produce one of the most lively accounts of early Mormon history to be written by a Gentile, found, despite himself, that his re-enaction of this great trek (even with the advantages of motoring) led him to identify strongly with the Mormon pioneers. It was as if something of their spirit and purpose infected him. As he approached the Salt Lake Valley, he recorded: 'my excitement was childish and palpable. It was singing in my ears and thumping through my veins ... And then, for the first time, I really *believed* in the Saints – not in their bizarre religion, but in what they represented: a collection of European townsfolk and villagers, who arrived in groups, not individually; who came not to escape, but to build.'[3] Ruthven's journey, and I'm referring to his passage from cynicism to empathy, is a testimony to the extent to which religious identity is forged through shared experience and the pursuit of a common goal.

My point, *pace* Bloom, is that the Mormons' early history is manifestly a catalogue of exile and persecution, marking yet another parallel between the Children of Israel and the Children of Lehi. Just as the ancient Hebrews fled bondage in Egypt, the

Mormons, under threat of violent annihilation, underwent an exodus all of their own. Through this ordeal, they developed a culture of resilience and self-reliance for which they are still renowned and which, from the distant comfort of their present-day theocracy, they continue to cherish. The population of Salt Lake City never appears more proud of its heritage than during the annual celebrations on Pioneer Day, while monuments to pioneers who never made it to Zion, like the handcart martyrs who froze to death in the mountains of Wyoming, take pride of place in the city's Temple Square. When I visited Salt Lake a couple of years back, the church had just taken to screening a full-length feature film called *Legacy*. In fact, this lavish Hollywood-style production following the fortunes and sufferings of a remarkably attractive New England family from their conversion in the east, through the early persecutions in Ohio and Missouri and the hardships of the pioneer trail, to their final homecoming in the west was being screened eight times a day to packed audiences of 600 a shot. Although Mormons are not especially known for their sentimentality, this overblown extravaganza could not have been more schmaltzy had Spielberg been in the director's chair. There was hardly a dry eye in the state-of-the-art IMAX cinema as the multi-national, multi-faith audience I sat with sniffed and snuffled their way through the joys and tears of pioneering.

I had the distinct impression that over and above being a tribute to the hard grit of pioneering, *Legacy* was a homage to the *idea* of pioneering or, rather, to pioneering as an American spiritual ideal. If the Mormons are quintessentially American, it is not because of their bogus mythology but because they exist as pilgrims in their own nation. Their almost alchemical transmutation of persecution and suffering into a perpetual effort to improve human destiny has, of course, been the *leitmotif* of every immigrant group to have alighted on American soil before or since, but none has stirred the crucible in quite so grandiose a style as the Mormons. Within only a few decades of arriving in Utah they had redirected their formidable organisational skills towards realising their dreams, and had built up and consolidated a genuine empire that embraced the whole of modern-day Utah as well as parts of New Mexico, Colorado, California and Nevada. Brigham Young named this territory Deseret, a term from the *Book of Mormon* meaning honey bee. The beehive, an emblem of industry, remains Utah's state symbol. Its insignia decorates highway signs and paving stones, the mastheads of newspapers, the ceiling of the great Tabernacle and the state and university seals. It is a constant reminder that the Mormons exist as a colony where every individual subscribes to an ethos of work for the good of the community. But the beehive is no less a symbol of Mormon autonomy, a badge of essential difference. Of the many paradoxes presented by Mormonism, the most curious is that, American as the Mormons are, authentic throwbacks to the Puritan vision, they are simultaneously and fundamentally unAmerican, even anti-American; a nation within a nation, proud and protective of their otherness.

Salt Lake City, state capital of Utah, is the humming centre of the beehive. Its wide tree-lined streets, banked by stately New England-style pioneer buildings and glassy monuments to modernity – hotels, banks and offices – are arranged on a grid and numbered outwards north, south, east and west from the Temple, in accordance with Joseph Smith's ground plans for

Zion. The Temple itself is an imposing structure, though not especially attractive. Four storeys high and crowned by six vaguely gothic spires, it took some forty years to complete because the huge granite slabs of its husk had to be hauled by oxen from a canyon thirty-five kilometres distant in the days before the Transcontinental railway branched into Utah. By day, the Temple is a sombre presence, its lacklustre grey exterior cold and uninviting, but when lit by night its spires glow enticingly like beacons calling in weary souls from miles around.

Salt Lake feels like no other American city. Notwithstanding its urban beat, big-business swagger, shopping centres, cinemas and restaurants, the whole place is pervaded by a sense of reserve, solemnity and conformity, pinched and crisped into stiffness by the alpine air of the surrounding Wasatch mountains. Edmund White described the feel perfectly; it's as if the city inhaled a sharp intake of breath and then refused to release it.[4] Although the Church's public affairs department likes to pretend otherwise, the line between religious and civil authority is more fantasy than living reality. With the State Legislature ninety per cent Mormon, the city's Gentile population has no real State or municipal powers. Smoking is forbidden in public places and restaurants are not allowed to serve alcohol. That said, however, there are designated areas where the Word of Wisdom may lawfully be jettisoned, mainly private members' clubs tucked away in the nooks and crannies of the city centre. An apostate friend of mine took me to one, the New Yorker, a plush basement dining club swamped in a nicotine fog, where the juices of Bacchanal flowed freely and the atmosphere effervesced with the kind of whispering camaraderie that must have enlivened the haunts of devil-may-care revellers during the prohibition era.

I decided to revise my impression of Salt Lake. Stepford, it seemed, was only skin-deep; the officially sanctioned underworld brought the place more into line with Margaret Atwood's *The Handmaid's Tale*. The difference is that, while Atwood's mandarins indulged their own weaknesses behind closed doors, it is the Gentiles whose foibles the Church is prepared to overlook. Any attempt to promote non-Mormon values from within its own ranks is instantly demolished. A couple of years ago, when a group of college students formed a gay discussion group – homosexuality being defined as a wilful rebellion against divinely sanctioned family values – the Church responded by banning all extra-curricular student societies. There are no half-way houses within Mormonism. It is a faith that demands total commitment from its adherents, and excommunication rather than forgiveness is the preferred corrective to behaviour deemed deviant. Adulterers, for example, or those daring to publicly criticise the Church, are immediately booted out.

The church offices, seat of all power in Salt Lake, occupy a twenty-eight-storey tower block adjacent to Temple Square. It's the tallest building in the city, a veritable watchtower from whose roof the whole of Zion may be surveyed. Dwarfing even the Temple, it rises up like a great corporate monolith to dominate every vista. From here, the church leadership rules over the Mormon drones through continuing revelation. The power structure is pyramidal, with the Prophet-President at its apex, flanked by the two councillors of the First Presidency.

151

Then, in descending order of importance, there's the Council of the Twelve (Gordon B. Hinckley's apostles), the First Quorum of the Seventy, the Second Quorum of the Seventy and the Presiding Bishopric. These upper echelons of the Mormon superstructure go by the disturbingly Orwellian title of 'General Authorities' (see plate 6). In the church almanac, row upon row of their smiling faces present a solid image of benevolent patriarchal power; exclusively male, virtually all Caucasian and predominantly over sixty. Only in 1978 were black Mormons admitted into the priesthood (previously, blacks ranked beneath Lamanites, having carried the curse of Ham down the centuries) and women continue not to figure at all. They are denied the Aaronic Priesthood bestowed without exception on every boy over the age of twelve.[5]

Although the forces of conservatism within the Mormon hierarchy are as tenacious as ever, conceding little to the social dynamics of the twentieth century, the Church is remarkably worldly. As Malise Ruthven has noted, the priests and Elders who move silently through the carpeted corridors of central HQ, sharp-suited and looking to the rest of the world like international bankers, are primarily executives of a gigantic corporate enterprise which manages an untold fortune. Its annual income from tithing alone is thought to exceed a billion dollars. In addition, the Church Corporate owns farmland and real estate across the States, presides over a small media empire – embracing everything from print through to radio, television and satellite stations – and has wide-ranging investments in the financial and construction industries, retailing, welfare and education.

The Church, in fact, has virtually become an advertisement

for itself. A honeypot of power and riches, it hardly has need of the *Book of Mormon* to attract more bees. People these days are far more likely to want to belong to a successful tribe than a Lost Tribe. And because they are prepared, in vast numbers, to forfeit personal freedom as payment for joining, the Church is able to continue growing at a spectacular rate even as it remains reactionary and intransigent.[6]

One might expect an institution whose principal concern is supposed to be with affairs spiritual to be diffident about its temporal successes, but the Mormons are not a demurring people. As enamoured of their own worldly achievements as anyone else, they pride themselves on having taken only 160 years to evolve from an inward-looking millenarian sect into an urbane and ambitious global presence. (It took the ancient Church Fathers over 400 years to make a comparable journey.) Press Mormon officials today about their millenarian origins and a mild embarrassment befalls them. They would rather talk about the high-ranking offices church members hold in the military, the FBI, the CIA and the government, their international business contacts, their hobnobbing with foreign dignitaries or their passionate patriotism. Indeed, they seem inordinately eager to portray themselves as the very model of the American establishment. Because the Church is famously propagandist, it is sometimes difficult to see the wood for the trees, but American establishment the Mormons are not. Nor will they ever be – despite appearances. Much in the way that the Church's rhetoric about salvation through Jesus Christ masks the fact that its complex theology, whatever else it may be, is not Christian – it is not even monotheistic – its establishment aura is just so much camouflage obscuring the real ambitions of the faith. Ultimately, these ambitions, which are earthly enough, may be viewed as subversive of the American establishment. But that very much depends on how faithful the Mormons have remained to the religion of Joseph Smith. And, in particular, to his singular vision of the kingdom of God, which assumed form at the precise point at which Joseph succeeded in turning himself into a messianic God in an extreme manifestation of that national paradigm we have come to call the American Dream.

Nauvoo, 1844. Within five years of quitting Missouri, the Mormons had built a thriving city on a picturesque hillside bend in the Mississippi River within the borders of Illinois. It had a city charter, its own militia, a population of 12,000 and a concentration of wealth accumulated through farming, brewing and manufactures second only to Chicago's. Nauvoo (a Nephite term meaning 'beautiful plantation') was Joseph's first and last attempt at building Zion. Like Salt Lake City today, the town was arranged on a grid with the Temple at its centre and, like today, the church leadership reigned supreme. In fact, by 1844 Joseph's rule was virtually autocratic. The prophet had heaped so many honours and medals and titles upon himself, he became a walking compendium of nineteenth-century oligarchy. He was 'Prophet, Seer and Revelator' of the Church of Jesus Christ of Latter-day Saints, Mayor of Nauvoo, Leader of the City Council, Lieutenant-General of the Nauvoo Legion, Judge of the Municipal Court, newspaper editor, temple architect, real-estate agent, registrar of deeds, trustee-in-trust of church finances, Presidential candidate and the husband of up to fifty (by some estimates) wives.

Joseph had always been vain, and the residents of Nauvoo soon grew accustomed to his wandering through the town dressed in full military regalia and parading the cavalry of the Nauvoo Legion at every available opportunity. Josiah Quincey, later Mayor of Boston, who visited Nauvoo in 1844 and noted Joseph's attachment to the impermanent things of this world, described him as a 'bourgeois Mohammed'.[7] But beneath all the fun of pomp and dazzle, Joseph had fallen seriously victim to his own self-awe. In a public letter to the Saints in 1842 he announced, 'I was ordained from before the foundation of the world.' As with so many messiahs grown intoxicated with a sense of their own unlimited power, his religious mission began to taken a turn towards *realpolitik*. The clearest evidence that Joseph expected secular authorities as well as Mormons to eventually bend to his rule comes from a sermon of this period in which he compares himself to the stone that smashes to bits the heathen nations in the Book of Daniel:

I am like a huge, rough stone rolling down from a high mountain; and the only polishing I get is when some corner gets rubbed off by coming in contact with something else, striking with accelerated force against religious bigotry, priestcraft, lawyer-craft, lying editors, suborned judges, and jurors, and the authority of perjured executives, backed by mobs, blasphemers, licentious and corrupt men and women – all hell knocking off a corner here and a corner there. Thus will I become a smooth and polished shaft in the quiver of the Almighty, who will give me dominion over all and every one of them, when their refuge of lies shall fail, and their hiding place shall be destroyed.[8]

The delivery of this philippic would not be the only time Joseph was to enlist Daniel in his cause. In a public speech delivered on 10 May 1844, he declared, 'I calculate to be one of the instruments of setting up the kingdom of Daniel, by the word of the Lord, and I intend to lay a foundation that will revolutionise the whole world.' What most of his listeners were unaware of at the time was that the kingdom of God had already been established.

Joseph's millenarianism had always been a mongrel thing, half pre-millennialist, in that he expected the world to end imminently, and half post-millennialist, in that his belief in human perfectionism fuelled his imperative to build Zion. It was a classic case of bet-hedging, contrived to allow for the possibility of the Millennium being realised irrespective of *when* the world ended. It's what philosophers would term a pragmatic compromise and it meant that Joseph was free to give whatever shape he chose to the kingdom of God. At Nauvoo, he chose to make the kingdom temporal, blending theology with politics, empire-building and arcane ritual. Without the empire-building the Kingdom might have remained symbolic; the 'keys to the kingdom of Heaven', bestowed on church elders in an elaborate Temple endowment ceremony, merely metaphorical; Joseph's theodemocracy, 'where God and the people hold the power to conduct the affairs of men in righteousness', just a futuristic ideal. But in 1843 Joseph petitioned Congress asking that Nauvoo be made a completely independent federal territory. The kingdom of God was taking on substance. As a concrete reality, it would need borders, diplomatic recognition and assured autonomy. It also needed a government. This Joseph catered for the following year when he created the

Council of Fifty. A board of fifty 'princes' constituting 'the highest court on earth', the Council was composed of men reared as militant democrats whom Joseph hand-picked to form the nucleus of a world government for the Millennium and whom he now asked to draw up a constitution for the kingdom of God. One of the first acts of this elect-among-the-elect was to crown the prophet 'king of the Kingdom of God'.[9] That same year, 1844, Joseph ran as a presidential candidate. Pragmatically, this was a move contrived to bribe politicians of all persuasions into taking affirmative action against anti-Mormon agitators, yet its symbolic import can hardly be avoided: in some corner of his mind, heavily hinted at in his sermon on Daniel, Joseph intended his theodemocracy to embrace the entire nation.

Whatever Joseph's plans for a revolutionary theocratic government, he never had a chance to set them in motion, for later that year he was shot dead in Carthage gaol by renegades from the Illinois militia. The Kingdom, however, endured long after the prophet had gone. In secret ceremonies in Salt Lake, the Council of Fifty crowned first Brigham Young, then John Taylor, kings of the kingdom of God. Thereafter, the progress of the Mormon monarchy becomes sketchy, largely because the mysterious activities of the Council are not recorded in the official church histories. However, as late as 1911, one of the Fifty addressed Joseph Fielding Smith in a letter as 'Prophet, President and King', making a mockery of Utah's statehood.

Over the past century, the Church has, with varying degrees of reluctance, had to abandon much of Joseph Smith's teaching. In its determined march into the American mainstream, it has repudiated plural marriage, exchanged democracy for republicanism, forsaken its early experiments in communism for a brand of hardline capitalism and grown fiercely patriotic. What remains tantalisingly open-ended, however, is what has become of the kingdom of God.

Leaders of the modern Church would have us believe that the kingdom of God has retreated into the murky realm of shadows, so that it is now both a shadow of its former self and a foreshadow on a corrupt world of the kingdom to come – a merely figurative entity. If this is what they really believe, then their avid pursuit of temporal glory is not just puzzling, it is a profanity. The Melchizedek Priesthood too, held in all fullness by every one of the General Authorities, is deprived of much of its clout, since Joseph was adamant that 'that Priesthood is a perfect law of theocracy and stands as God to give laws to the people'.[10] And yet the kingdom of God cannot exist as Joseph conceived it in current Mormon practice, because without plural marriage the Saints cannot complete their 'eternal progression' towards god-hood. And without being mortal gods they are not fit to inhabit the kingdom of God. It is no wonder that fundamentalist Mormons feel justified in thinking that the leaders of the Utah Church have made one too many a compromise with Gentile America.

There is but one solution to this problem, however, though it is nothing short of insane. Yet to all intents and purposes the Mormons have embarked on it with gusto and a studious dedication. If they cannot build a temporal kingdom of God whose government is the only legitimate legislative authority in the world and the only monarchy with divine right to reign, then they will obliterate the competition. In all seriousness, the Mormons plan nothing less than to demolish all self-appointed law-givers and monarchs anointed by those without Priesthood power. And they will proceed in precisely the manner Joseph would have done. On that fateful day in 1844 when the prophet announced his intention to lay a foundation to revolutionise the world, he went on: 'it will not be by sword or gun that this kingdom will roll on ... the power of truth is such that all nations will be under necessity of obeying the Gospel.'[11] In short, and crazy as it may seem, the Mormons fully intend to convert the world. As my apostate friend in Utah put it, making reference to the Mormons' energetic programme of baptising the dead into their faith in order to release their souls from the spirit world (a value-free purgatory of Joseph's invention): 'they want the whole world, dead or alive!'

Looking at the Mormon Church from the outside in, its most visible and vocal champions are its missionaries. Temple Square in Salt Lake City is swarming with them, mainly primly dressed and impeccably polite young women who refer to each other as 'Sister' and who can barely contain their desire to 'share' their love of Jesus with unsuspecting tourists. In fact, the Mormons, who do not hold with the doctrine of original sin, the idea of eternal damnation or the absolute separation between God and man, no more believe in traditional Christianity than they do in American democracy, but the message of salvation through Jesus Christ delivers them converts swiftly and effectively. From Temple Square, the missionary population radiates out to cover the entire globe. At any one time the Church has 50,000 full-time missionaries stationed in the field – a substantial army by any standards, whose movements are meticulously coordinated along a chain of command that extends from the Mission Presidents, based off-shore, right through to the General Authorities. One gets the sense that the President of the Church himself takes a keen interest in their progress.

Although missionary work is highly valued by evangelical groups of all persuasions, none organises its missionary operation on anything like the same scale, nor regards spreading the word as quite the same order of good deed. The missionaries, young men and women in their late teens and early twenties, refer to their two-year missions as 'callings', that is to say, as direct commands from on high, and families save for years so their children can serve missions much in the way that Jewish families save for bar mitzvahs. Through the missionary calling, moreover, Aaronic priests progress to Church Elders and so begin their ascent of the Mormon hierarchy. If there exist such beings as 'career Mormons', missionary work is the way to go.

Individual missionaries must be prepared to accept a posting anywhere in the world and they are admirably prepared for the task by intensive language-training courses at the Brigham Young University in Provo. After English, Spanish and Portuguese, the most commonly spoken languages in the international Church are Tagalog, Japanese, Samoan, Cebuano, Llokano, Korean and Tongan. No island, however isolated, is beyond the ken of the Saints. It is entirely owing to the missionaries' hard work that the Church is currently flourishing across Latin America, with around a million members in Mexico, and almost as many in Brazil. There has also been a dramatic growth in membership in Chile and Peru, not to mention Africa, the Caribbean and Asia. All in all, there are now more Mormons living outside the United States than within it.

Today the Church numbers some 10 million (not including

the dead, baptised by proxy, who effectively count as stand-by Mormons who will enter the kingdom of God come the Millennium). By the year 2000 the Church estimates that worldwide membership will have swelled to 11 million. But how many members will there be in 2010? In 2050? And in 2070? Time is not an issue for the Mormons, even if Utah abounds with Saints whose reflex response to wars and rumours of war, oil crises, earthquakes and economic collapse is to purchase mountains of canned foods and store them in what the real-estate agents euphemistically call 'fully furnished basements'. Crass millenarianism is not the way of the church leadership, who, slowly and surely, are building the kingdom of God. They will not cease and they will not falter, for they firmly believe that both the world and the future are theirs. Moreover, it is not inconceivable that they are right. What will determine their success on this course, however, is ultimately a matter not of numbers but of demographics.

The recent shift in the cultural tectonics of the Church presents the Mormon leadership with the greatest challenge the faith has so far had to face this century – multi-culturalism.[12] The Nephite legacy has always been understood to be peculiarly American, as American as is the Church's pioneer heritage, and the Mormons further believe that New Jerusalem will eventually be built on the continent, in Independence, Missouri, the hallowed 'centre place', where the Church, incidently, has recently been buying up land. This mythology, embracing both sacred history and future destiny, cannot but sit uncomfortably with the present international make-up of the Church. One only needs to visit Salt Lake to view its cosmopolitan constituency; the place is full of Koreans, Tongans, Africans and

Japanese, many of whom make the pilgrimage in order to get married in the Temple, only to wind up staying. To date, a sort of feeble apartheid seems to exist, judging by the list of church wards in the Salt Lake phone book, which contains separate entries for 'Tongan Wards', 'Laotian Wards' or 'Vietnamese Wards'. Yet if the Church is serious about being a global faith, it will soon have to turn to examining its attitude to race – its own as much as any other. The days of 'white and delightsome' Caucasian rule are fast coming to a close, and it ought not to be long before the constitution of the General Authorities begins to reflect the ethnic and national diversity of church members. In short, the Church will have to de-Americanise itself. In spiritual terms, this will not be easy, for the problem is this: how can the whole world be made to feel as emotively about so exclusively American a faith?

While Mormon historians and archaeologists have been exercising themselves over this question lately, their piecemeal answers are far from satisfactory. It is as though even the intellectuals haven't quite grasped the scale of revisionism that needs to be got under way. They argue, for instance, that the Jaredites landed not in North America but in Central America or South America, in an attempt to attend to the identity problems of their Latin members. Or they seek to justify Polynesian claims to Nephite descent by citing the last chapter of *Alma*, which tells of Nephite splinter groups who sailed off into the 'west sea', never to return. But there are only so many internationalist readings the *Book of Mormon* can bear. It is, after all, the product of a man who never travelled outside America. More fruitful perhaps is the approach of President Hinckley, who is encouraging the lay clergy to spiritualise and thereby universalise the concept of pioneering. Time has yet to tell whether his strategy will work. And while there are no guarantees that his successors will continue to pursue it, one may be certain that they will abandon it only if they manage to devise a more sure-fire means of ensuring their own survival. Ever pragmatic, the Mormons remain, on this score at least, unswervingly loyal to Joseph Smith.

6. THE PROPHETIC CLOCK

In the Judaeo-Christian tradition, history and time walk hand in hand, they are eternally and intimately entwined. The one has no meaning without the other: numbers and events are partnered for life. As J. B. Priestley put it in his eloquent meditation *Man and Time* (1964), we are 'time-haunted'.

Priestley was speaking for modern man, imprisoned by 'the inescapable beat' of passing time that locks us into forward motion, contains our every action and impoverishes the concept of eternity by turning it into 'a vast helping of passing time'. He hankered for the Great Time of the ancient civilisations, a mythological time, a time of the gods in which creation, magic and power co-existed. It is what the Aborigines refer to as eternal dream time. It is 'all-at-once' instead of 'one-thing-after-another' – a lyrical eternal present that we like to imagine once had concrete reality in the hazy and impossibly distant past of prelapsarian Eden, in the Summerians' paradisiacal Dilmun or the Golden Age of Hellenistic lore.[1] Though unable to reach this time in any real sense, we might perpetually circle it through the ritual observation of astronomical cycles, which have their terrestrial counterpart in the seasonal or agricultural

164

year. In this sense, it is a time whose beginning may be for ever symbolically relived within cosmologies which insist that the value of moving forward lies in the idea of return.

What Priestley felt simply nostalgic about, today's mystery-mongers – equally disillusioned with the products of passing time – are determined to resurrect. Chief among them is Graham Hancock, whose best-selling *Fingerprints of the Gods* (1995) unearths all manner of cryptic mysteries touching on everything from the myth of Atlantis to the riddle of the Sphinx. The book contains such a jumble of long-forgotten esoteric material, drawn from ancient Egypt, Bolivia, Mexico and Peru, that it is not immediately clear whether any organising principle is in operation. Only in the conclusion does Hancock refer to his having 'an urgent mission'. This, it turns out, is to calculate the advent of the 'Great Return'. What eventually transpires, after ploughing through 450 pages of astronomical and geological puzzles, mathematical progressions, and disquisitions on primitive art, archaeological ruins and early map-making, is that Hancock is not only convinced that the lost traditions and beliefs of prehistory open the door onto a profound hidden knowledge of the cyclical nature of time, but that he embarked on his intellectual quest for the sake of our souls. The Great Return, he argues, might be the only thing that can save us from ourselves.

Of course, salvation was the nub of the Judaeo-Christian version of things, and if Jews and Christians sneered at the way impious pagans went about in a circle it was because they believed that the present, eternal or not, held no prospect of it. Since *being* implied only a kind of stasis, they made a massive investment in *becoming*. Fulfilment belonged to the future and passing time became the vehicle that would carry them towards it. Jews and Christians therefore severed the concept of time from myth and ritual, binding it up instead with history, making it real. No longer an abstract concept that existed in its own right, time became something that only had meaning as it was experienced. It was, in effect, enslaved by history. This sort of time required a different calendar, one that began not with the sun's or the moon's position in a particular cycle, but with an event, the creation of the world, say, or the birth of Christ. In other words, it became necessary to count in order to know where you were. The Bible serves as an immutable blueprint for this model of time, revealing a deterministic and linear view of human history that stretches from the Creation to the Last Days. Between being switched on and switched off, time's relentless beat is marked by a periodised succession of never-to-be-repeated events: Adam and Eve were banished from the Garden of Eden once and for all; humanity all but perished in the flood only once; Christ died for our sins only once; and he will return to complete his work only once. Every event is unique and preordained.

The obvious problem with the scriptural scenario is that human history, with its undeniable curvature – its peaks and troughs, cadences, contours and revolutions – does not much resemble the straight line alongside which mankind is supposed to march steadily onwards towards fulfilment. But the Bible has two in-built solutions to this difficulty. One is that it simply insists that history works in a cumulative fashion. Guided by the hand of providence it conspires for the good, and though in times of misery and despair it appears to stray from its path or retrace its steps, its every turn is predetermined and its underlying course, hidden perhaps from faithless eyes, is a meaningful progression towards fulfilment. The fact that Christ was understood to have fulfilled all the messianic typologies of the Old Testament may be seen as proof of just this. The other biblical remedy for the disparity between what history looks like and how it ought to look is apocalypse. For all its veiled language and wilful opacity, apocalypse unravels the essential mystery of precisely how divine will traces a straight line through the vicissitudes of human history. It is a device for measuring history.

With a keen sense of melodrama, apocalypse outlines the historical narrative from curtain rise to curtain fall, introducing us to the main players, building suspense around critical scenes and dividing the drama into a number of acts. At its most fundamental level, it narrates a three-act play, with turning points situated at the flood and final destruction to mark the sole instances of divine intervention in world history. But because it goes about this task by tracing the procession of generations or kingdoms through a succession of ages, understanding history through apocalypse is rather like peeling successive layers off an onion. On the outside is the visible world of events, which, when correctly interpreted, discloses a story about the progress and reverses of peoples and nations. Strip that away and you arrive at an eye-watering interior tale of the troubled relationship between God and mankind.

Different apocalypses stretch the basic three-act play over different numbers of epochs or ages. Enoch, for example, divides time into ten cosmic weeks, each heralding a new generation. Two run from the creation to the flood, five run from the deluge to the present, leaving three to unfold before the final judgement. In the Jewish apocalyptic tradition ten ages appear to be the norm. Even Daniel's four empires, succeeded by the kingdom of God, fit this ten-age schema since they relate only to post-diluvian times. And most of the Sibylline Oracles follow suit. Baruch's apocalypse sounds the only dissonant note, picturing twelve periods of alternating 'bright' and 'dark', the last and longest blanket of night signalling the boundless reign of evil before the world is brightened for ever.

St John's Revelation, with its rounds of seven, offers an alternative taxonomy of time compatible with dividing world history into seven millennia, the last being Christ's terrestrial reign. Originally part of Hellenistic astrological lore, the idea of seven cosmic epochs of 1000 years' duration, each taking its character from one of the planets, found its way into Jewish and Christian traditions. Here, it was stripped of its pagan symbolism and reinterpreted in the light of Genesis using the Psalmist's metaphor 'for a thousand years in thy sight are but as yesterday when it is past'. The new understanding was that the world would endure for 6000 years, analogous to the six days of creation, while the seventh day of rest was taken to refer to God's kingdom on earth.[2] Allowing Genesis to contain a prefiguration of world history made the Bible look seductively symmetrical, with both beginning and end pointing in the same direction, foretelling of things to come. Not surprisingly, commentators on apocalypse exhibit an inordinate fascination with historical time and its structure.

Over the years, successive generations of biblical scholars, prophets, millenarians and mystics who defy categorisation have tried to map historical events onto this primal narrative with an empirical zeal that insists on a one-to-one correspondence between actual events and apocalyptic fiat. The exercise involves trawling the past in search of fulfilled prophecies, the seven seals, trumpets or vials of wrath, the four doomed world-kingdoms, the demise of the whore of Babylon or the reign of Antichrist. It is a form of navigation, a plotting of historical coordinates that give you your bearings in time. Presented with their combined efforts, one encounters an interpretive labyrinth full of competing and, often, partially overlapping historical identifications, unexpected twists and turns and definitive boundaries that mysteriously shift. Even the most theoretically straightforward mappings seem to admit innumerable variations. Take the example of Daniel's 'four kingdom, four beast' progression.[3] The ancient sage was good enough to name the first as Babylon, but he left the job of assigning the rest to the vivid imaginations of following generations. In the Jewish context of Selucid persecution, Babylon, Media, Persia and Macedon were unchallenged representatives of the infernal succession. However, following Titus' destruction of the Temple in AD 70, Rome seemed to beg inclusion and, for the sake of its accommodation, Persia and Media had to be squeezed together into the second kingdom. Later, Jewish mystics responded to the Mahometan threat and the trials of the Inquisition by denoting Turkey or Spain as the fourth kingdom, identifications made possible through a prior compression of the Greek and Roman empires into a monster third kingdom of Hellenism.

While Jews were busy squeezing and squashing empires, Christians were engaged in indefinitely extending Rome. After the city fell to the Goths, its fourth kingdom candidacy was initially prolonged through a blurring of boundaries with Byzantium. Any new wicked power, meanwhile – Saracens,

Lombards, Huns, Vandals and so on – was then piled into the feet and toes of the Danielic statue or the horns of the fourth beast. Later, Catholic heretics and leaders of the Reformation further elongated Rome by pronouncing the Roman Church co-extensive with the defunct empire (a mapping that simultaneously labelled the pope as Antichrist) and assimilating its various satellite nations into feet or horns. Some Reformation commentators thought the Turks wicked enough to displace Rome, while the Germany of Charles V became a popular fourth kingdom choice among Counter-reformation agitators. More often than not the cause of theology served as a vehicle for political propaganda. In Tudor England, for example, Spain, as public enemy number one and principal aide of the papal kingdom, popularly played the reviled 'little horn' to Rome's fourth kingdom. But by the end of the seventeenth century enmity had shifted to Bourbon France, where Louis XIV's Revocation of the Edict of Nantes licensed ruthless persecution of Huguenots. From the safety of his Dutch exile, Huguenot prophet Pierre Jurieu became a tireless promulgator of anti-Bourbon invective. His *Accomplishment of the Scripture Prophecies* (1687) prophesied that the ten-horned beast of Rome would fall as its successor kingdoms gradually withdrew support. Already Sweden, Denmark, England and some German states had seen the error of Catholic ways; next France would break its papal bonds. Jurieu's prediction that the French withdrawal would commence between 1710 and 1715, with 1785 marking 'the glorious reign of Jesus Christ on the Earth', helped whip up a millenarian frenzy after the Revolution of 1789. One could go on in this manner, tracking the fourth kingdom's ever-changing guise down to the present day. Suffice it to say that Daniel's infernal succession remains as useful a means as ever of smuggling political propaganda into grand historical schemes under the cloak of theology, Ronald Reagan's demonisation of the Soviet Union as the 'evil empire' being a case in point.

Thus far, I have cited only the mappings of Futurists, who believe that Daniel's apocalypse contains the scheme of world history until the end of time. Praeterists – those who insist that Daniel's prophecies, like those of the rest of the Old Testament, apply only to history before the birth of Christ – have had ideas of their own. In praeterist schemes the four kingdoms usually culminate in the original Roman empire, with its various emperors or provinces crammed into feet and horns. But a variation on the praeterist theme developed the notion that Daniel's prophecies applied to Jews alone, chronology notwith-standing. The implication was that the longed-for fifth kingdom would be realised with the restoration of the Jews and that the fulfilment of this prophecy was somehow prerequisite for the Christian Millennium. Thus, in his *Letter to the Jews* (1794), Joseph Priestley could sincerely write, 'may God make you the most illustrious as you are now the most despised, of all the nations of the earth'. Similar noble sentiments, underscored by self-interest, led nineteenth-century adventists in England and America to celebrate the formation of the Universal Israelite Alliance in 1882 with a prophetic flurry that was to be echoed by fundamentalists this century after the founding of the state of Israel.

One might well ask how it is possible for the straight line of divine intent to be preserved amid such abundant interpretive convolutions. Yet, contrary to what might be expected, the providential plan emerges intact not because of historical fact but in spite of it. Millenarians, prophets and biblical commentators may be as attentive to accurate historical detail as the most meticulous antiquarian, but they display no humility before the chronicle. Playing fast and loose with the historical record, they mould it like potter's clay, first into one shape, then another, in order to obtain the right fit with apocalypse. Rome's extraordinary, almost cartoonish, extensibility demonstrates how far the historical canvas can be stretched from one apocalyptic pole to the next, while empires that thrived for centuries are habitually compressed into comparatively insignificant apocalyptic watersheds. Microscopically enlarged and telescopically condensed by turn, the whole of the past can seem to be at the mercy of an apocalyptic feel-good factor.

In fact, although apocalypse functions as a topographical aid, allowing a mapping of history to the prophetic scenario at precise points in time, it doesn't much matter where you situate the individual historical markers, so long as when you join the dots you get a straight line. There is a certain seductive charm to the whole business, not least because, with the exception of human progress, which passes for the work of Antichrist, apocalypse's benchmarks – the rise and fall of nations, social revolutions, famines, plagues and natural catastrophes – chime with our secular sense of what counts as important historically. Indeed, secular history can justifiably be accused of being just as much a product of straight-lined myopia. In the habit of relating the past as an epic story, secular historians rely on a selective vision that effectively concertinas the vast sweep of history so that only a robust handful out of the superabundance of past events sit on its ridges. This privileged row of epoch-making moments is then strung together to form the principal plot, while the bulk of world-historical happenings sink into oblivion in the concertina grooves. Though secular history attempts to get at the underlying order in the apparently disordered sphere of events, it should not be confused with sacred history, whose linearity is of an entirely different order – a product of divine fiat not human perspective. World history conforms to an unbending programme because the whole of it is preordained, none of it could have been otherwise. Contemporary events slot into the same inflexible schedule, their outcomes are predetermined: the future is all mapped out for us, its joys and miseries already prepared. All this rather takes the steam out of history, rendering untenable the domino model of cause and effect that underpins secular history and denying mankind the power to change things for better or worse. The mythic overlay of apocalypse imposes on the world of events a supra-temporal significance, weaving history instead into a tapestry of signs and signifiers. In so doing, it completely overturns the accepted order of things, making the myth reality and history the allegory.

Sacred Arithmetic and the Jehovah's Witnesses

The sense that apocalypse documents a hidden reality extends to mystical numbers. These are accorded the same relationship to dates as the apocalyptic narrative bears to history – which is to say, they have existential validity. Nothing has provoked more thumbing through Daniel, Revelation and the various other apocalyptic passages of the Bible than the idea that embedded within their riddle-like verses there lurks a timetable for the end of the world. The logic of apocalypse makes the idea irresistible, since, if history unfolds in a predetermined fashion and prophecy is understood as literal, it follows that the messianic hour, the start of the Millennium and the date of the Last Judgement must be fixed and can therefore be computed. Calculating precisely when the world will end has preoccupied a long line of number-crunching prognosticators, from the second-century Sibyl who predicted the return of Nero as Antichrist in 195, to William Miller – nineteenth-century architect of 'The Great Disappointment', the barbed title given to the failed advent of 1843 for which Miller had roused unprecedented excitement – and beyond. Along the way it has beguiled theologians such as Joachim of Fiore, the twelfth-century Calabrian abbot who devised a hugely in-fluential system of apocalyptic ready-reckoning; exercised mathematicians such as Isaac Newton and John Napier of Merchiston, inventor of logarithms; engrossed astronomers, astrologers, archaeologists and pyramidologists; and led mystics on a merry dance along paths strewn with auguries, runes, omens, portents and other such supernatural props. Apocalypse has furnished them all with a numerical means of ascertaining the final hour, and between them they have generated an impressive list of projected ends; 195, 500, 948, 1000, 1260, 1420, 1588, 1666, 1763, 1785, 1819, 1843, 1866, 1903, 1914 and 1975 among them. Each end has been fervently anticipated and then bitterly mourned. But then millenarians are not only resilient in their convictions – not to mention resourceful when it comes to *post hoc* rationalisation – but always willing to return to their sums.

No sect in modern history has been more obsessed with numbers or preached millenarianism longer and more consistently than the Jehovah's Witnesses. Like the Mormons, the Jehovah's Witnesses are indigenous to America, though their sizable constituency now extends to about 3 million worldwide. Their faith may best be described as a radical Adventism, in that eschatology is the very point of their existence. Ever since the Witnesses were incorporated in the 1870s, chronology has been their abiding passion and the establishment of a millennial theocracy their ultimate goal. Individually, however, their aims are modest, for they aspire to be no more than 'faithful and discreet' slaves of the all-powerful Jehovah. Yet notwithstanding their boasted humility before the Lord, when Armageddon comes they, and only they, will attain this bizarre distinction. What makes the Witnesses especially fascinating is that they not only exhibit an all-consuming longing for the end of the world but insist that the end-time has already come.[4]

The Witnesses' original mathematical groundwork was laid down by Charles Taze Russell (1852–1916), a pastor who had migrated through Presbyterianism, Congregationalism and Adventism and emerged unsatisfied with them all. In the early 1870s he succumbed to the seductions of mystical numbers and set about devising his own timetable for the end of the world. First he dated the Second Coming to 1874 (by running Daniel's 1335 days of waiting for God's blessing from the fall of the Ostrogothic empire in 539). The year was to have marked the start of escalating global troubles culminating in cosmic destruction in 1914. Nineteen fourteen acquired its momentous significance from Russell deeming it to be the end of the Gentile Dispensation – that stretch of 2520 years representing God's promise to Moses to punish the Jews seven times for their sins for failing to keep his covenant. Russell ran the 2520 years (a 'time' being generally understood to mean 360 years) from Jerusalem's fall to Nebuchadnezzar in 606 BC. Meanwhile 1878 (then 1881) was given as the date when the faithful Elect, that is the 144,000 Saints of Revelation, would be raptured from the earth as the churches of the world began to crumble. Although Russell thought that the established clergy were false shepherds, the movement's inherent anti-clericalism did not achieve its full-blown form until the 1930s, when the Witnesses ruled that no Christians, barring themselves, stood a chance of salvation.

Nineteen fourteen presented them with a mixed bag of apparent confirmations and outright failures. On the one hand, the outbreak of the First World War seemed to prove that the pastor's chronology was sound. Russell himself experienced a surge of vindicatory excitement; on 2 October he declared, 'The Gentile Times have ended; the kings have had their day.' On the other hand, Christ was nowhere to be seen, the churches stood steadfast, refusing to crumble, and nobody was being raptured heavenward. Russell, who had already postponed the Second Coming so that it collided with his end-date, now adopted the ingenious argument that 1914 represented the crowning of Christ as king of heaven. Having thus rescued his chronology from the problem of evidential disconfirmation, he proceeded to argue that the first resurrection of Revelation, whereby the biblical patriarchs, saints and martyrs were scheduled to rise from the dead, would commence in 1918. This was Russell's last legacy to his disciples, for he died in 1916 before the world ended, leaving the problem of finding explanations to his successors.

Although the Witnesses have since piled chronology upon chronology, tangling numbers into ever more complicated systems, they have not reneged on Russell's basic mode of time-keeping. Instead they have busied themselves with a tinkering that has served merely to extend it. Looking back on the century from our present vantage point, we can see that the Witnesses have calibrated the whole of it in terms of sacred arithmetic. The detailed mathematics is too tedious to include here, but two further dates merit attention because they cast light on how the Witnesses have managed to deal with repeated disappointment.

After Russell's death, the movement passed into the hands of his legal advisor, Judge Joseph Rutherford, an autodidact who arrogated to himself the roles of chief chronologer, sole interpreter of the scriptures and all-powerful President of the Watch Tower Society. Having styled himself thus as Jehovah's earthly channel, he took to transmitting messages directly from on high, the most significant being that the world would end in 1925. Although Rutherford proclaimed the end in good faith, he had equipped himself well for possible failure. As soon as he assumed charge of the Witnesses he had conducted a commu-nist-party-style purge of moderates. When the world did not end in 1925, the new hardline leadership took a firm grip of the situation and argued that they had clearly been granted time in which to properly prepare themselves for Armageddon. To this end, the Witness rank and file were remodelled into an army of evangelisers. Instead of constituting congregations, classes or ecclesias, under the new military-style leadership they became 'companies' and 'company servants'. Full-time mission-aries were referred to as 'pioneers' and 'sharpshooters' in the spiritual war against the Devil. Having pledged themselves to combat evil, the Witnesses had by 1930 made a thorough enemy of the world. The world, for its part, was not long in coming to regard them with near-equal hostility because, for one thing, the Witnesses refused to salute the flag and to stand for the national anthems of demonic national powers. And, for another, in 1932 they abandoned a long tradition claiming that the Jews had a role to play in Jehovah's plan. In that they had already condemned Christendom to eternal damnation, they now smugly assumed identity as the only Israel of God.

In the 1940s and 1950s the Witnesses managed to rehabilitate themselves somewhat before the public. This was largely because in the face of Nazi persecution they had fought for their right to believe and worship what and how they chose. For a while they had really become the righteous victims they always imagined themselves to be. Paradoxically, at the very same time that they came to be seen as champions of religious freedom, the Watch Tower Society began to establish a system of 'theocratic law' that was illiberal in the extreme. It instituted a privileged clergy class of 'kingdom heirs' who belonged to the 144,000 Saints of Revelation. (Outside of the new aristocracy, the vast majority of Witnesses continued to enjoy a guaranteed passage into the Millennium, but only as members of the 'great multitude' [Rev. 7: 9]; they would hold on beyond the end, though in a less glorious manner than the Elect.) And Church courts were empowered to conduct inquisitions in which Witnesses could be 'disfellowshipped' for disobedient behaviour such as openly challenging the sect's teachings, drinking, committing adultery and, from 1961, accepting blood transfusions.

The next wave of eschatological excitement came in 1966, when President Frederick Franz announced that the world would end in 1975. Here was a magic number that could be extrapolated from Pastor Russell's original calculations, which dated the day of creation to 4025 BC. Anyone who cared to do their addition would soon realise that 1975 was the fateful year 6000 of the world and the start of the seventh day of mankind's existence. There was a spectacular growth in membership over the next few years, even as the coming end demanded that Witnesses sever virtually all worldly connections. Many sold their businesses, cashed in their investments, dropped out of college and ceased associating with non-Witnesses altogether, in eager anticipation of their final vindication. All the harder, therefore, was their fall when the world failed to end. The Witnesses were devastated. There had long been an undercurrent of cruelty present in Witness practice; the banning of birthday parties as pagan celebrations must have blighted many a childhood, while the idea that death is preferable to receiving a blood transfusion is utterly inhumane. In the fiasco following 1975, this streak of cruelty surfaced again. Addressing a large audience of Witnesses in 1976, President Franz asked, 'Do you know why nothing happened in 1975? It was because you expected something to happen.'

No more dates have been ventured since 1975. Indeed in 1995 the Witnesses announced that no more ever would be. This was not a move of retreat, however, but of stunning confidence. It was the ultimate defence of Russell's chronology, whose absolute limit had been reached in 1975. The pragmatically minded, determined to wring further mystical permutations from it, could of course challenge Russell's arithmological competence. But notwithstanding their utter lack of numerical resources, the Witnesses refuse to allow anyone to breathe new life into their mathematics. In 1982 they disfellowshipped Swedish Witness Carl Olaf Jonsson for suggesting that 606 BC was not the year in which Jerusalem fell to Nebuchadnezzar. The question we need to ask is why? The answer is more than a little disturbing, for the Witnesses simply no longer need numbers: their prophetic clock has stopped ticking. The battle of Armageddon is almost upon us. In 1958 the Watch Tower oligarchs insisted that the end of world would come before the generation who were alive in 1914 died. It is an edict that Franz ratified after 1975. Since the youngest person alive in 1914 is now fast approaching their mid-eighties, the last battle cannot be much longer delayed.

As Harold Bloom argues, the Witnesses are not much inclined towards spirituality. They have developed nothing so sophisticated as a theology; if anything, given their fierce anti-intellectualism, their beliefs ought properly to be grouped under the heading dogma. But viewed from the outside in, the chief distinguishing feature of the Jehovah's Witnesses is not their dogma – their slave-like submission to their all-powerful sovereign ruler or their 'heavenly hope' for salvation – but their intense and virulent hatred of the world, which, for almost a century beyond its expiry date, has done nothing but groan on. In its war-like eagerness to see the world destroyed, the Watch Tower leadership continues to exhort its followers to battle: 'Put on the complete suit of armor from God', they cry.[5] Soon the day will come when they will be able to help Christ's heavenly legions ruthlessly squash into the ground governments and monarchs, the university and the market, the Church and any other temporal institution you care to name. To the extent that hate is their foremost passion, the Jehovah's Witnesses are the very embodiment of D. H. Lawrence's 'Patmossers', those weaklings who despise the powerful because they lust after power themselves. They may well only desire to be like Mathew's 'faithful and discreet slave', but never has slavery been more exalted.

Despite carrying a dismal record of repeated failure, an obsessive interest in prophetic numerology is not confined to the sectarian outreaches of Christianity. During the Second World War, the Cold War, and both during and after the Gulf War, mainstream millenarians aligned with one or other of America's fundamentalist denominations regularly put eschatological prophecy through the numbers mill. Based on different calculations involving Israel's modern history, the Californian television preacher and prophecy writer Charles Taylor made a series of predictions of the world's end taking place in 1976, 1980, 1988 and 1992. A more intriguing example is former NASA engineer Edgar Whisenant's *88 Reasons Why the Rapture Will Be in 1988*, which recruited all sorts of numerical proofs based on readings of Daniel and Revelation. There are many reasons (though perhaps not as many as eighty-eight) why Whisenant's booklet sold in excess of 2 million copies, but the principal one is that it provided mathematical back-up for the what Moral Majority denizens were repeatedly expressing in narrative terms. The tacit understanding at work in both cases was that 1988 stood at exactly one biblical generation's remove, that is forty years, from the return of the Jews to the Holy Land.[6] Mystical mathematics is, in fact, American to the core, part and parcel of the nation's inheritance from the Puritan Pilgrim Fathers. Its continuing popularity amongst millenarians is a modern-day reminder that arithmology was an essential component of Protestantism's self-understanding.

A History of Human Folly?

The Reformation was a hey-day of prophetic commentary. After Luther had put Daniel to use in identifying the pope as Antichrist, a stream of prophetic commentaries poured from Europe's presses. These were stuffed with historical digitations dating both the binding of the beast (understood as the Millennium) and the 1260 days of papal apostasy along a sliding scale that extended from the birth of Christ to the conversion of Constantine. By placing the Millennium in the past, early Reformation commentators found numerical justification for their conviction that they were living in the 'little season' of anti-Christian domination when papists were busy amassing the armies of Gog and Magog for a final crusade aimed at snuffing out the true Protestant church. The end was clearly imminent, and it was not the interim end of millennial respite, but the eternal bliss that would succeed the Last Judgement.

While Reformation theologians were quite happy to calibrate the past in term of sacred numbers, when it came to futurology a more cautious mood prevailed. The business of making predictions was regarded at best with suspicion and at worst as the work of the Devil – or at least of his minions, astrologers. Although no one doubted that the Reformation was itself an

eschatological event, theologians preferred to cast their speculations about its likely fate in allegorical terms and John Bale's
clever reading of it in a self-consciously Augustinian light was,
at least for English Protestants, the definitive word on the
matter. In *The Image of Bothe Churches* (1548) Bale brought his
experience as a bishop, dramatist and bibliographer to bear on
his depiction of world history as a tale of conflict between the
Church of Christ and the soon-to-be-overthrown Church of
the Devil, or, to use Bale's own terminology, 'that adulterouse,
cursed and malignant church [of] hipocrites'. Like Augustine's
two cities, only one of the two Churches was destined to survive
the end of the world. In this morality play, the Church of
Christ was, of course, the fledgling Protestant Church, currently
under pain of exile like the woman in the wilderness, but
shortly to be adorned as a bride in anticipation of her spouse's
second advent and her final deliverance.

Within only a few decades, however, futurology was in vogue
amongst even the most conservative of biblical exegetes. The
decisive factor in bringing about this shift was a changing
attitude to the Book of Revelation. In the early sixteenth
century, the apocalypse of St John the Divine was still clawing
its way towards respectability. Commenting on Revelation in
his 1522 preface to the hugely influential *Deutsche Bibel*, Luther
confessed, 'my spirit cannot accommodate itself to this book',
but by 1530 he steeled himself into giving it lukewarm com-
mendation.[7] Though doubts lingered about its canonicity and
apostolicity, against these the tortuous progress of the Reformation seemed in itself to proclaim the book's validity. In the
1540s new translations of Revelation by the respected contin-
ental theologians Andreas Osiander and Philip Melancthon

further enhanced its reputation and, before long, biblical commentators threw futurological caution to the wind.

One of the first to do so was John Foxe (1516–87), the renowned martyrologist. Within various editions of his *Acts and Monuments*, he offered a variety of end-time options, 1564, 1570 and 1586. In 1586, just before his death, Foxe deferred the world's end one more time. In an unfinished commentary on Revelation, the *Eicasmi*, posthumously published by his son in 1587, 1594 was ventured as the auspicious date. Foxe had arrived at this date through a fairly elaborate series of computations. He began with the forty-two months (1260 days) of beastly tyranny, which became 294 years by reckoning each month as seven years. These years – 'the declining tyme of the church and of true religion' – denoted the era of persecution that extended from Christ's ministry to Constantine's defeat of Licinius in AD 324. The Millennium, or binding of the beast, then slotted in here so that its close in 1324 could mark the start of the forty-two months of witnessing. Foxe viewed this period as a parallel era of persecution in which the Protestant Church was engaged in the final struggle to establish God's truth in the face of rampant and violent papal denial. By adding these 294 years to 1324, 1594 emerged as the date for cosmic denouement.

Foxe's interpretive slant, weighted as it was towards persecution and martyrdom, voiced the religious mood of the day. As Richard Bauckham has argued in *Tudor Apocalypse* (1978), the Tudor apocalypse was a theology of persecution and history. As such, it was essentially pessimistic, with champions of the Church of Christ seeing no release from the trial of suffering until Judgement Day brought them deliverance. In stark contrast, the Stuart apocalypse was fundamentally optimistic, articulating a theology of revolution and hope. With sufficient distance from the Anabaptist débâcle at Münster, Protestants came to believe not only that they might actively aid God in the overthrow of Antichrist, but that they would reap the benefits of so doing in an earthly Millennium. In exegetical terms, this about-turn was given expression by reading verse 20 of Revelation as progressive rather than recapitulative, so that the Millennium could be shunted up into the future. As Tudor gloom gave way to Stuart hope, daily expectation of the End was gradually replaced by a daily expectation of the Millennium. A conviction that the best part of St John's prophecies was yet to unfold gave Stuart commentators fresh impetus for futurological speculation. The turning point came with the defeat of the Armada in 1588. Understood as a foreshadow of Armageddon, Spain's humiliation seemed to prove that Protestants stood a fighting chance of overthrowing their popish persecutors. The message was that activism paid off, that the Sword was as good a witness to God's truth as the Word or the Cross.[8]

Of the post-Armada commentators, John Napier and Thomas Brightman were the most influential, though Napier could not quite bring himself to part ways with the Augustinian legacy of placing the Millennium in the past – in spite of his optimism. Brightman's calculations, on the other hand, manifest quite literally the transition from despair to hope that Bauckham discusses, in that they contain a bizarre exegetical compromise; two Millenniums instead of one. The first ran from Constantine to the loosing of the Ottoman Beast and the second immediately followed. Thirteen hundred, the crucial year that saw one

Millennium out and another in, marked, according to Brightman, both the start of the Roman Antichrist's downfall and the first resurrection of Revelation, which he understood as the revival of biblical preaching. Writing some 300-odd years into the Millennium, he believed that the next 700 years would bring the final perfecting of the revived Church, the conversion of the Jews and the terminal wilting of Antichrist.[9]

The first commentator to make a clean break with the ever-weakening hold that Augustine exerted on Protestants in respect of apocalypse was Joseph Mede (1586–1638). As a result, this mild-mannered, stuttering academic, a lecturer in Greek and fellow of Christ's College, Cambridge, was the unlikely popular choice for exegetical guru of the Civil War era. Mede pointed out that it did not make sense for the papal apostasy to begin during the Millennium. Nor was Brightman's ostentatious solution to the problem acceptable; there could only be one Millennium and it was most definitely in the future, albeit the not too distant one. In 1628 Mede wrote gaily to Archbishop Ussher that if the papal apostasy was reckoned from the deposition of Augustulus, the last Roman Emperor, in 476, then the second advent and Millennium would come in 1736, 'which is just the very year when the 1260 years of the Beast's reign will expire'. In his *Apostasy of the Latter Times* and *Key of Revelation* (both published in Latin in the 1620s and in English in the 1640s) he ventured further chronological speculations, variously dating the start of the papal apostasy to 365, 395, 410 and 450, to arrive at a number of millennial options, 1625, 1655, 1670 and 1710. Mede was more interested in the mathematics of extrapolating the line of divine intent than in the ultimate earthly destination of its terminus: of the Millennium itself he wrote, 'what it means and what shall be therein, Posterity will better understand'.[10] Though he was no radical, much political capital stood to be made from his apocalyptic as a consequence of its sanctioning a revolutionary rupture between past and future.

Ahead of the Civil War, a wave of millenarian expectation broke over England, accompanied by a flood of futurological literature that generated a proliferation of dates for the second advent, including 1641, 1645, 1648, 1649, 1650, 1657, 1660 and 1665.[11] Among the most influential of these texts was *The Personall Raigne of Christ Upon Earth* (1642) by Puritan exile John Archer, who, by taking the number of the beast, 666, to be of chronological import, ear-marked 1666 as the apocalyptic hour. This was to be the *annus mirabilis* of the century, cherished by Russian dissenters and the German prophet Koffer. It was a date that struck hope and terror in the hearts of Fifth Monarchy Men (so named after Daniel's fifth kingdom), and whose approach caused such expectation across Europe that it led the Jewish would-be messiah Sabbatai Zevi to publically declare his mission. In England, the Civil War seemed to have actualised Armageddon, but the surge of euphoria that attended it was destined to be short-lived. Very quickly, the triumph of the New Model Army under Cromwell and the regicide of 1649 were unmasked as the heralds not of New Jerusalem but of New Münster. Only the most militant revolutionaries and wild sectarians, like the Fifth Monarchists and the self-proclaimedly sinless Ranters, persisted in thinking that good would come out of Charles I's execution, but even many of them later came to see Cromwell's reign of saints as a sham Millennium – the deliverer rapidly transformed into Antichrist. By the time 1666 arrived, flanked by fire and plague, Cromwell was dead and the monarchy restored. What was supposed to have been the Millennium was revealed to have been nothing more than a revolutionary blip, and most millenarians, chastened by the holy wars, interpreted the natural catastrophes that sandwiched their *annus mirabilis* as divine punishment for getting things so wrong. Milton's *Paradise Lost*, part apologia, part resignation and part belligerent protest, followed in 1667.

Before long, however, the seductions of apocalypse proved irresistible once again. The Glorious Revolution which replaced papist James II with the Protestant William of Orange sent millenarians scuttling back to the sacred texts to show that the millennial prophecies had all along pointed to 1688–9. But it was the ghost of Brightman not Mede that hovered over their scribbling hands, for they maintained that the Millennium would come about through gradual religious and political reform, not by engaging in violent combat with the hosts of Antichrist. As a revolutionary ethos was displaced by a quietist post-millennialism, good Christians on the eve of the Enlightenment resigned themselves to the fact that they would simply have to wait and hope and trust. For the time being at least, futurology went into recession.

Although interest in apocalypse went underground in the eighteenth century, assuming a place in the shadowy world of freemasonry, occultism, illuminism, mesmerism and the mystical spiritualism of Jacob Boehme and Emanuel Swedenborg, it resurfaced in the wake of the French Revolution, breaking through the rationalist veneer of polite society to hold radicals and conservatives alike in its thrall. Like the Reformation, the Revolution was understood to be an eschatological event. For

Republican polemicist Joseph Priestley, who, inspired by the new American constitution, envisaged the Millennium as 'a proper kingdom ... the object of which will be the happiness of the subjects of it', it was one of the 'signs of the times', specifically, the earthquake of Revelation 11: 13. The numerologists too were busy making millennial calculations. James Bicheno, a dissenting minister, Jacobin and Newbury schoolmaster, ventured 1819 as the date for the second advent. He reasoned that the Revolution of 1789 marked the end of the 1260-year papal apostasy. It was a forerunner of the End, which would arrive thirty years later, when Daniel's 1290 days of evil tyranny were due to lapse.[12]

By now it should be obvious that sacred arithmetic is a very different animal from everyday mathematics. To begin with, it has a limited repertoire of integers to play with – a cluster of mystical numbers drawn principally from Daniel and Revelation – and only one genuine axiom. This is the day–year theory, hailing from Psalm 90: 'For a thousand years in thy sight are but as yesterday when it is past, and as a watch in the night.' Furthermore, unlike secular mathematics, it has no pure form, no abstract existence whereby addition, subtraction, multiplication or division are capable of producing meaning. It only has applied uses as it relates to history. In spite of appearing to involve the most convoluted computations, its operations are in fact fairly straightforward. The beauty of the internal logic of sacred arithmetic is that only one date or event need be fixed in order to uncover what historian Ernest Sandeen has called 'a prophetic Rosetta Stone', the code-cracking key that unlocks the secrets of past and future, so allowing a precise timetabling of the entire apocalyptic scenario. That said, however, by using sophisticated computations, selectively ignoring the day–year theory, and by indulging in fanciful historical manipulations involving Gnostic and Sibylline sources, for example, almost any end date may be nominated. The point is that, unlike real mathematics, sacred arithmetic is a highly subjective science. And therein lies its strength, for millenarians are far less concerned with getting it right than with providing numerical justification for the apocalyptic significance of their own historical moment. In essence, their enterprise is that of introducing the plausibility of numbers to the wilder shores of apocalyptic speculation.

The Catholic side of the story is much more straightforward, in that the vast bulk of Roman arithmologists owe their inspiration to a single patron, Joachim of Fiore. In the eleven years following 1190, Joachim received visions in which the concealed meaning of the whole of the scriptures was revealed to him. This secret knowledge allowed him to formulate a reading of the development of history which recast the basic three-act apocalypse as an ascent through three successive stages, each presided over by a member of the Trinity. The first age, or Age of the Father, ran from Adam to Abraham; the second age, or Age of the Son, from Elijah to Christ; and the third age, or Age of the Spirit, was inaugurated by St Benedict. Each age was further divided into seven periods ruled by the saintly fathers, with Joachim reserving for himself a role corresponding to that played by John the Baptist in the second age. The third age of love and peace was millennial in character, a new-fangled paradise in which there would be neither wealth nor property, neither law nor sin. Mankind, possessing only spiritual bodies, would exist in voluntary poverty, undertaking no work and bowing to no Church until the Last Judgement dawned. Joachim expected the transition to the third age to begin in 1260, which marked the end of the three years that the true Church had spent in the wilderness, and identified his own inspired writings with the Everlasting Gospel of Revelation 14 which would be preached 'unto them that dwell on the earth, and to every nation, and kindred, and tongue, and people' (Rev. 14: 6). They would be the 'Third Testament' that supplanted the Old Testament of the first age and the New Testament of the second.

Historians of religion rightly regard Joachim's exegetical efforts as one of the greatest uncondemned heresies. An earthly reign of the Holy Ghost in a third status was at loggerheads with Augustinian orthodoxy, particularly since it implied that the ecclesia was a temporary administration that would vanish amid the death pangs of the second age. Indeed, Joachim spoke of an Antipope whose tyrannous reign would hasten its demise. Such a vengeful theology was the product of his profound disenchantment with an increasingly corrupt and power-hungry Church which, over time, had come to identify itself with Augustine's City of God, bending his original concept of an invisible city of the just to flatter its own worldly ego. In the wake of the failed advent of the year 1000, Joachim's doctrines furnished millenarians with new inspiration. They held particular appeal for sectarians as convinced as was Joachim of the Church's wicked and despotic ways. But the papacy soon wised up to the uses to which the abbot's writings could be put and was quick to condemn the work of Franciscan propagandists such as Peter Olivi and John of Parma, who insisted that St Francis was the Adam of the new age and that they were already living the reformed monastic life of that glorious dispensation. Bernard McGinn and Raoul Vaneigem have further argued for Joachim's centrality in the cosmology of numerous medieval counter-Catholic sects, Lollards, Hussites, Taborites, Cathars, and the Brothers and Sisters of the Free Spirit among them.[13] Each believed that it had inaugurated the blessed dispensation of peace.

Notwithstanding, perhaps even as a result of, Church suppression, Joachite doctrines continued to thrive in the underground world of popular religion for centuries to come, his notion of a messianically incepted new age having particular appeal. Lodowick Muggleton spoke of three ages or commissions, of the Father, the Son and the Spirit, and prophesied that the last commission, to which he and Reeve were witnesses, would begin in 1652. Anabaptist messiah Jan Bockelson divided mankind's earthly residence into ages of Sin, Persecution and Vengeance. In 1599 Thommaso Campanella, astrologer to the pope, was arrested in Naples for raising a revolt aimed at instituting a utopian new age, the City of the Sun, in which an era of Love would supplant those of Power and Wisdom. David Lazzaretti, the messiah of Monte Amiata, claimed that there had been kingdoms of Grace and Justice and that the world was in a state of transition which would herald the kingdom of the Holy Ghost. Generally speaking, Joachim's writings were a limited resource for Protestants because although they were clearly anti-papal they were not sufficiently Christocentric. Some Protestants nonetheless leaned on them to a degree, and one, Giacopo Brocardo, developed a thorough-going Joachism which hailed Luther as the Adam of the new age.

In terms of world-historical schema, Joachim's ideas have

served as the principal conduit between sacred and secular history. In fact, history seems to be full of three-step narratives; the Stone, Iron and Bronze ages of archaeologists, the Golden, Silver and Bronze ages of speculative mythologists and the triumvirate of Ancient, Medieval and Modern eras that trisect western civilisation. However ubiquitous, though, the trinitarian model of history is only strictly Joachite if it is fundamentally progressivist – so that each stage represents a move towards the better – but at the same time features a cyclical element that brings each age to a declining close. The philosophical history of Giambatista Vico, for example, fits snugly within Joachite thinking. Vico spoke of ages of Gods, Heroes and Men. The first was paternalistic and violent, the second age thought might was right and self-destructed, while the third age, herald of reason and civilisation, was prone to over-sophistication and therefore in need of divine intervention to reinstate primitive innocence. Auguste Comte and Karl Marx both invoked Joachite schemes, but stopped short of the providential climax. Comte elevated positivism to quasi-religious status by picturing historical progress as an ascent through theological and metaphysical ages to the present scientific one, while Marx famously modelled human social development on primitive communism, class society and a final communist millennium. In our own era, D. H. Lawrence spoke of epochs of Law, Love and Comfort, and Marshall McLuhan, in *The Guttenberg Galaxy* (1962), posited three stages of human communication; a primitive age that relied on oral traditions, an age of printing that led to rational and detached information exchange, and a glorious age of free-flowing and intimate electronic communication. In view of today's World Wide Web, McLuhan looks very much like a prophet. But the most notorious Joachite visionary of modern times has to be Hitler, spurred by dreams of a thousand-year Third Reich.

Part of Joachim's enduring appeal is that, despite the simple, some might say reductive, elegance of his historico-spiritual scheme, it retained sufficient links to the sacred texts for it to share the intellectual kudos of the scholastic and arithmetically ambitious Protestant commentaries. Not so with naive apocalypse, which made capital out of a reflex fight-or-flight crowd psychology, spinning tales of terror from signs of the times drawn not from the annals of history but from the book of nature. This is the mass-market end of apocalypse, unashamedly populist and unfailingly effective: it uses mystical numbers to mystify and to frighten, not to clarify. It is also the tradition to which the hysterical Sister Marie Gabriel is heir.

Solar eclipses, comets, novae, earthquakes, volcanic eruptions, floods and other freak productions have all acquired symbolic depth in the hands of millenarians working the vein of naive apocalypse. In the 1570s, a decade teeming with popish plots and scares, the German lawyer Sheltco à Geveren produced a slim volume entitled *Of the Ende of the World*, which went through four English editions in 1577 alone. Yet it was not the shady activities of the Roman Antichrist that concerned him so much as the comet of 1577 and the 1572 nova in Cassiopeia, which 'returning now declares, that Christ returns agayne in might'. His belief that the 'inclination of the starres' was designated by God to be 'Clockes of his eternall counsail', rather than sending him to the scriptures, led him to pay his respects to the Bohemian astrologer Cyprian Leowitz, who had pointed a trembling finger to the conjunction between Saturn and Jupiter that would take place in 1583. By way of shoring up the apocalyptic clout of this auspicious event, he listed a number of papal abominations that had coincided with past conjunctions. Making no distinction between canon and almanac, he blended a loose interpretation of history with popular astrology to arrive at the conclusion that 1593 was year 5555 of the world and an appropriate End in view of providential 'shortening'. In fact, he seems to have had some sort of mystical attachment to the number 5 and its multiples: 'every five hundred years there happen wonderful alterations both in religion and Common Weales.' Just in case the End arrived sooner, he quoted some pop-prophetical verses composed by the mathematician Regiomontanus which set the date for global destruction at 1588.

Although the ascription of eschatological significance to natural wonders could not claim the pedigree status of historical exegesis, it was not without canonical basis. Luke, Mark and Matthew all foretold of convulsions and commotions in nature: 'great earthquakes shall be in divers places, and famines and pestilences; and fearful sights and great signs there shall be from heaven' (Luke 21: 11); 'the sun shall be darkened, and the moon shall not give her light, and the stars of heaven shall fall' (Mark 13: 24–5). Consequently, any celestial anomaly, terrestrial catastrophe or medical scourge was fair game. When the fire of London followed hot on the heels of the plague in 1666, a rash of pamphlets appeared urging impious, dissolute metropolitans to repent and mend their ways while heaping blame on every conceivable enemy of true religion. One cynic, who had grown impatient with prophetic moralisers, remarked:

'The Quakers say, it is for their persecution. The fanatics say it is for silencing and banishing their ministers. Others say, it is for the murder of the king and rebellion of the city. The clergy lay blame on schism and licentiousness, while the sectaries lay it on imposition and their pride. Thus do many pretend to determine the sin aimed at in this punishment.'[14]

A similar outpouring flowed from press and pulpit in the aftermath of the Lisbon earthquake of 1755, which destroyed two-thirds of the city and claimed over 100,000 lives. The Bible scholar and Jansenist, Laurent-Etienne Rondet, twinned the earthquake with the sixth trumpet of Revelation sent to punish heretical Protestants and Jesuits, while the Chevalier de Olivera, a Portugese diplomat and Protestant convert, saw it as a castigation of Rome's idolatrous adoration of images and cruel Inquisitional tactics. The Lisbon clergy responded by burning his effigy as well as his book before blood-thirsty crowds. In London, where two earthquakes had struck only five years earlier, Lisbon sparked a lively trail of fire-and-brimstone preaching. George Hoare, later Bishop of Norwich, told his parishioners: 'Thou also perish. Behold me smoking! Remember and REPENT. This is the short but very full sermon that Lisbon in ruins preaches to London in sin.' For very different reasons, Voltaire wrote a poem of commiseration. The last line of its first printing, later changed, was a thinly veiled attack on the '*tout est bien*' philosophy of Leibniz and Pope. With no superstitious connotation intended, it read, '*le mal est sur la terre*'.[15] Another scoffer was Adam Smith, who mocked the summoning of 'the invisible hand of Jupiter' to explain natural catastrophes as the handy catch-all of a vulgar theism based on such primitive sentiments as 'surprise' and 'wonder'.[16]

The mixing of Christian sources with all kinds of superstitious hocus-pocus made for a potent apocalyptic brew, even if it delivered a greater proportion of panicky squeals to heads bowed in repentance. But for critics of apocalypse such a happy marriage between orthodoxy and heterodoxy meant that with the greatest of ease the computations of ecclesia and academy could be lumped in with divination, sorcery and witchcraft. In Ben Jonson's *The Alchemist* (1613) the worldly Sir Epicure Mammon 'talk'd of a fifth monarchy I would erect, with the Philosopher's Stone', and in *Leviathan* (1651) Thomas Hobbes dismissed 'Prognostiques of time to come' as 'Conjectures upon the Experience of time past', lining up a row of culpable pretenders to revelation that began with modern-day prophets and enthusiasts and ended with astrologers, necromancers, thaumatologists and conjurors. There is a distinctly contemporary ring to Jonson's humour and Hobbes's ire, perhaps because in many ways we still see the world through the eyes of the Enlightenment, when, if prophecy was not associated with the occult branches of illuminism, it was popularly considered as part of folklore. *The Prophetical Mirror* (1795) is just one of many books that garnered extracts from the writings of Jurieu and Robert Fleming, the Civil War enthusiasts, divines like Archbishop Ussher and academics like Joseph Mede, Henry More and Isaac Newton, and set them alongside the home-spun prophecies of Mother Shipton and Robert Nixon, 'who was but a kind of ideot'.

A detailed history of the two-way traffic between apocalypse and mysticism falls into that straw-man category of fascinating, yet-to-be-written books. But if we imagine turning to the index of such a tome, we should be able to find there Nostradamus, Jacob Boehme, Madame Blavatsky, George Gurdjieff,

Krishnamurti, Edgar Cayce and Jeane Dixon, as well as a host of crypto-Christian astronomers, astrologers, wise women and miracle-mongers. One of the most bizarre instances of cross-pollination that I have come across is the apocalyptic pyramidology of Morton Edgar, whose thesis, in short, was that the 'Great Pyramid of Gizeh scientifically, symbolically and prophetically corroborates the philosophy of the divine plan of the ages'. With no sense of cultural trespass, let alone anachronism, this majestic testimony to the sophistication of an ancient Near Eastern civilisation was claimed as a monument to Christianity.

In the grip of a digital obsession, Edgar measured every possible circumference, plane, area, angle of inclination and diagonal of the pyramid, before proceeding to imbue his figures with apocalyptic significance using an ingenious analogue of the day–year theory which, in taking one pyramid inch to represent a historical year, put an entirely new gloss on the relationship between space and time. He found the area of the pyramid's main square to be 144,000 square inches (one for every Saint Elect) and that the length of the horizontal passage indicated the 7000 years of world history. By ascribing 'date-levels' to different horizontal slices through the pyramid, he was able to read off successive ages. Not that such computations were straightforward; the duration of the age of Adam, for example, he obtained from the 'difference between the two inclined heights of the ancient floor-beginning and the north edge of the basement sheet of the descending passage above natural rock level'. However, his most significant discovery was finding that the area of the pyramid's secondary square was 95,750 inches, which is 1915 × 50, the secret here deciphered being that 1915 marks the start of Christ's millennial reign. The fact that Christ was not around when Edgar was writing in the early 1920s was of no consequence, for he had borrowed from Charles Taze Russell, founder of the Jehovah's Witnesses, not only the idea that the Gentile Dispensation ended in 1914, but also the notion that Christ's millennial reign would begin with his heavenly coronation.[17]

Academic and ecclesiastic number-crunchers have always been alert to the dangers of non-Christian contamination and have had no compunction about fighting back to defend their territory. Swiss Reformation theologian Heinrich Bullinger, for example, declared that in Revelation we have 'an absolute and certayne prophecie of thynges to come, that we need not to have the prophecies of Methodius, Cyrill, Merline, Briget, Nothard and certain triflers'. In an attempt to dissociate apocalypse from all things tainted with spookiness, sober exegetes rallied behind the sacred texts to insist that they were both lucid and rational. Thomas Brightman claimed that they dealt with 'evident arguments' not 'obscure signs', and Enlightenment exegete Richard Hurd opined, 'the prophetic style is ... a sober and reasonable mode of expression'. However, the most celebrated advocate of the rational character of prophecy is Sir Isaac Newton.

Newton's furtive and long-term interest in apocalypse is well known. Less generally acknowledged is the fact that his approach to prophecy was a direct extension of his approach to the laws of motion. The same rational method that had allowed him to tease out natural laws from unruly nature could, he believed, be applied with similar success to the Bible. His was a two-pronged approach, arithmological and semiotic. In a manuscript paper, 'On the Language of the Prophets', he set out his view that all the prophets wrote in the same 'mystical language', whose relationship to the natural and political world was analogical or 'hieroglyphical', like that of the ancient Egyptian priests. To get at the hidden truths of prophecy, all that was required was a commonsense matching of signs to their correct signifiers. Though there was nothing esoteric in claiming, for example, that a new moon represented a people's return from exile, at root, Newton's conviction that myths, fables and prophecy embodied real truths stemmed from his far from rational belief in the *prisca sapientia*, the ancient wisdom granted by God to mankind through revelation.[18]

On the mathematical front, Newton was more consistent. He clung fiercely to the 6000-year chronology, adopting Archbishop Ussher's conclusion that 4004 BC was the Day of Creation as the basis of his own computations. Giving short shrift to his atheistical Royal Society peer Edmund Halley, who calculated from the salting of the sea that geological time had to be measured in hundreds of millions of years, he produced an account of creation that sought to throw the weight of science behind Genesis. He even exercised his formidable mathematical powers on the science of mystical mathematics, his posthumously published *Observations on the Apocalypse of Daniel and Revelation of St John* (1730) containing pages of tedious historical calculations. According to Voltaire, Newton wrote his commentary 'to console mankind for the great superiority he had over them in other respects'. Voltaire, like most enlightenment Newtonians, preferred to draw a veil over his mentor's theological predilections: it was the Enlightenment after all and a progressivist post-millennialism – inaugurated by Robert Boyle's *The Excellency of Theology* (1674) – that held scientific achievement to be proof of human perfectibility was the order of the day. If the religion of progress has a birthday, Boyle's book is a strong contender for marking it. No matter how sensible Newton's forays into prophecy might have been, they were quite simply not sensible enough for his disciples' liking.

Aside from a youthful (and paranoiacally private) flirtation with futurology, Newton aligned himself with the time-honoured tradition of thinking futurology presumptuous, even Promethean. God had, after all, commanded: 'It is not for you to know the times or the seasons, which the Father has put in his own power' (Acts 1: 7). He adopted a praeterist stance towards Daniel and, while he allowed himself licence with Revelation as far as the past permitted, he wrote in his *Observations*:

> The Folly of Interpreters has been to foretell times and things by this Prophecy ... By this rashness they have not only exposed themselves, but brought the prophecy also into contempt. The design of God was much otherwise. He gave this and the Prophecies of the Old Testament, not to gratify men's curiosities by enabling them to foreknow things, but that after they were fulfilled, they might be interpreted by the event, and his own Providence, not the Interpreter's, be then manifested thereby to the world.

Censuring the stealing of God's thunder is commonplace in apocalyptic commentaries. Even where predictions *are* ventured, such protests as Newton made often crop up as disclaimers, apparently hinting at disingenuousness or false modesty. Yet, depending on how chronological speculation is framed, there need be no contradiction in dabbling in futurology while believing in the inscrutability of God. Wise commentators who made the leap from fulfilled prophecy to about-to-be-fulfilled prophecy presented their end-time computations as humble 'conjectures'. Some fudged the problem of brazen specificity by offering a number of alternative likely dates, or, as Brightman had done, by leaving sufficient clues along the chronological treasure trail to make it possible for the close reader to extrapolate the numerical reasoning. In such cases, it was the norm for commentators to qualify their entry into the forecasting market with some statement to the effect that of course no one could possibly know the mysteries of the divine mind. Still, their legacy was to bequeath to posterity a catalogue of failed advents.

A Never-ending Story

Any temptation to dismiss the history of millenarianism as a history of human folly ought to be resisted on the grounds that such an evaluative judgement would be a category mistake: like expecting sacred arithmetic to obey the logic of everyday mathematics. It is because apocalypse has its own internal logic – one, moreover, which insists on the greater power of myth over fact – that eschatology has managed to survive centuries of disconfirmed predictions. Apocalypse is ineluctably myth-driven. There must be a temporal end to the world because we believe in one, whether as a consquence of our need for consonance or because without it life would be meaningless. This is why the history of millenarianism, like the sacred texts it draws sustenance from, is fundamentally recapitulative: every generation produces its own interpretations of history and its own apocalyptic chronologies. The peculiar and ironic result is that, against its own insistence on finality, apocalypse is a never-ending story. Like a soap opera, it is for ever lurching from one narrative cliffhanger to the next, one time-suspending crisis to another. Every failed ending is rapidly followed by *post hoc* rationalisation; blame is attributed to arithmological error or to a misreading of the signs of the times, while millenarians the world over habitually persuade themselves that they will have to endure even greater evils before the tide turns. As Frank Kermode has observed, the End cannot be discredited, only postponed. The practical outcome is that the science of mystical numbers is continually refined and historical identifications continually revised in order that belief in an appointed End might be sustained.

Ever since the biblical prophets took turns updating and interpolating the Book of Isaiah, revisionism has been the lifeblood of millenarians. It is effective because apocalypse trades in symbols, because Daniel's kingdoms and Revelation's cast of eschatological heroes and villains possess innate fluidity and malleability, and because mystical numbers are exactly what they claim to be: mystical. Thus one set of historical and chronological mappings may be washed away by the flow of time and succeeded by another set without calling into question apocalypse's authority. Apocalypse allows millenarians to be pragmatists, albeit persistent ones; for, whatever disappoint-ments they have to endure, they never give up the cause. Foxe, you remember, was constantly having to catch up with himself, rearranging his apocalyptic signifiers, proffering one end-date after another and reinterpreting the significance of each of them once they had passed. James Bicheno, who produced several editions his *Signs of the Times* in the 1790s, all pointing to 1819, found himself in 1817 having to account for the inconsequential end of Armageddon, Napoleon exiled and the pope and his demonic helpers restored. This done, he swiftly pronounced 1864 to be the new year of doom.

What brought William Miller down was his rigidity. Ransoming his credibility to passing time, he staked everything on the year 1843 and lost. Miller is an important figure in American millenarian history. A New England farmer turned prophet, he spearheaded a millenarian movement that rekindled East Coast revivalism on a scale not seen since Jonathan Edwards engineered the 'Great Awakening' of 1740 and that led, in his own day, to the birth of Adventism. Embarking on an intense course of Bible study in 1816, Miller emerged two years later with an apocalyptic timetable culminating in the advent of 1843. Although he offered fifteen mathematical proofs for his reasoning, his Rossetta Stone was an assumption that the seventy weeks for the abolition of sin had been fulfilled in the Passion. Moving backwards, he calculated that the seventy weeks must therefore have begun in 457 BC (490–33), from which time a forward projection of Daniel's 2300 days of desolation yielded 1843.

Miller was not much of a missionary; however, his skills at the pulpit rapidly won him followers more zealous than himself, who soon put in place a powerful publicity machine. They established a circuit of regular camp meetings all over New England, some of which are reputed to have attracted crowds of 10,000, while their mini-publishing industry ensured that Miller acquired a healthy following on both sides of the Atlantic. Once 1843 was under way, Miller, complying with pressure from his more militant followers, proclaimed that since the biblical calendar was based on the Jewish year the deadline for the Second Coming should be extended to spring 1844. Then, in 1844, two of his most ardent supporters, Samuel Snow and George Storrs, switched to a Levitical festal calendar and set the date for 22 October. Though Miller dissociated himself from the activist splinter group formed by Snow and Storrs, he ended up taking the blame for their failed advent as well as his own and spent his remaining years a ruined man. At its peak, the Millerite movement claimed 50,000 supporters, many of whom sold their businesses and homes in anticipation of Christ's glorious advent – actions which grew into fabulous rumours that would become part of American folklore, of Millerites convening on mountaintops in white ascension robes. Christ's failure to materialise devastated the movement. One of its historians, Francis Nichol, quotes one believer, Hiram Edson, recounting now they 'wept and wept'.[19]

The Adventist embarrassment of 1843 saw millenarian historicists at their most dispirited and paved the way for the ascendancy of futurist interpretations of apocalypse. Historicists such as Edward Irving, founder of the Catholic Apostolic Church, Henry Drummond, ringleader of the millenarian confraternity the Albury Group, and Alexander Campbell, who broke away from the Baptists to lead a millenarian congregation calling itself the Disciples of Christ, are just some of Miller's British contemporaries who believed, as he did, that Revelation recapitulated most of Daniel and that its prophecies were being fulfilled in contemporary Europe and America. Drummond, for example, claimed in 1827 that the first fifteen chapters of Revelation had been fulfilled. Futurists, most notably John

Nelson Darby, co-founder of the Plymouth Brethren, rejected any harmonising of Daniel and Revelation on the grounds that none of the events in Revelation had yet been fulfilled. Their position was consistent with acknowledging the immanence of the End but not its imminence. Darby was responsible for formulating the theology known as Dispensationalism, the central tenet of which is the secret rapture of the Church. He taught that the prophetic clock had stopped at the foundation of the Church, leaving Christian prophecies unfulfilled, and that only the rapture would restart it. Arguments and counter-arguments were thrashed out in the multitude of millenarian journals of the day, and by and large the futurists triumphed.[20]

Historicism, however, was not snuffed out. In North America, for example, former Millerite Ellen Harmon White experienced visions after 'the Great Disappointment' of 1843–4, which revealed to her that the time had been right but the event wrong: the 2300 days fulfilled in 1844 marked the cleansing of the heavenly sanctuary, so Christ's coming would not be far off. This was the beginning of Seventh Day Adventism, and the arithmological eschatology of Charles Taze Russell was not long in following it. An altogether quirkier case is that of English-born Michael Baxter, a disaffected Irvingite, missionary in Canada and founder of his own prophetic journal, *Our Hope*. Baxter managed to predict a series of incorrect dates for the Second Coming from 1861 to 1908, the most outlandishly precise being 12 March 1903 between 12.30 and 2.30 p.m. The steady drip of historicist commentaries has continued to the present day – Jon R. Stone's bibliographical *Guide to the End of the World* (1993) cites literally hundreds of them. Though the majority have barely caused a millenarian ripple, they testify to a permanent undercurrent of apocalyptic thought, a seemingly perpetual anxiety about the shape of history and the progress of time and, not least, the extraordinary resilience of millenarians.

While failed prophecy is evidently to blame for the disappearance of many an adventist sect, in more subtle ways it also explains the institutionalisation of others. After the initial disappointment comes the deepest kind of soul-searching. Hiram Edson, the Millerite who was prone to tears, reflected: 'My advent experience has been the richest and brightest of all my Christian experience. If this had proved a failure, what was the rest of my Christian experience worth? Has the Bible proved a failure? Is there no God, no heaven, no golden home city, no paradise? Is all this but a cunningly devised fable?' It was because Millerism could not answer such questions that it died; it lacked not only depth and adaptability, but theology. As it happens, Edson became one of the founding fathers of Seventh Day Adventism. A more sophisticated millenarianism has the capacity to diffuse the impact of failure, allowing the *raison d'être* of a sect to be diverted from end-time preoccupations and channelled into other quests. In the case of the Mormons, Joseph Smith developed an extraordinary theology that allowed his followers to dispense with end-time anxieties once and for all. By contrast, the Jehovah's Witnesses have dealt with failed prophecy through a combination of means, balancing *post hoc* rationalisation, both chronological and historical, with a redistributing of priorities, so that in the immediate aftermath of a failed advent emphasis is placed on ministering.

In view of millenarianism's chequered history, and especially the degree of numerical flexibility that apocalypse readily admits, it is impossible to regard the anticipation of great things or monumental destruction from the year 2000 with anything other than a jaundiced eye. Despite being the end-product of a whole string of mystical computations, the year has a fundamental arbitrariness about it, heightened rather than diminished by centuries of digitations. In the Jewish (and Chinese and Islamic) calendar it is not even significant; neither more nor less importance attaches to the year 5760 than to 5759 or 5761. Besides, Jews count more by way of celebrating their survival than as a means of arriving at the end. Their religion is predominantly framed around remembrance rather than expectation.

Yet, bearing in mind the same millenarian history, we may be sure that millenarianism will not disappear should the passing of the year 2000 fail to bring about the end of the world. Millenarians might be temporarily dejected, but they will return to the sacred texts, the stars, the pyramids and whatever else might be made to serve their cause, and begin their mission anew. Some sects will disappear, others will consolidate their identity in new areas. In all likelihood, before the year 2000 even arrives many will have set their sights on new, more distant horizons, leaving the year 2000 to the bureaucrats and heritage moguls, exhibition organisers, millennium commissions, builders of ferris wheels and domes, champagne *assembleurs* and even to the enterprising tourist companies offering trips to Patmos.

7. BEYOND THE END

'The question put by a wise man is half the answer.'
Jacob Emden, eighteenth-century rabbinic scholar

'What if this present were the world's last night?' asked John Donne. Of all the questions one might address to the apocalyptic imagination, none is more tantalising. Whether approached individually or collectively, as an imaginative exercise, or as a challenge to redefine the world we live in, it has the effect of producing a marvellous concentration on the moment at hand. This is as it should be, for if this present were the world's last night, then this present becomes everything. To get a sense of the overwhelming burden that is placed on the present once the future is annihilated, consider the terminally ill. Disabused of the illusion of their own immortality by the simple cancellation of their tomorrows, many find the courage to ignore what they are condemned to lack and devote the precious time remaining to squeezing the last drop of joy out of life. They will strengthen existing bonds with their nearest and dearest, make that trip to Timbuktu they have long dreamed of, write the book they always suspected lay within them. The necessity of a limit makes them reach for the limitless. Others, perhaps feeling unable to square up to such a significantly enhanced today through arriving at a pinnacle of self-definition, desire to seek oblivion all the faster, to lose themselves before life itself is lost. Either way, the whole drama of their individual existence must be brought to a point of resolution.

When the whole drama of human existence needs to be brought to its resolution in the here and now, the demands made on the present are formidably greater. For if this present is to become everything to history, then this present has to contain the whole meaning of time. It needs to expand ahead of itself, trespassing over traditional temporal boundaries in order to swallow up everything that the future is customarily thought to hold. In its systematic appropriation of the world to come, it must succeed in a most extraordinary task, that of absorbing the process of redemption, because Donne's question robs the human story of its usual chance to hide its point in the realm of tomorrows. Ideally, this emergency dilation of the here and now ought also to give us a glimpse of life beyond the end, since if this present is the world's last night we need to find some way of putting the future behind us. Though a certain degree of abstraction is needed in order to think these ideas through, the conceptual leap is not as great as one might imagine. It merely calls for a more subtle approach to Donne's question.

In an essay expounding on the folly of millenarianism written in 1951, C. S. Lewis employed Donne's question to great effect. After roundly censuring those who persistently venture dates for the end of the world against strict scriptural injunction, he suggested, in an apparent *volte-face*, that the doctrine of the Second Coming nonetheless fails if it does not make us perpetually ask 'what if this present were the world's last night?' It was naive and crass to ask 'when?', since one could never know, but essential and rewarding to muse on 'what if?' In recommending that we view each day as though it were our last, Lewis sought, as a good Christian, to remind us that ours is a temporal existence; death, both personal and global, is inevitable, therefore we should exist in a constant state not of anxiety but of preparedness, striving all the while to be good.[1] Consciously or unconsciously, in the service of his abiding beliefs, Lewis made good strategic use of Donne's question. Exploiting its innate oddity, he obtained maximum mileage out of the fact that it grants us all the certainty of global annihilation without the pain of its actuality and all the thrill of rupture without loss of continuity; the fact that, in effect, it delivers the End as a non-event.

Picking up where Lewis left off, Donne's gentle interrogative seems to raise as a matter of speculation the idea that the end of the world might come imperceptibly, stealing upon us under cover of a non-event to bring things to a halt with an inaudible last gasp. The theory has a certain appeal, a teasing attraction, but what does an invisible, intangible End look like? The question is both forbidding and compelling: forbidding, because it forces us to abandon preconceived ideas about bangs and explosions, and compelling, because it invites us to imagine what an apocalypse could potentially be if it lacked almost all external signs. If it were not heralded by trumpets, for instance, flagged in by extravagant pyrotechnics or, even more curiously, if it left no visible traces behind it. And if the end of the world *did* come in this manner, insensibly and without warning, there is the issue of whether we would necessarily recognise the event for what it was. These are peculiar thoughts to acclimatise to, but if we set them in the context of some of the more inscrutable avenues of biblical speculation they can to some degree be normalised. If Christ can come like a thief in the night, why not the end of the world?

As it happens, the concept of a silent apocalypse does have a religious precedent. In the Jewish mystical tradition, there is a vein of Kabbalistic thought that postulates a secret redemption in which the Messiah redeems time without leaving a symptom detectable *in* time. According to the Lurianic Kabbalah, the soul of the Messiah has been subject to a regular cycle of transmigration since the beginning of time, ever since it left the body of Adam and then David and migrated who knows where. Successive descents of this soul were seen to be dependent on and transformative of the state of the world, where in every generation there is only one righteous man disposed to receive it. The redemption, therefore, will not come all at once but in stages, some of which will be inwardly hidden in the spiritual worlds and others of which will be more apparent. The idea of a gradual and secret redemption is profoundly radical in that it does not somehow seem to amount to a miracle. Rather, as the logical result of a process already immanent, the redemption becomes symbolic – the symbol *replaces* the event. Maimonides, the greatest of medieval Jewish philosophers, was himself drawn to the idea that dominion of the world could pass from the Tree of Knowledge of Good and Evil to the Tree of Life without struggle, silently. In his opinion the redemption would not change the natural order.

Like C. S. Lewis invoking a 'what if?' in order to deflect misguided millenarians from asking 'when?', such mystical embellishments on the theme of redemption were the result of clever manoeuvrings around biblical injunctions. One such injunction dating from the first-century Mishnah, which Gershom Sholem quotes in his monumental study of the Kabbalah, is so all-embracing in its prohibitiveness as to have the effect of stimulating conceptual innovation. It reads: 'Whoever ponders on four things, it were better for him had he not come into the world: what is above, what is below, what was before time, and what will be hereafter.' As might be expected, it was duly ignored.[2] One gets the sense, reading Sholem, that the entire Kabbalistic tradition was born out of a need to push against the restrictions placed on speculative thought by the combined rabbinically championed forces of the Talmud, Mishnah and Midrash. Against the practical religion of mainstream Judaism it set the deeply held esoteric conviction that a true theology requires knowledge of what is secret or hidden. Interestingly, ideas concerning a secret redemption not only endured, diffusing and recombining over time, but turned out themselves to have practical application, particularly when they were taken up within some of the more imaginative strands of millenarian thinking. On occasion, they have even succeeded in becoming orthodoxies of sorts.

John Nelson Darby's doctrine of the secret rapture of the church is a case in point. Moving on from the Plymouth Brethren to found Dispensationalism, Darby developed a line of apocalyptic theorising that has come to dominate mainstream British and American millenarianism, largely by forming the basis of the *Scofield Reference Bible*, a key fundamentalist text. At its centre is the doctrine of the secret rapture, which, in order to discourage arithmological guessing games, teaches that the second advent will occur intangibly. It will be perceived only by those who participate in it, the Faithful Elect who will be raptured from the earth via a mode of supernatural trans-vaporisation that instantaneously deposits them in heaven. For Darby there would effectively be two second comings, the first in which the church gets magicked heavenward at an unexpected moment, and the second in which Christ will come in the usual manner, heralded by trumpets and flanked by his angelic host to precipitate the programme of events described in the Book of Revelation.

In other guises, the idea of a secret redemption has been turned to the purposes of sects further from the mainstream. A traditional speculation whose *leitmotif* is intangibility can readily be put into practical service when promised advents disappoint or when eagerly awaited dates of destruction produce no brimstone. In the first category belongs the insistence on the part of Joanna Southcott's followers that their messiah, Shiloh, did indeed enter the world, spiritually, when no evidence of his foetal existence was found in his mother's decaying cadaver, while in the second category we can locate the conceptual ingenuity of original Jehovah's Witness Charles Taze Russell. Russell argued that the Greek word *parousia*, which the King James Bible translates as 'coming', also means presence. Thus he came to believe that before the battle of Armageddon Christ would be 'invisibly present' prior to his revelation. Numerological reasoning convinced him that the Lord would return, unmanifest, in 1874 and that the world would end in 1914. Passing time has not erased his prophecies, for the Witnesses continue to believe Christ to be 'invisibly present' on earth, going about his work unperceived, and have accordingly restyled 1914 as 'the beginning of the End'. This latter idea is decidedly Lurianic, in that, instead of the end coming as an explosive all at once, it is assumed to come upon us incrementally, creeping and invisible at first but gathering momentum to reach a loud and spectacular crescendo.

What distinguishes Darby, Russell and the Southcottians from their Kabbalistic forbears is that they really did believe that their present was the world's last night. In all probability, they would have preferred to have been justified in their views by vindicatory earthquakes, fireworks and thunderbolts. It was only because the end failed to happen or did not happen as it ought to have done that they fell back on intangible redemptions and imperceptible ends. Yet, at least in the case of Russell and the Southcottians, what they accomplished through their strategic use of the silent apocalypse was a most difficult task: that of redefining the present *as though* the end had occurred. That way, they brought the meaning of history to a resolution in the here and now despite external evidences. The extent of such an achievement may be appreciated just by following through the mind-bending, time-bending difference it ought, technically, to make to everyday life. It implies that we would awake one morning to 'find' that the world had ended even though things looked the same. We would have passed through the end and still be left with this world. Its meaning, however, would be completely different, paradoxically transfigured. Whatever else might be made of the notion of a new era dawning imperceptibly within our era, this *Gestalt* shift should be acknowledged as a conceptual triumph for millenarianism –

a way of thinking about the world that is so often accused of the most naive literalism.

Supposing there were secular versions of this sort of approach to the present which went one step further than their millenarian originals and asserted that the end had *actually* happened – that the silent apocalypse had already gone by undetected and that we were now living beyond the end. What would life be like on the other side of the apocalypse? How would we square our existence with the promised Millennium? What meaning would we attach to the passage of time? And what becomes of history? In 1925 T. S. Eliot ventured gloomily some way along this road with *The Hollow Men*, which is premised on the idea that the advent of mass culture brought history to a definitive close. Playing parodic havoc with modernity's self-promoting promise to usher in paradise, Eliot saw us for ever stranded not in a new Eden but in 'death's other kingdom', a muted world of 'Shape without form, shade without colour,/ Paralysed force, gesture without motion'. In this dead land bereft of 'lost Violent souls' and therefore bereft of hope-enlivened struggles to find meaning in life, there were only 'hollow men' – men who couldn't dream, who talked nonsense and whose heads were stuffed with straw.

In Huxley's Epsilons, Ortega y Gasset's 'mass man' and Elias Canetti's 'baiting crowd', Eliot's hollow men yielded philosophical counterparts in a way that his suggestion that history had ended never did. We have had to wait for the dawning of postmodernity and the advent of a humanity definable by its consumer choices for there to be renewed interest in the end of history. The fullest treatment of the subject comes from American political scientist Francis Fukuyama, who, in complete contrast

216

to Eliot, finds relief in the idea that directional human activity has ceased. In *The End of History and the Last Man* (1992) he set out to convince us that the event (or non-event) that placed us beyond history, turning us into post-historical beings or Last Men, was the disintegration in 1989 of the eastern bloc and the subsequent conversion of the splinter nations into liberal capitalist democracies. For Fukuyama, this mode of self-government represents the highest form of human social development. Beyond it there can be no further evolution. It will simply spread horizontally until it embraces the entire globe. It is the velvet apocalypse.

Broadly speaking, Fukuyama's arguments belong to that category of speculative thought known as universal or philosophical history, which concerns itself with history's hidden meaning – with meta-history. In its more optimistic guises, universal history simply transposes the Christian belief in the perfectibility of the soul on to the sphere of human action to conjure up an end-time fantasy in which history resolves itself and is mercifully abolished. Rightful credit for founding the discipline lies with St Augustine, but universal history is more familiar to us through the writings of men like Condorcet, Voltaire, Kant, Hegel and Marx. The field even has its own cult figures, like Teilhard de Chardin, the French zoologist and spiritualist who earlier this century fantasised about history culminating with humanity finally confronting and approving of itself in an arena of heightened self-consciousness he called the 'noosphere'. Universal history relies on the assumption that history proceeds purposefully, albeit often haphazardly, towards a single goal. In other words, there is an end-point at which its meaning finally becomes apparent. Passing this point has a transformative effect, so that beyond the moment of arrest and revelation there lies a post-historical landscape of millennial bliss. For Condorcet, the bliss was quite literal, for he believed that the consummation of history would occur with the realisation of human happiness. Marx thought that history would come to an end by finally breaking away from contingency, false consciousness and material constraint. And Hegel, building on the legacy of Kant, believed that through a tortuous succession of revolutionary jumps history would reach its ultimate destination with a full recognition of the 'absolute world spirit'. With the exception of Condorcet – inoculated against history by a combination of his faith in human perfectibility, progress and the onward march of *bonheur* – these thinkers tended to view history as a snare in which humanity is entrapped, an encumbrance that enchained and weighed down the human spirit. The struggles of history were thus really struggles to escape history.[3] Although Fukuyama appears to share this loathing of history, with its pointless wars, multiple injustices and bloody insurrections (a view given one of its most economical expressions by Kurt Vonnegut: 'History, read it and weep'), he differs from his noteworthy predecessors in several important respects.

In the first place, he sees history as culminating in a socio-economic order rather than in a fundamentally psychic one, as though the end of history was merely about arriving somewhere without knowing why. In this sense he is truly a philosopher of the market, an apologist for unseen forces and self-limiting ambitions. More importantly, in halting history at democracy he takes for an end what others would classify as a means. For Marx, for example, the value of bourgeois society lay in its purposiveness, its directionality. The democracy it engendered was about process, something which though based on a philosophical goal was not shaped to be a philosophical goal in itself. Democracy cannot aspire. It exists not so that citizens can become something but so that they can get on with their lives, attending to matters of physical security and material plenty and enjoying little pleasures without having to exert themselves in striving for them. By taking the democratic means of living for an end, Fukuyama effectively brings history to a close with private concerns. Crucially, there is no transformation beyond the end, because liberal capitalist democracy rules out the grandeur of transformations in favour of just being. This is not to say that such a society is static, rather that its dynamism is self-limiting. Its ability to produce wealth, for example, only serves to increase the number of ways to just be. Even its pursuit of self-understanding, achieved via psychoanalysis and its derivatives, ends in self-acceptance. This is a critical departure from the universal histories of old, which, however secular in content, were sufficiently Christian in form to envisage the end of history as transformative and life beyond the end as genuinely fulfilling. It also explains why Fukuyama needs to summon up the Last Man, for he cannot help wondering whether human psychology will eventually rebel against a state in which becoming is no longer a question and boredom is the only danger.

In reaching for the last man, Fukuyama inevitably calls up the spirit of Nietzsche, who, when modern democracy was but a beginning, foresaw that if it ever became an end, hope for mankind would be lost. *Thus Spake Zarathrustra* contains the clearest articulation of Nietzsche's view that in democracy man capitulates to weakness. Everybody wants the same and there-fore is the same. There is no real individuation, no striving and no exertion, only last men, numbed by the masterless slavery of rational consumption and preciously preoccupied with intro-spection and self-preservation. When Zarathrustra tells the crowd that the last man works merely to entertain himself, avoids all strife, is assiduous about tending to his health and solicitous of his material well-being, they cry, 'Give us this last man ... Turn us into these last men!' They do not care that although the last man sleeps soundly his life lacks meaning. Or that he is as uninspired as he is untormented. Thus Zarathrustra is left alone in his poetic belief that 'One must still have chaos in oneself to be able to give birth to a dancing star'. Refusing to accept that democracy's liberation of mediocrity was what several millennia of history had really been about, Nietzsche called for the return of the strong who lived and died by absolute values, the *Übermensch* or overman who understood that man had to surpass himself. These were men who would inaugurate a new aristocracy, by force if necessary.[4]

Fukuyama is absolutely clear about which, out of boredom or bloodshed, is the lesser evil on our horizon. But he only manages to reject Nietzsche's critique of the last man by arguing, rather lamely, that becoming is not entirely out of the question in liberal capitalist democracy. This most fundamental of human desires, he maintains, can find some outlet in the competitive ethos that makes such a society run. We can strive to excel in business, science, literature, in scholarship or in sport. Fukuyama's attempts to rescue the last man from a Nietzschean contempt have been overlooked by commentators eager to point out that he was wrong about the consummation of history, that what he took for its end was merely its temporary suspension. It is true that within a few short years the former eastern-bloc nations found themselves once again embroiled in history, their descent into the process being marked by the reappearance of tribal warlords, the resurgence of religious fundamentalism and old ethnic rivalries, thriving black-market economies and the outbreak of civil war – in short, by every kind of inequality that liberty has the potential to unleash. Liberal capitalist democracy proved, indeed, to be only a means. But taking satisfaction in his failed prediction is rather like dismissing millenarians because they keep getting the date wrong for the end of the world. What is interesting about them, and, by extension, about the secular millenarianism of Fukuyama, is the millennial desire. Fukuyama *wants* history to end because he actually believes that the last man's existence is desirable. And if the post-historical landscape he admires falls short of the millennial ideal, it is because, as an apologist for democracy, he believes that transcendence exacts too high a human cost. The irony is that in making a positive case for the last man he need not have troubled himself to argue that history had ended, since the last man's great talent is to pretend that it has.

Thus while history continues moving towards its destination, whatever that might be, the last man persists. Evidences of his existence abound, surfacing in our fear of and resistance to the historical process and in our patent obsession with self-preservation, which is the tangible form by which reason grasps the post-historical promise of immortality. One need only reflect, for instance, on the influence of fitness culture in the western world to know that the last man is alive and well and busy displacing the process of becoming from a social goal into a physical ideal. The stress on the body beautiful, fetishisation of youth, excessive preoccupation with healthy eating, exercise and cosmetic relief from ageing, all point to the fact that in the realm of the imaginary the body is now more than a temple, it has been remodelled as New Jerusalem – the locus of our desire to escape the effects of time. This presence of the last man *within* history rather complicates the standard picture of his psychology. Because he has emerged before the great consummation and yet behaves as though history were already behind him, he is effectively in denial. This is why his insistence on working beyond the end looks suspiciously like its opposite, end-aversion. Unlike Nietzsche's last man, today's last man still fears the end. His denial of history and focus on self-preservation are as much ways of resisting the end as of existing beyond it. It is as if by pre-empting closure he is doing his best to turn time into a medium without direction in the hope that somewhere along the way the end will simply get lost.

In Mary Shelley's much underrated and still under-read novel *The Last Man* (1826), the business of functioning beyond the end achieves just this. First history ends, giving birth to the last man. Then the last man uses his post-historical existence to cheat time out of effecting the only other end it can, his eventual death. As with all Shelley's novels, this relentlessly bleak tale contains a strong autobiographical element, in this case the author's identification with her central character, Lionel Verney. Cast as the last member of the human species, Verney is the sole survivor of a global holocaust – the only man to have travelled beyond history. In her more melodramatic moods, Shelley was prone to viewing herself in this light. 'I may well describe that solitary being's feelings, feeling myself as the last relic of a beloved race, my companions extinct before me', she confided to her journal while writing the novel.[5] In one sense she was not over-dramatising matters, for when Percy Shelley and Lord Byron perished, history too terminated in her world. The poets had been at the centre of an intense group of people who expressed their hopes through mutual friendship and experimental lifestyles. In that they sought to redefine the structure of the family, practised free love, championed radical politics – everything from revolutions to vegetarianism – their life activities were about making history. Appropriately enough, both Percy Shelley and Byron are reincarnated in *The Last Man* as history-makers, characters with social ideals, political power and military ambitions.

Framed within an acid reworking of the apocalyptic myth spiked with sarcasm and irony, and set in the twenty-first century, the novel's bare plot is that a mysterious plague mercilessly lays the species to waste. Last-man-to-be, Lionel Verney, chronicles the disease's virulent progress from beginning to end, charting how each successive stage of its horrible ravagings produces ever more desperate behaviour among the fast-diminishing band of survivors. Every gain for the plague is a loss for mankind, until selfishness and brutishness rule the 'failing remnant' – 'each was eager to be among the elect, and clung to life with dastard tenacity'. At this point, an epidemic of prophetic madness breaks out; an old and batty astronomer emerges from his den of arithmetic to announce the distant approach of a paradisiacal state, thus 'prolonging his prospect through millions of calculated years', and a 'self-erected prophet' tries to further his ambition for personal power under cover of preaching repentance, winning the ignorant, low born and weak to his mean cause. As the species dwindles to nothing, Verney comes to understand the crushing meaning of providence: 'truly we were not born to enjoy, but to submit and to hope', he says. His own salvation, if to be granted life in the midst of pointless death may go by that name, transports him into an intolerable future empty of another human soul, a cruel, parodic anti-paradise whose very contemplation leaves him inconsolable, wishing the world to have been his tomb rather than his prison. One cannot help feeling that in suggesting that being singularly spared is tantamount to damnation Shelley found a barbed way of delivering a rebuff to the Romantic notion that salvation could be found in solitude and solipsism.

At the centre of the novel is an almighty eschatological struggle shrunk to fit the individual psyche. It takes the form of a conflict raging in Verney's head between his stoic readiness to meet his fate and his equally strong desire to avert it. Put more simply, but no less quixotically, he longs to die and yet he wants to live for ever. He does not, however, make the millenarian mistake of thinking that the one automatically follows the other, that death is somehow not really an ending, merely a rite of passage. That error falls to the self-erected prophet, who is in many ways Verney's mirror image, reflecting back the apocalyptic Last Emperor to his last man and seeing a gateway where Verney anticipates only a 'dread blank'. By juxtaposing these characters, Shelley was able to locate the quest for immortality at the forefront of the last man's concerns while also contrasting two very different routes to obtaining it.

The prophet, as you might expect, tries to seize a portion of the world to come by styling his own 'fanatical party' as 'the Elect', convincing his followers that they are the mortal immortals or 'remnant' of Revelation for whom the agonising throes of death are no more than the rapturous birth pangs of everlasting life. This is an outrageous presumption, made more outrageous by the fact that it is *only* presumption, and just to prove that the prophet is as mortal as anyone else, Shelley has him murdered by a disillusioned apostate and his stricken body left to rot. What seemed to gall her most about the doctrine of special election, which she judged to be 'pernicious', was its anti-democratic thrust; the prophet would hog the whole of eternity to himself and was 'violent in his hate of any who presumed to share with him his usurped empire'. Verney's meritocratic bid for immortality is, by contrast, rather anodyne – he writes his autobiography (which doubles up as the text of the novel). But you get the sense that his was the journey from lastness to everlastingness that Shelley wished to recommend. She even bestowed a quasi-religious status on his writings by inventing the secondary fiction that the entire narrative was part of a prophetic text found in the cave of the Cumaean Sibyl. Another dollop of religious symbolism and it would have become the Everlasting Gospel.

Interestingly, if you remove the spiritual overlay you are left with a post-historical bid for eternality so eminently sensible and apparently obvious it belies its own strategic sophistication. Verney himself is barely conscious of the fact that by binding his own essence into something that will not only endure but outlast him he effectively gains a foothold on posterity and is thereby able to begin putting the future behind him. Of these pragmatic dealings with immortality he merely says, 'I will leave a monument to the existence of Verney, the Last Man.' In a sense, this is all that needs saying, since the word monument, from the Latin *monere*, to remind, does an extraordinary amount of work in this context. A whole constellation of connotations assumes a bearing. Monuments are reminders, physical marks or matters of record, sepulchres and objects of commemoration. They speak of durability and solidity and stubborn resilience; through them we possess an almost mechanical means of attenuating existence, a kind of rack for stretching history. Moreover, what the word monument omits to signify, Shelley herself supplies, and that is paternity. Near the beginning of the novel, before the plague has even raised its serpent head, Verney discovers the value of writing, specifically of writing biographies – 'I became as it were the father of all mankind. Posterity became my heirs'. It is an early lesson that serves him well at the end of time, when he is denied the means of natural succession, when his inheritance on earth has been cut off (and, to extend the analogy, he himself has been castrated), and he uses it to fabricate a descent of sorts for himself.

As archetypes of last men, Verney and the prophet ought to strike a chord of self-recognition within us. Culturally, if not personally, and not merely because the apocalyptic vortex encircling the year 2000 holds us in uncomfortable proximity to a much-feared end, but because we have begun thinking just as practically about securing our own immortality. In the opening chapter of this book I talked about the various ways in which the idea of finitude, filtered through the distorting lens of millenarianism, colours our dealings with the future. My argument was that, against the grain of common sense, our strongest convictions about our own decline arise not from a contemplation of the past but from our anxieties about the future. Now, in turning to the idea of everlastingness and to the different ways in which we have taken up negotiations with eternity, we need once again to turn our assumptions around by 180 degrees; for the future, that traditional realm of transcendence, is now the place to which only those convinced of their own special election and a few sundry New Agers attach their hopes for immortality. The rest of us, last man every one, appear to be investing them in the past.

Back to the Future

Time and again observers of contemporary culture have singled out retrospection as the dominant mood of the late twentieth century. Indeed, our passion for digging up relics, the tireless popular consumption of rediscovered ancient wisdoms, the constant revising and novelising of recent history and our near-devotional attitude to commemoration – think of the bowed heads, solemn speeches and revived minutes of silence – seem to suggest that if in the nineteenth century history attempted to pass itself off as a science, in the twentieth century it aspires to become a religion. Sceptics will no doubt point out that in the shadow of the century's end it is only to be expected that we should seek security in the nostalgic embrace of the past, like children clinging for dear life on to their mothers' skirts because they are afraid to face the unknown. But never before has there existed such a frenzy for preservation and conservation. Again, a comparison with the end of the nineteenth century springs to mind; as pessimistic, mournful and decadent as was the last *fin de siècle*, it gave birth to an industry that represented daring, expansion and globalisation. I am, of course, referring to the tourist industry. Today, the end-of-century industry that hugs that forward-looking ethos to itself is the heritage industry, and the values *it* embodies are conservatism, contraction and localisation. Along with the environmentalist movement, from which it takes its leading ideology – that of recycling – the heritage industry insists that we not only learn from the example of the past, but that we carry it with us into the future, preserved in aspic for all eternity.

It does not matter a bit that the past which the heritage industry is busy recreating is an ersatz one; that the stately homes, theme parks, museums of industry, Tudor villages, folk festivals, medieval banquet weekends and historical walks which cater to an increasingly popular passion for consuming the past are merely totems of a longed-for authenticity that reality somehow fails to provide. What counts is the objective existence of the past, its concrete manifestation in the here and now, and the fact that we have managed, literally, to rescue the bygone from oblivion. The same kind of self-congratulation under-writes the soft end of the retrospective impulse that has turned us into avid collectors of memorabilia, lovers of period-piece cinema, builders of family trees, restorers of relics and con-sumers of retro-chic, be it distressed furniture, warehouse conversions or the modern history-bound novel. It is as though we no longer trust memory to compensate for the loss of the past. And if retrospection has replaced memory, perhaps, in some sense, heritage has replaced history. According to French sociologist turned errant intellectual Jean Baudrillard, our determination to relive the past, albeit an antiseptic version of it, has actually reversed the course of history.

In a provocative and mischievous work of cultural diagnosis, *The Illusion of the End* (1992), Baudrillard argues that history is thrown back on itself by our 'mania for origins', obsession with relics, archives, monuments, memorials, biographies, complete works, and the sententious rigmarole of marking anniversaries, armistices, jubilees and centennials in an endless cycle of commemoration. Courtesy of an additional retrogressive thrust supplied by our compulsion to instantly historicise contemporary events by means of super-exhaustive news coverage, we are now, he contends, receding post-haste from an imagined imminent end and heading into a future stuffed full of 'simulacra' made to resemble the past we were supposed to have left behind. In essence, we have entered a time warp that has deflected the course of history from its traditional linear trajectory. Instead of shooting us up to New Jerusalem on the straight and narrow, or plummeting us down into apocalyptic decline, history now takes the form of an asymptotic curve or parabola, which is to say, it climbs, peaks and then descends, effecting a reversal as opposed to a consummation. As a result of this 'baleful curvature', it is boomeranging us back in the direction from whence we came, carrying us beyond the end without having taken us through it. However outré the thesis – and Baudrillard is notorious for his love of sensation – he is surely right to see in our retrospective neurosis the loss of an elemental joy in the reality of history: we no longer delight in the historical process because it is too pertinent a reminder of our responsibility for what the present has become.

Yet even our fetishisation of a replica past dusted off and spruced up to look like new has more to do with repentance than with nostalgia. Take the 1989 bicentennial of the French Revolution, an orgy of expensive pomp, parades, self-righteous speechifying and monument-building, complete with a re-enacted storming of the Bastille. Its sole purpose was to affirm that present-day France is *not* a place in which revolutions are acceptable. History is thus disinterred, only to be impaled again on the altar of simulation. Another example would be the British Conservative government's great show of contrition in returning the Stone of Destiny (memorably described by Ian Bell in the *Observer* as 'that unprepossessing lump of homeward bound, regal Caledonian rubble') to its rightful Scottish custodians in 1996, thereby issuing a clear signal that devolution was *not* – at least, as long as they remained in office – on the political agenda. Baudrillard is wonderfully enigmatic on the subject: 'It is as though history were rifling through its dustbins and looking for redemption in the rubbish.'[6] This sly reference to Trotsky's dustbins of history, which serve the cause of forgetting because nothing comes back out of them, insists that even Marxist metaphors for progress go into reverse.

If we turn from history to nature, we find the same obsessions with repentance and resurrection infusing an elaborate rescue fantasy. The natural world must be preserved, conserved, memorialised and recycled, extended beyond its sell-by date in defiance of time, just like the residues of the past. In the interests of superannuation, there has been a frantic creation of preservations and reservations, botanical gardens, national parks, protected waters, sacred forests, sanctuaries and zoos (which, thanks to a miracle of public relations, are no longer regarded as torture chambers but as havens of conservation). Nietzsche once said that now God is dead mankind's greatest sin is against the earth. It is a message that environmental pundits everywhere take very seriously, because now God is dead the earth will sit in judgement of mankind. Utterly at home within this grid of religious reference, the self-styled eco-saviours of the earth chastise us for mismanaging our God-given dominion of nature. Like the apocalyptic messengers of ancient times, they are impassioned by a need to announce, to spread the word far and wide, repent and be saved. Their rhetorical spin relies on a Green version of the Fall, as though the state of our moral health could be read directly off the natural world. Both are polluted, exhausted and depleted, and both, therefore, are endangered. Hellfire awaits us in the form of an environmental disaster, unless we are prepared to put the Earth First, making reparations for our sins through the sacrament of conservation. For all its transparency, the Green argument has struck a seam of guilt. But, as with most matters relating to the human conscience, this has been sublimated into something else. In this case it is an anxiety about things disappearing. Thus nature, like the past, must be made to endure.

By virtue of simply enduring, the preservations of history and nature may be seen as the inanimate equivalent of the last man who just is. They exist, and within that property resides their entire meaning. However, the strange space which they inhabit underscores that existence with a kind of indelibility the last man has yet to achieve. It is a space belonging to the expanded present of the post-historical imagination, in which time ceases to have meaning. Within it there is no decay, no corruption and no forgetting. If the present we inhabit now could be infinitely stretched, it would approximate that space. Lionel Verney understood this much in fashioning a monument out of the raw materials of his own life. We, however, have the whole world at our disposal. All of it is potentially heritage-to-be. All of it can have a posthumous existence, a hereafter in the here and now. Taken to its limit, the world could be turned into a museum in order that we might banish time from our lives once and for all. We would then have created a place of immunity from the end of the world, a place in which recycling ensures continuity and where durability stands in for eternity. Such a world as this would pay rich homage to our late twentieth-century understanding of heaven on earth. It would even have effected a transcendence of sorts, since the business of prolonging the survival of things ordinarily destined to perish affords us an empirical, tangible means of going beyond the temporal.[7] In this sense, our icons of everlastingness serve as secular counterparts to the images of non-transience that populate the religious imagination – the everlasting deities with infinite minds, incorruptible paradises, immortal souls, interminable torments and endless cycles of transmigration and reincarnation. But if preservation holds out the promise of transcendence, what it actually achieves is merely technical; immortality without the gift of salvation. It is the same order of achievement as getting beyond history without having passed through the end: there is no transformation.

On a small, experimental scale, we already possess a prototype museological cosmos in the shape of Biosphere 2. Sitting at the feet of the implausibly pink Santa Catalina Mountains in the middle of the Arizona Desert, near Tucson, this paean to the ethos of recycling is a sight to behold. A gigantic structure constructed from plate-glass sheets held together in imaginative polygonal contortions by steel girders and rising in places to heights of ninety-one feet, it covers three and a half acres of land and houses a variety of natural environments or 'biomes'. There is a miniature rainforest, marshland, arable farmland, an expanse of desert scrub imported from the Biosphere's barren surrounds, and an ocean, twenty-five feet deep and holding 900,000 gallons of sea water (see plate 7). To the extent that the biosphere's ecosystems were designed to be totally self-sustaining, the complex is entirely sealed off from the outside world. Airlocks provide the only means of entry above ground, while a 500-ton steel liner separates the biomes from the earth below. The problem of desert heat causing the atmosphere inside the biosphere to expand is taken care of by a pair of enormous steel lungs situated on either side of the complex, which inflate and deflate in uncanny imitation of the breathing process. In ecological terms, the living museum of Biosphere 2 is the perfect model of what is known as a 'closed system'.

In and around Arizona, though, it is still referred to by the colloquialism that attached to it at its opening in 1991 – 'the human zoo'. That was when an eight-person crew consisting of four men and four women was sealed into the complex to begin a two-year survivalist mission. The idea was that, cocooned off from the rest of the world, the 'Biospherians' would be locked into a relationship of mutual dependency with nature that had not existed since Adam and Eve tended the Garden of Eden. It is an idea that appealed to Christian sentimentalists and environmental romanticists in equal measure, though the Biospherians were neither looking back with the former nor forwards with the latter. Rather, they were pioneering travellers in the expanded present of post-history, where it is possible to leave planet Earth and yet still remain on it. In this realm outside of space and time, the mythic dimension of their mission took on a hyper-real quality, as though Biosphere 2 had unearthed a piece of long-forgotten archaic paradise and replanted it in the present. It was an impression deliberately calculated to prick the conscience of a fallen species whose relationship with nature had degenerated into one of disrespect and exploitation.

Biosphere 2 owes its existence to two men: John Allen, a metallurgist by training and something of a seeker by vocation, who dreamed the project up, and Texan oil billionaire Ed Bass, who, in the mid-Eighties, put up the $150 million needed to realise it. Over the six years of planning and construction, Allen used his considerable charm to cull the expertise of top-ranking scientists from around the world. It was largely due to the collaboration of such venerable institutions as the Smithsonian, the Yale School of Forestry and the Royal Botanical Gardens at Kew that Biosphere 2 was the toast of the scientific world on its completion. But the day international TV crews filmed happy Biospherians clad in shiny red boiler-suits entering the airlock to begin a new life was destined to be its greatest. Within weeks, there were rumours afoot intimating that the scientific credentials of some of the Biospherians were not what they ought to be. The disturbing revelations about Allen's personal history which followed prompted most of the scientists associated with the project to retract their good will. Eighteen months on, the dream was over. Oxygen levels in the Biosphere had fallen dangerously low, the cockroach and ant populations had run riot and, with none of the world's leading scientists on hand to devise remedies, the crew were pulled out haggard and undernourished.[8]

Although a second crew went into the Biosphere in 1994, the survivalist bubble had already burst – and not just because the original mission was perceived to have failed. The term 'survivalism' had narrowed to become almost exclusively associated with gun-toting white supremacist militia groups who seclude themselves from the world and take pot shots at passers-by or else plant home-made bombs in government buildings. It had become an undesirable tag. At the same time, Biosphere management was in a state of disarray, principally as a result of souring relations between Allen and Bass. Before the end of the year, Bass fired Allen and nine other project managers and, as law suits began to fly, terminated the second mission, announcing that Biosphere 2 was to embark on a new phase of experimentation under new management.

It is curious that John Allen, a man unusually skilled at putting the future behind him, was unable to do the same with his past. His colourful *curriculum vitae* makes for fascinating acquaintance, especially since he disclosed so little of it to the world-renowned scientists whose help he had recruited. More to the point, it places Biosphere 2 in a rather unflattering light. His story may be easily summed up as a gradual drift from mainstream conventionality to the outer fringes of social acceptability. After taking a metallurgy degree from Colorado University and a business degree from Harvard, the Oklahoma-born impresario embarked on a sequence of un-American adventures. He walked across North Africa, hung out in Laos, dallied with Buddhism and imbibed the teachings of Greek-born mystic G. I. Gurdjieff. Then in the mid-Sixties he resurfaced in San Francisco as Johnny Dolphin, beat poet. At the end of that decade he formed a theatre troupe, the Theater of All Possibilities, and together they decamped to Santa Fe, New Mexico, to live on a commune and do a lot of primal screaming. According to various visitors, Allen's leadership at Synergia Ranch, where Bass was a sometime resident, was cultish and routinely involved meting out verbal and physical violence. His outlook was also becoming increasingly apocalyptic.

Before I learned any of this, I had met up with Allen in London at his Institute of Ecotechnics, the organisation from which some of the original Biospherians, theatre troupe members, obtained bogus scientific certification. The building doubles up as the October Gallery, an exhibition space in the heart of genteel Bloomsbury. Tall and with rugged Mount Rushmore features, Allen, now in his sixties, cut an imposing, even intimidating, figure. He signally failed to answer any of my questions about Biosphere 2 directly, regaling me instead with a crypto-philosophical monologue about closed systems, the five kingdoms of the earth and the self-sufficiency of biomes, while drawing complicated diagrams representing the spread of corporate responsibility that had allowed Bass, his one-time devotee, to oust him from power. I understood none of it, so I had bought *Space Biospheres*, the book he wrote in 1986 to promote interest in his project. This slim volume contained the information I had been looking for; namely, that Biosphere 2 was conceived as a dress rehearsal not for eco-sensitive living but for space colonisation. Allen was convinced that the earth was doomed. Long before the sun burned out, he argued, mankind would see to its own obliteration through

236

nuclear holocaust, global pollution or the mere conceit of overpopulation. 'The major motivation behind creating Biosphere 2', he wrote, 'is to assist the biosphere to evolve off planet earth into potential life regions of our solar system, and eventually throughout the galaxy and cosmos'.[9] Mars, which he thought bore an uncanny resemblance to Earth, was his favoured destination, closely followed by the moon.

I suspect that if Bass were quizzed today on the matter of his investing in Martian real estate he would be more than a little embarrassed. Indeed, since he parted company with Allen in 1994 he has worked hard to transform Biosphere 2 from a temple dedicated to sci-fi eco-spiritualism into a rigorously functional research lab. As a sign of his commitment to funding 'proper science', he went into partnership with Columbia University's Lamont–Doherty Earth Observatory, whose directors subsequently appointed a team of Ivy League scientists to run various research projects based at Biosphere 2. Their tenure began in January 1996. When I visited the complex shortly after the handover, they were busy flushing the system with carbon dioxide with a view to discovering whether or not we really have anything to fear from the Greenhouse Effect, ignoring peer group criticism suggesting that state-of-the-art biospherics need utilise nothing larger than a goldfish bowl. Visitors are not permitted inside the complex, for which disappointment they are inadequately compensated by a PBS documentary featuring Alan Alda interviewing earth scientists and a quick circumnavigation of the complex under the blazing sun. Up close, the biosphere somehow loses its mystique, begins to look like the oversized greenhouse it really is. I longed to see Biospherians at work inside, but our tour guide, who had a goatee beard and a pierced tongue, toed the management line, saying, 'Having them out was a breath of fresh air for the scientific experiments.' Surely they *were* the scientific experiment? So desperate is Biosphere 2 to play down its survivalist past that its staff are not even able to credit the vision, dedication and courage it took to boldly go where no man had gone before and actually test whether a capsule world might support human life. Perhaps, after all, it is fitting that this imaginative leap should have been taken by a theatre troupe, especially one committed to exploring all possibilities.

In many ways, Biosphere 2 inhabited by human beings worked best as theatre. On its verdant stage was enacted a drama of life and death, wholly unscripted, improvised from moment to moment. At times it was comical, as when, for example, the Biospherians noticed that their skin had turned orange because of the high levels of beta-carotene in their diets, and at times tragic; months of arduous agricultural labour resulting in a crop failure would leave the crew dejected for weeks. Moreover, while most theatrical productions are incapable of sustaining a long run, this one consistently drew huge audiences. Day upon day, for eighteen months, thousands of people made the trek into the desert just to have the experience of peering through the glass at Biospherians. It is a sensitive point with current management that today's visitor figures are paltry in comparison. Mounting a predictable defence, the public relations team dismisses the record-breaking visitor figures of old as the product of a mindless theme-park mentality, as though it were a blessed relief to be no longer plagued by gawping, gasping, camera-clicking hordes. In this, they radically underestimate the degree of curiosity people had

238

about a way of living so steeped in mythic significance its attractions cannot be explained away by the desire to buy the T-shirt and the mug.

Indeed, Biospherian practice took shape within an idiom deeply inimical to the idea of consumption. It gave concrete form to a prelapsarian vision of humanity as beings who take nothing from the earth and put nothing back. In Biosphere 2, as in paradise, there was no addition and no subtraction. There is an element of asceticism in play here, reminiscent of the kind of fascination Christians exhibited in the Middle Ages for the issue of whether or not angels could eat or excrete. If they did, they left no evidential trace of having done so. Angelic purity thus manifested itself as a form of self-erasure, something the Biospherians were not quite up to emulating. However, they achieved the next best thing, with the individual not so much erased as blended seamlessly into the environment, quietly operating a system of exchange that left the whole unchanged. In essence, what captured public imagination was recycling as a way of existing in the world and not merely as something you do with empty wine bottles. In one sense, it was a *modus vivendi* that ought to have felt familiar. Despite the clash between ideals of zero growth and of unlimited growth, its cyclical, self-sustaining dynamic nurtured aims as modest in their way as liberal capitalist democracy – equally self-limiting, and equally unfriendly to the idea of becoming. Transformation is therefore debarred from us regardless of whether we attempt to live like angels, leaving the world apparently untouched, or decide to eat, drink and shop because there is nothing more substantial to be had. One could argue that this is no bad thing at a time when transformation tends to present itself to us in the shape of a monomaniacal thug with a semi-automatic trying to shove the Millennium down our throats.

To the extent that we seem to be processing the world around us with a view to separating what can and cannot be made to endure, in *lieu* of mourning what has already gone we have begun to mourn what has yet to be lost. Or, more accurately, whatever cannot be projected into the expanded present of post-history. This grieving reveals itself most clearly in the current vogue for obituary writing which encompasses a whole slew of books recently published heralding the end of everything from architecture to the family to the nation state. Among them, John Leslie's *The End of the World* (1996) weighs up the odds of human extinction, George Brockway's *The End of Economic Man* (1991) predicts the death of free-market capitalism, and Jeremy Rifkin's *The End of Work* (1996) foresees the global economy shrinking the labour force to a tiny élite, leaving the rest of us twiddling our thumbs. One could go on: there's Neil Postman's *The End of Education* (1996), Peter Toon's *The End of Liberal Theology* (1995), Claudio Narajo's *The End of Patriarchy* (1994), David Carson and Lewis Blackwell's *The End of Print* (1995), and many more. My favourite is the late French historian Jean Gimpel's crazed *The End of the Future* (1995), which trumpets an apocalyptic message of universal decline caused by a fatal slowing down in the rate of technological progress. The second millennium, argues Gimpel, belonged to the west. Concorde and plastics were its culmination. But we have squandered our inheritance, turned our backs on the supersonic and sublimely synthetic (the electronics revolution is dismissed out of hand as a drain on human productivity), in favour of a return to trams and river buses, linen and bricks. One Spenglerian cycle has ended in regression. The next millennium will belong to China. Gimpel is the first to admit that his prophetic track record is poor. He confesses that in the 1930s, convinced of the end of the written word, he tried to become a film director and that in the 1950s, when he thought the motor car's days were numbered, he took flying lessons. Before he died, he came to believe that air travel would soon be a thing of the past.[10]

Of course, substantial differences exist between these books. Some are more gimmicky than others, some more apocalyptic, while Gimpel's is off the seismograph. But insofar as they constitute a genre, they all take the view that the contemporary world is a frightening place, either because established structures have been destabilised by their inability to keep up with the rapid pace of global change or, and this is a distinctly millenarian position, because the technological innovation we take to be a sign of our progress is in reality the instrument of our undoing. If one were searching for a likely progenitor of this fad for obituary writing, Fukuyama's *The End of History* appears to be the obvious candidate. And, in terms of publishing phenomena, it is. But Fukuyama's thesis is about culmination and cessation, not disappearance. As employed by his imitators, the 'End of' tag functions instead to label as obsolete anything bearing the taint of impermanence and to consign it to the dustbin of history for good. In this regard the obituarists echo the kind of pessimism about the possibility of progressive cultural change associated with French structuralist thought. Long before the first 'End of' book entered the bestseller lists,

Michel Foucault heralded the End of Man, and Barthes and Derrida announced the 'death of the author'.

In *The Order of Things* (1966), Foucault characterised man as the central fiction of the human sciences. His radical scepticism about the reality and authority of man implied that man could just as easily be eroded by the human sciences as formerly he was constructed by them. He could be dissolved, disintegrated, made obsolete. This sort of anti-humanism is indebted to an understanding of history that denies humanity any motive force in its development. Building on the work of thinkers like Louis Althusser, who took Marxist historical materialism to a logical conclusion and defined history as a 'subjectless process' made neither by man nor for man, it goes on to undermine the notion that man is a subject at all. And it recalls the secular eschatology of anthropologist Claude Lévi-Strauss, who wrote in *Tristes Tropiques* (1955): 'The world began without man and will end without him.'[11] Like Rousseau before him, Lévi-Strauss romanticised a paradisiacal pre-human order which mankind had managed to contaminate with its passion for progress. Blithely unaware that progress is in fact corruption, modern man deludes himself that he is better than his uncivilised ancestors. For Lévi-Strauss, human development reached its pinnacle in the Neolithic age. Ever since, mankind has been in decline. Soon it will disappear. What we have here is a kind of universal history, but in reverse gear. It proclaims that instead of proceeding to a point of culmination, history is moving towards a nadir. Instead of crowning the achievement of mankind, it will end in bringing about its dissolution. The end of history, therefore, will coincide with the end of man. There is a conspicuous current of self-loathing running through this argument, not dissimilar to that found in catastrophe tales or in the conspiracy theories beloved of millenarians, except that here it is history that is doing the conspiring, slowly but steadily plotting our downfall.

In terms of how the last man might react to this prospect of his own imminent disappearance, the 'death of the author' has crucial bearing. By claiming that man is no more able to fix meaning in the world than to shape the events unfolding within it, this obituary made him as irrelevant to literature as he had become to history. This is not the place to debate the ins and outs of theoretical deconstruction, but to point out that within the framework of cultural relativism traditional belief in the immortality of texts is undercut by the notion that the meaning of texts is by definition temporal, subject to a constant round of erasure and reconstitution; an endless refraction through the multiple viewpoints of multiple readers. The implication is that no Gospel is everlasting. Thus the twentieth-century last man, unlike his nineteenth-century predecessor – unlike Lionel Verney – has the route to immortality through authorship closed to him. Perhaps this explains why our obsession with self-preservation is overwhelmingly focused on the body.

Heavenly Bodies and Heavenly Hope

And so we return to fitness culture and health clubs, the plastic surgeon's table, macrobiotics and the anti-ageing industry, to all the myriad means by which we chase after immortality in the here and now. Somehow and in some way we are determined to squeeze ourselves into the expanded present of post-history by making ourselves durable. At one end of the spectrum we will press into the service of this goal anything that will turn back the clock and lead us back to glorious youth. We will incorporate silicon and collagen, imbibe homeopathic elixirs, work out in the gym and learn to nurture the child within on the therapist's couch. At the other end lies the pursuit of longevity, where all sorts of medical technologies may be wheeled in to prolong the human lifespan: pace-makers and hip replacements, dentures and organ transplants. To view our dedication to self-preservation as symptomatic of a loss of faith in an afterlife goes some way towards unravelling the complex expectations now brought to bear on the body. But it is not enough, because it seems to imply a form of abdication and a lack of imagination that do little justice to the scale of our physical ambitions. To begin with, we need to discard as outdated a Nietzschean understanding of the last man as a coward who hides behind self-preservation because he hasn't the courage to aim for transcendence. Today's last man sees self-preservation as a *means* of transcendence. This is largely by way of last resort, since those traditional routes by which the human desire for becoming finds expression appear to be blocked; history, for example, has stagnated, politics has forsaken vision for management and, while we have grown disillusioned with the idea of a single ethics for all, we have failed to find alternatives to this outlet for elective self-improvement. Frustrated by the difficulties or impossibilities of going beyond ourselves in the context of the social body or the body politic, we have retrenched our desire for becoming in the body corporeal. It is as if, in some collective sense, we have suddenly remembered that the verbs to breathe and to aspire share a common root.

However, there is a yet deeper level of material investment that reveals itself in the extent to which we have asserted the importance of the body over the soul. Whereas in former times we feared the corruption of our souls, we now fear the corruption of our bodies. Anxieties about environmental pollutants and toxins, the overuse of fertilizers and pesticides, and our surreptitious intake of food additives abound. And forms of wilful self-destruction like over-eating, smoking, drug abuse or alcoholism are regarded almost as sinful. Imperatives to maintain the body's primal purity are no longer encoded simply in aesthetic terms; they are explicitly moral. This is one of those occasions when it feels as though one *fin de siècle* is actually screaming its anguish to another, for our moral duty to our bodies is something that Wilde's Dorian Gray was unable to learn. Fiction's archest aesthete makes a Faustian pact with his own portrait, whereby he gains eternal youth and the ageing that ought to befall him works its cruel changes instead on the exquisite canvas. Once secure of his forbidden fruit, Dorian Gray contrives to lead a dissolute life without the bloom of youthful innocence ever leaving his cheeks. But he gets his just desserts when in a fit of rage he destroys his horribly disfigured avatar and instantly comes into his miserable inheritance, as ugly as it is overdue. The play on visibility and concealment in Wilde's novel resonates today, for in the same way that environmentalists attempt to read the psychic health of society off the natural world, it is increasingly the case that the inner core of an individual is thought to manifest itself on the body's surface. The body beautiful is presented to us as wholesome and good, while the overweight and the under-exercised are written off as morally complacent. At the same time, body-culture gurus working in everything from competitive sports to meditative yoga have appropriated the language of perfectibility once reserved for describing the progression of the immaterial part of ourselves. Explorations of physicality are now exalted as journeys of self-discovery. As the new uncharted territory, the body is a place where we are able to realise in the fullest sense who we have the potential to be: it is a site of revelation.

This way of thinking seems to stem from conceiving the soul as something that can conceivably be detected with extreme difficulty, like the quark. It effectively spiritualises the body. It renders flesh and bones sacred in order that the body durable can rise to an epiphany modelled on the image of the saints, whose blessed flesh refused to decay in the grave.

No group reveres the body corporeal more than cryonicists, that small band of scientific optimists who elect to have themselves, or sometimes just their heads, deep-frozen in liquid nitrogen immediately after their deaths. Far from being an alternative to burial or cremation, cryonics represents a new departure in the funereal arts, for it is undertaken in the conviction that death is reversible. Cryonicists have every expectation that we will soon possess the knowledge to bring people back from a state of frozen suspension into life, health and perhaps eternal youth. In the meantime, all their energies are concentrated on perfecting the means of preserving the human body indefinitely and without deterioration, in imitation of the saintly ideal. Since psychologist Jim Bedford attained the posthumous distinction of becoming the first man to be frozen, in California in 1967, some seventy people have taken the first step towards conquering death and placed themselves in cryonic suspension. Awaiting the call to everlasting life, their corpses are currently being stored at temperatures of minus 196° C in four non-profit-making cryonics institutes across the United States. The Alcor Life Extension Foundation in Scottsdale, Arizona, is the largest of these organisations, home to thirty-four suspendees or 'cryonauts'.

A further 406 people are signed-up Alcor members, which means they have donated their bodies to the foundation under the Anatomical Gift Act and, in order to meet the costs of $50,000 for a 'neuro-suspension' (head only) or $120,000 for a 'whole body' suspension, have taken out life insurance policies naming Alcor as their beneficiaries. When their final hour comes, a team of technicians will be poised by their side ready to pack them in ice and inject them with organ-preserving fluid the moment they are pronounced legally dead. Then, laid in a rubber 'mobile rescue cart', their corpse will be rushed by ambulance to Alcor's operating theatre and subjected to a heart bypass operation to drain it of blood. That done, it will be perfused with glycerol, which minimises mechanical damage to the body's cells by virtue of not expanding on freezing. If the member is signed up for a neuro-suspension, their head will be cut off with a bone saw and stored alongside others in a concrete vat filled with liquid nitrogen. Whole-body suspendees, meanwhile, are further cooled in a silicone oil bath before being transferred to a tall stainless steel barrel or dewar. The success of this process is thought to depend on speed: the faster a member is cryonically treated, the less ischemia – chemical poisoning as a result of cellular disintegration – sets in. With this in mind, many of Alcor's members make living wills exempting them from life-support services and autopsies, which will delay and probably undermine the effectiveness of their suspension. And most members secure sympathetic doctors and morticians in advance because, whilst there is no law against cryonics, its supporters are still having to battle for social acceptability.[12]

Steve Bridge, President of Alcor when I visited Arizona in 1996, is quick to defend cryonics as a scientific practice. 'We are not in the business of resurrection,' he told me. 'I think that what we are dealing with are people who, by tomorrow's medical criteria, will just have been in a long coma.' He cited the fact that cardiac arrest and drowning used invariably to be fatal, whereas these days stopped hearts and collapsed lungs are usually treatable: 'Death is just one of those things we haven't learned to solve yet.' Bridge has a suasive manner with the argument that death is not absolute, merely a matter of degree. But despite his ingenious logic (what would one call it, futuristic retrospection?), the only reason why cryonics is not in the business of resurrection is because reanimation is not yet a possibility.

It is, however, a dream that is continually fed by technological advances in artificial intelligence, robotics, genetics and cybernetics. And by nanotechnology, the projected science of constructing machines so minute they use individual molecules as operational components. In *Engines of Creation* (1986), Eric Drexler claimed that with such technology at our disposal matter might be manipulated atom by atom and, eventually, new worlds might be built from scratch. Including a chapter on cryonics by way of providing a near-future context in which nanotechnology could be applied, he spoke of tiny computers the size of small proteins being dispatched into the thawing bodies of cryonauts to effect the on-site cell repair that would be prerequisite for reanimation. For the first time, the chilly rite of passage into tomorrow that had seemed like a far-fetched whim from the fringes was clothed with the aura of possibility. In 1989 Alcor carried out a survey of its members and found that over two-thirds of the respondents had read Drexler's book. Of these, one-third said it was the most important book they had read in their lives. Up there with Drexler on the list of life-changing reads was Ayn Rand's *Atlas Shrugged* (1957), which suggests that a keen interest in science combined with belief in the titanic force of human will power is the key to the cryonicist mind. Beyond that, the survey confirmed that the archetypal Alcor member works in a computer-related industry, is highly educated, financially secure, optimistic, Caucasian, male, aged between thirty and fifty, and believes, moreover, that reanimation will be feasible within a hundred years.

Bridge is unusual among cryonicists in having formerly worked as a children's librarian, but he has always been a sci-fi junkie. In fact, it was at a sci-fi party in the mid-Seventies that he first encountered cryonics: 'I was telling this guy that it had to be hypothetical and he said, "No it's not. I've frozen two people." It was like this mind-twisting jump, as if the front door had opened and aliens had just walked in.' Bridge's interlocutor was Mike Darwin, who served as President of Alcor in the Eighties. These days, Bridge appears to be less scrupulous about separating fact from science fiction. He likes nothing better than to wax futuristic about possible reanimation scen-arios and his talk is peppered with sci-fi neologisms, cloning, prosthetic enhancements, nanotechnology and cybernetic rewiring: 'I'd like to come back as a full body, though I might swap it for a robotic one depending on what models were available. Obviously, I want to be smarter and faster. I don't want to wear glasses or get tired and I'd like to be able to see for ten miles, visit the moon and zip around the galaxy.' Although Bridge is as keen to see tomorrow as any of Alcor's charges, his head is not so much in other worlds that he can no longer think pragmatically. For one thing, he is taking precautions to preserve his identity in case his eventual defrosting causes a personality meltdown: 'I've asked all my friends to save my letters and I've stored a huge amount of stuff on computer disks over the years. I have access to a lot of who I am, so if I come back minus my memory I can regain part of it by reading about who I was.'

For all the futuristic fanfare, visiting Alcor's premises makes the intrigues of tomorrow's world seem extraordinarily remote. Tucked discreetly away between the luxury bungalows of north Scottsdale, the building looks like any other red-brick office block. Inside, however, the atmosphere is strangely evocative of H. G. Wells's *The Time Machine* (1895). Fronting the outfit is a wood-panelled reception, carpeted and sedately furnished. Old-fashioned brass desk lamps cast a soothing light and the walls are hung with solidly framed photographs of Alcor's residents looking as they would have liked to be remembered and, one presumes, as they wished to return. The nineteenth-century feel extends to the operating theatre behind, a white, windowless room containing a crudely functional steel bed, over-hung by giant lightbulbs and witness to many grisly goings-on. To one side stands the mobile rescue cart, a home-made confection resembling a rubber bath tub with attached tubing, pumps and dials – the product, one imagines, of the frenzied labour of some nutty professor. It all seems untrustworthily low-tech, like yesterday's vision of tomorrow.

At the back, the building opens out on to two cavernous rooms. In one is the silicone oil bath which looks like a large 1950s refrigerator laid on its back. Above it, a hoist is suspended from the ceiling so that freeze-dried corpses may be fished out of the bath and gently lowered into dewars. The other room is the cryotorium. This is Alcor's inner sanctum, home to the famous dewars and the concrete vat containing the severed heads. A flotilla of liquid nitrogen canisters is a reminder that cryonauts need constant tending, since the primordial soup of the future has a way with evaporation. Mike Perry, Alcor's caretaker, actually sleeps in the building so as to be available at all hours to replenish the ten to fifteen litres lost each day. With a Ph.D. in mathematics and scientific optimism enough for the entire staff at CERN, he is one of cryonics' most zealous champions: 'I believe it is the rightful destiny of mankind to be immortal.' Like thermos flasks (whose vacuum-insulated construction they share), the dewars give nothing of their contents away. Lift their lids and they simply smoke, enticingly. The only clues to their function are the Alcor insignias pasted on their flanks like taxonomic labels depicting a phoenix rising in glorious red flames from the ashes. Inside them, Alcor's cryonauts are suspended in a senseless limbo, literally the sleep of the dead, and there they will remain – at least that is the intention – until resurrection day dawns (see plate 8). When the technical team of the Westinghouse Electric and Manufacturing Company sealed the archives of their day into their time capsule back in 1938, they could hardly have imagined that the time-capsuling of human beings was only decades away, or that death would have become a waiting game rather than an end.

Cryonics is the crowning madness of our rational quest for immortality, not because it desires to transcend death, but because it entertains pretensions of doing so physically, biologically, by means of artificial survival. It is hubristic, yes, but it is also strangely mundane – an infinitely attenuated lifespan offering no more vitality, no more process, than an infinitely stretched present. In seeking to combat death, cryonics has merely put in its place the living death of museological existence, the 'esprit de corpse' of post-history. Curiously, the assumptions, motivations and technical considerations underpinning cryonics link up directly with the issues about immortality and resurrection that preoccupied theologians in the Middle Ages. Will we return to this world physically intact? With our bodily organs in place, with all our distinctive features, illnesses and handicaps? Will resuscitation preserve our identities, our memories, idiosyncrasies, desires and neuroses? And if the body is reassembled anew, who will come back, the child, the adult, or the old woman or man?[13] Cryonics answers these questions definitively, for it intends to bring us back just as we are. In its pursuit of literal everlastingness, it seeks an immortality that pre-empts the end rather than transcends it, leaving no room for metaphor. If it succeeds, we will have become adepts at resurrection, but there will be no salvation, only technological enhancement: we will be improved rather than transformed. Eternity will have degenerated into the production of artificial limbs. This is what happens when paradise regained is treated simply as a mechanical function of death postponed.

These days, there is not much evidence of a millennial impulse driving cryonicists, more of the selfish gene. But for Robert Ettinger, the visionary behind the deep-freezing of human beings, a belief that we would arrive in paradise by crossing the Rubicon this side of the apocalypse was a central component of his thinking. A former physics professor at Wayne State University, Detroit, Ettinger is the author of cryonics' founding text, *The Prospect of Immortality* (1964). He has been a tireless propagandist for his cause ever since he set about gathering like-minded techno-optimists around him by founding the Immortalist Society in 1967, followed, in 1976, by the Cryonics Institute, Alcor's Michigan-based counterpart. His book is remarkable for the degree to which it mixes no-nonsense realism with an elaborate romance that casts cryonics as a modern-day version of the alchemical quest for eternal life. Less remarkable is its tendency to borrow from science fiction. 'We will remodel', 'we will repair', he wrote. 'You and I, the frozen, the resuscitees, will be not merely revived and cured, but enlarged and improved, made fit to work, play and perhaps fight, on a grand scale and in a grand style.' This sort of talk deserved the fate it met with in television's *The Six Million Dollar Man*.

But while Ettinger indulged a fantasy of an earth filled with super-strong, super-virtuous cryonauts – Nietzsche's *Übermensch* made real – it was not primarily in a biological or eugenic ideal that he invested his hope. Rather, the most conspicuously hopeful dimension of his thinking was social. The difference is that the scientific imagination clings to the idea of immortality as a means of reconciling humanity to death, while the social fantasy takes flight from the idea that without it we cannot reconcile ourselves to life, to the intolerable necessity of having to achieve everything within constraints. Thus Ettinger maintained that our cryonic passage into the future would be a 'door into summer', heralding a Golden Age of heroism and tolerance, peace and plenty. 'Neither greed, nor lust, nor ambition will in that society have any recognisable similarity to the qualities we know. With the virtually unlimited resources of that era, all ordinary wants will be readily satisfied.' Using a standard libertarian argument, he reasoned that once individuals possessed indefinite lifespans, the pursuit of self-interest would coincide with the interests of bettering society. 'The result is wonderful: we have lost our souls, but gained heaven.' Ultimately, for Ettinger, cryonics was science's answer to Christian perfectionism, with the freezer era ushering in 'an age of brotherly love and a living Golden rule' rendered compatible with the secular American Dream through the symbolism of consumer culture. Paradise, he said, would be 'king-sized and chocolate covered'.[14] Yet his very admission of a social goal serves to point up cryonics' limitations. As Ettinger saw it, the problem was this: will it be the selfish and weak who are frozen? And the brave and dignified who spurn it? One might add: would we get bored? Would we lose a sense of moral obligation? Will we start to long for death like the Wandering Jew of myth? For now, we have no way of knowing, nor will any amount of technological foresight help, since mechanisms of social change are beyond its purview. But we might make a good guess, for technical salvation suffers from the same drawbacks as liberal capitalist democracy: it has no interest in aspiring. So it may well be that tomorrow's immortals will be as disappointing as Swift's everlasting Struldbruggs, who Gulliver expected to be rich, wise, virtuous and just, only to find that 'they were not only opinionative, peevish, covetous, morose, vain, talkative, but uncapable of all natural friendship, and dead to all natural affection'.[15]

At one point in his book, Ettinger described cryonics as 'a Pascal's wager based on a faith in science': if it works you gain everything and if it doesn't you lose nothing. Such was his own faith that he ventured his freezer programme at a time when a frost-bitten toe was considered incurable. While this bravura attests to the extraordinary fertility of Ettinger's imagination, it says a good deal more about the character of scientific optimism. Even today, cryonicists are able to sustain themselves on very little. Nanotechnology, for example, is still in the nursery. A recent issue of *Cryonics*, Alcor's in-house magazine, which has almost 1000 subscribers, reports that IBM researchers in California have only just succeeded in engraving their company logo on to the surface of a frozen nickel crystal using individual xenon atoms. Then there is their stubborn resolve in the face of on-going criticism from cryobiologists. While cryonics is predictably denounced from the pulpit and from elements within the legal network, its most unforgiving foes are cryobiologists, those members of the medical profession who work in the field of organ transplants and preservation. In spite of intensive research into deep-freezing living tissues, they have not yet managed to revive so much as a frozen kidney. Technooptimism, however, needs only the merest trace of promise on which to thrive, a hint of possibility here, a hint there. Out of a moon landing, it will dream of Martian colonisation, time travel and communing with extraterrestrials. Tripping off the Internet, it will envisage virtual worlds, the delights of techno-sex or the birth of a classless, genderless, global economy. From a spangle of such pin-heads of resolved problems thrown on to the blank canvas of the future, techno-optimists will happily busy themselves joining the dots.

At its limit, such exuberant free associating can border on the mystical, looking to all intents and purposes like a species of New Agery. The Californian-based Extropian movement, for instance, prophesies the dawning of a radical new era of unbounded, technologically enabled freedom. Many of its proponents are so high on science that they have upgraded their names by deed poll to things like Max More, Tom Morrow and Will Excel. In this they have noteworthy precedent: science's first apologist, Joseph Glanvill, titled his eulogy to the Royal Society *Plus ultra* (1688), or 'more still'. Extropy (a term coined in contradistinction to entropy, the nineteenth-century's scientific codename for cosmic doom) is concerned with everything that could conceivably help human beings surpass themselves. In the words of British-born extropian theorist Max More: 'Extropians have a specific conception of transhumanism, involving certain values and goals, such as boundless expansion, dynamic optimism, intelligent technology, and spontaneous order.' This capsule definition comes from a condensed manifesto for Internet users that More updates intermittently. In it he goes on to give more definite shape to the dreams of extropians. They look forward, for instance, to the day when we will attain complete control of our emotional responses through the genetic or viral manipulation of human neurochemistry; when we will have abolished ageing and involuntary death; when we will be able to buy intelligence-boosting drugs at the supermarket or use computerised brain implants as cognitive aids; when we can have designer bodies courtesy of computer-assisted molecular restructuring, or no bodies at all, by 'uploading' an individual's pattern of consciousness on to computer disk. More's rallying cry reads: 'No one will punish us for opening Pandora's box, for equipping ourselves with wings of posthuman intelligence and agelessness ... Life and intelligence should never stagnate; it can re-order, transform and transcend its limits in an unlimited progression. Let us progress on into a posthuman stage that we can barely glimpse.'[16] It's a rousing finale. Bluntly paraphrased, it says that it is in human nature to go against nature. Accept that and you become a citizen of the new universe.

As with cryonics, the ethereal castle-building of extropianism rests on the barest of foundations. The vision of neurochemical mastery, for instance, simply grafts a fantasy of control on to the reality that psychiatry has given us mind-altering drugs like Prozac and Deprenyl. And projected sallies into the world of prosthetics, cybernetics and synthetic on-line existences wildly extrapolates from recent research in which signals have been successfully passed back and forth between a neuron *in vitro* and a field-effect transmitter. We have been here many times before, at this critical juncture where the establishing of a fact triggers the unfurling of endless possibilities. If it induces a feeling of *déjà vu*, it is because the outer limits of scientific optimism afford us insight into the workings of real science. Real science progresses in just this manner; it casts fishing lines into the unknown, hooks up some strange creature and then tries to walk on water to reach it. The psychological aspect of this process is something that Francis Spufford has done much to illuminate. The scientific imagination, he argues, feeds off the unactualised. Every time a technological vista opens with the promise of new beginnings, it is spurred into the manufacturing of trains of untested possibilities. Some of its predictions will be utilitarian and some theoretical, while others will range from the bizarre to the grandiose. Spufford understands the essentially romantic pull of possibility, for he says that it is precisely because we cannot know whether or not our scientific and technological anticipations are accurate that 'modest results and frankly utopian results can have equal likelihood in our minds, and are rolled together intoxicatingly, almost lyrically'.[17] For this reason, science appears to be full of awesome prospects. In times as gloom-ridden as our own, an awesome prospect is a rare and wonderful thing because it encourages a form of hope. It also allows us to remember a way of asking 'what if' which is inquisitive and fearless because it belongs to a beginning, to a moment when limits seem to exercise no tyranny and the only desire is a hunger for expansion.

It is often remarked of the late twentieth century that faith in science has replaced religious hope. But what does that really mean? If it were merely a matter of appropriating goals, then the scientific faith would find its ultimate expression in Frank Tippler's plainly ludicrous attempt to style astrophysics as the new theology. Tippler contends that the Omega Point, Roger Penrose's projected destination of spacetime, is God. It is eternal, explains the whole of history, past, present and future, exists beyond space, time and matter, and is the transcendent source of all life. The universal wave function, in the meantime, is the Holy Spirit, while the human soul most closely resembles a self-programming universal Turing machine. By his own reckoning, Tippler is all soul – a code-cracking Turing machine programmed to solve the problem of eschatology: when the apocalypse comes, he argues, the Omega Point will resurrect us all.[18] No: science cannot *replace* religious hope, it can only offer as an alternative the thrills, both exciting and terrifying, of possibility. And possibility is not the same as hope, just as heritage is not history and indefinite self-preservation is not immortality.

Possibility is about what we can resolve. It looks like hope and appears to be concerned with our prospects because its sights are firmly set on the terrain of the future. But, unlike hope, which implies a submission to the idea that the future is something that comes upon us, it seeks to empty the future of its consequences, to reel it into the here and now bit by bit by confining it to an array of predicted outcomes. The future is thus predetermined not because some higher intelligence has co-opted it into its plot for humanity, but because possibility stakes a material claim on the unactualised. Possibility allows no room for the uncertainty of becoming. It cannot supply what we need to awaken us from the torpor of a life after expectation has been curtailed.

In one sense, all our efforts to annihilate the future, our debasement of hope into possibility, deferral of death and resistance to history relate to Pascal's wager, but in a way that Robert Ettinger neglected to consider. For the thing about Pascal's wager is that if you bet on the non-existence of God, as secular society has done, the stakes are higher. Everything we would stand to win in a designed cosmos needs to be relocated. One could imagine various ways of doing this, the most effective perhaps being to fill the old metaphors with new meaning, as Marx did, for example. But motivated by a nervous desire to pre-empt the end, to get beyond it without passing through it, we have felt it necessary to cash in the winnings and relocate paradise, immortality and eternity in the present. In the process losses have been incurred, since without history we condemn ourselves to an absence of destiny; without death we lack the moral incentive of impending judgement; and without hope we lose the chance for transformation. If we are to reclaim hope, then, we have to accept that hope has a cost which a belief in technological possibility lacks. It is not cumulative; it thinks that we can, after a while, have our hands full, so that if we wish to reach for the next object of hope we must first put something down. If we are to have genuine hope, then we must begin to let the past die; which means giving up on preservation and remembering how to forget. We must surmount our edgy inability ever to leave the present, break the deadlock of our crammed, anxious stasis, learn to relax a bit. And we must embrace an uncertain future that is beyond our comprehension even if that means admitting the prospect of a terrifying end – after all, it is not as if our attempts to obliterate the future have resulted in a culture that is free of fear.

Hope is not just a spiritual idea: it is apocalyptic. It is future-oriented because it is born of despair and fear. It may not insist on a complete rupture between this world and the world to come, but it does allow for the future to be radically different in a way that possibility cannot because it places limits on our expectations. Once again, the antiquated, pedantic, literal and clunking apparatus of apocalypse appears to have application to contemporary secular culture. It not only comprehends our fears, it makes them productive by encouraging the nurturing of hope. So long as the Christian apocalypse remains in prospect, we can make peace with passing time and have real hope for a real future. Better still, perhaps, is the Judaic solution, which perpetually postpones the world's end in the interests of the moral tension that results. It suggests that in order for us to live fully the apocalypse must never arrive – nonetheless we must always be apocalyptic and always hope that it will. Put another way, it's about making clever equations that allow hope to be strung across time so that each moment is imbued with expectation. Such as: the hope for the Messiah *is* the Messiah. It is a question of retaining the desire without the paradigm. This is why the proverbial rabbi of Jewish lore who is busy planting a flower when an ecstatic pupil announces that the Messiah has arrived is able to finish planting his flower before going to check the report. He experiences no urgency because he already possesses the Messiah in the hope for him. In Christian terms, an equivalent understanding suggests that what millenarians truly want is the hope embodied in the Millennium and not the Millennium itself.

Either way, the implication is that to live just before the end is the best place to be, because there hope is at its peak. And if the apocalypse is indefinitely delayed, so much the better. Long live the *fin de siècle*! As we advance towards the year 2000, we need to turn the hourglass over and approach the twenty-first century with renewed dread.

NOTES

Preface

1. Quotations from Heaven's Gate members were printed in articles in the *Observer* and the *Daily Telegraph*, 28, 29 and 30 March 1997. Full transcripts of the Solar Temple documents can be found in *Gnosis Magazine*, winter issue, 1995.

2. Italo Calvino, *Six Memos for the Next Millennium* (Vintage, London, 1996).

1. Prospecting the Future

1. Herman Kahn and Anthony Wiener, *The Year 2000, A Framework for Speculation on the Next Thirty Three Years* (Collier Macmillan, Toronto, Canada, 1969); John Naisbitt and Patricia Aburdene, *Megatrends 2000*, (Sidgwick and Jackson Ltd, London, 1990).

2. *The Letters of D. H. L.*, edited by George Zytaruk and James T. Boulton (Cambridge University Press, New York and London, 1981), Volume II, June 1913–October 1916.

3. Benoit B. Mandelbrot, *The Fractal Geometry of Nature* (W. H. Freeman and Company, Oxford and San Francisco, 1977).

4. Immanuel Kant, 'On a Newly Arisen Superior Tone in Philosophy' (1796), reprinted in *Raising the Tone of Philosophy, Late Essays by Immanuel Kant,* edited by Peter Fenves (Johns Hopkins University Press, Baltimore and London, 1993). The book also contains a transformative critique of the essay by Jacques Derrida: 'On A Newly Arisen Apocalyptic Tone in Philosophy'.

5. David Loye, *The Knowable Future, a Psychology of Forecasting and Prophecy* (John Wiley and Sons, New York, 1978).

6. Almost any United Nations Publications report of recent years will suffice to make the point. Robert Heilbronner, *Business and Civilisation in Decline* (Norton, New York, 1976); *An Inquiry into the Human Prospect, Looked at Again for the 1990s* (Norton, New York, 1991); *Visions of the Future, the Distant Past, Yesterday, Today, Tomorrow* (Oxford University Press, Oxford and New York, 1995); Rupert Sheldrake, *The Rebirth of Nature, the Greening of Science and God* (Century, London, 1990).

7. E. C. Zeeman, *Catastrophe Theory, Selected Papers, 1972–1977* (Addison-Wesley Publishing Company, Reading, Massachusetts, 1977). See also Tim Poston and Ian Stewart, *Catastrophe Theory and its Applications* (Pitman Publishing, London and Boston, 1978), and Roger Lewin, *Complexity Theory, Life on the Edge of Chaos* (Phoenix, London, 1993).

8. Julia Voznesenkaya, *The Star Chernobyl* (Quartet, London, 1987). The wormwood–Chernobyl connection is regularly exploited by doomsayers such as Rupert Sheldrake.

9. Ian Cotton, *The Hallelujah Revolution* (Little, Brown, London, 1995). On the rise of Pentecostalism in America see Harvey Cox, *Fire from Heaven, the Rise of Pentecostal Spirituality and the Reshaping of Religion in the Twenty-first Century* (Addison-Wesley Publishing Company, Reading, Massachusetts, 1995). See also

Notes

Janice T. Connell, *The Visions of the Children, the Apparitions of the Blessed Mother at Medjugorje* (St Martin's Press, New York, 1992).

10. Arthur Kroker and David Cook, *The Postmodern Scene, Excremental Culture and Hyper-aesthetics* (Macmillan Education, Basingstoke, 1988); Roy Porter and Sarah Dunant, eds, *Age of Anxiety* (Virago, London, 1996).

11. George Steiner, 'Totem or Taboo', in *No Passion Spent, Essays 1978–1995* (Faber and Faber, London, 1996).

12. Press coverage of the siege was extensive on both sides of the Atlantic. Here, I have made use of reports in the *New York Times*.

13. *Armageddon in Waco, Critical Perspectives on the Branch Davidian Conflict*, edited by Stuart A. Wright (University of Chicago Press, Chicago, 1995); Christopher Keep, 'An Absolute Acceleration, Apocalyptism and the War Machines of Waco', in *Postmodern Apocalypse, Theory and Cultural Practice at the End*, edited by Richard Dellmora (University of Pennsylvania Press, Philadelphia, 1995).

14. Michael Barkun, 'Reflections after Waco, Millennialists and the State', in James K. Lewis, ed., *From the Ashes; Making Sense of Waco* (Rowman and Littlefield, Lanham, Maryland, 1994).

15. Pope John Paul II, *Tertio Millennio Adveniente, Apostolic Letter of his Holiness Pope John Paul II to the Bishops, Clergy and Lay Faithful on Preparation for the Jubilee of the Year 2000* (Catholic Truth Society, London, 1994).

16. The story of the end of the first millennium is best told in Henri Focillon's *The Year 1000* (Harper Torchbooks, Harper & Row, New York and London, 1969).

17. Paul Boyer, *When Time Shall Be No More, Prophecy Belief in Modern American Culture* (Harvard University Press, Cambridge,

Massachusetts, 1995); Timothy Weber, *Living in the Shadow of the Second Coming, American Premillennialism, 1875–1982* (University of Chicago Press, Chicago, 1987). For America as a millennial nation see Charles L. Sarford, *The Quest for Paradise, Europe and the American Moral Imagination* (University of Illinois Press, Chicago, 1961); Ernest L. Tuveson, *Redeemer Nation, the Idea of America's Millennial Role* (University of Chicago Press, Chicago, 1968); Ruth Bloch, *Visionary Republic, Millennial Themes in American Thought 1756–1800* (Cambridge University Press, Cambridge, 1985). For background on the Reagan era see Steve Bruce, *The Rise and Fall of the New Christian Right, Conservative Protestant Politics in America 1978–1988* (Clarendon Press, Oxford, 1988).

18. William C. Weinrich, 'Antichrist in the Early Church', *Concordia Theological Quarterly*, Volume 49, 1985. Gregory C. Jenks, *The Origins and Development of the Antichrist Myth* (Walter de Gruyter, Berlin and New York, 1991).

19. Paul Boyer, *When Time Shall Be No More*; The Reverend Michael Wieteska, 'Intimations of Empire, the Great Powers in Prophecy', distributed by the author.

20. Norman Cohn, *Warrant for Genocide, the Myth of the Jewish World Conspiracy and the Protocols of the Elders of Zion* (1967) (Serif, London, 1996).

21. David Icke, *The Truth Vibrations* (Aquarian Press, London, 1991); *The Robot's Rebellion* (Gateway Press, Bath, 1994); *and the truth shall set you free* (Bridge of Love Publications, Isle of Wight, 1995). The Magazines *Open Eye* and *Greenline* keep a close watch on Icke's far-right associations.

22. Umberto Eco, *Foucault's Pendulum* (Secker & Warburg Ltd, London, 1989).

23. Norman Cohn, *Cosmos, Chaos and the World to Come* (Yale University Press, New Haven, 1993).

2. The Ultimate Destination

1. Frank Kermode, *The Sense of an Ending, Studies in the Theory of Fiction* (Oxford University Press, Oxford, 1966).

2. Victor Turner, *The Ritual Process* (1969) (Penguin, Harmondsworth, 1974).

3. See Robert P. Carroll, *When Prophecy Failed, Reactions and Responses to Failure in the Old Testament Prophetic Traditions* (SCM Press, London, 1979).

4. For background on the literary structure of apocalypse see Paul D. Hanson, *The Dawn of Apocalyptic, the Historical and Sociological Roots of Jewish Apocalyptic Eschatology* (Fortress Press, Philadelphia, 1979), and Norman Cohn, *Cosmos, Chaos and the World to Come.*

5. Ander Hutgård, 'Bahman Yasht, A Persian Apocalypse', in J. J. Collins and J. H. Charlesworth, eds, *Mysteries and Revelations* (*Journal for the Study of Pseudepigrapha* Supplement, JSOT Press, Sheffield, 1991).

6. Yigael Yadin, *Bar-Kokhba* (Weidenfeld & Nicolson, London, 1971).

7. Michael A. Knibb, *The Qumran Community* (Cambridge University Press, Cambridge, 1987). The most complete translation of the Scrolls is Geza Vermes's, *The Dead Sea Scrolls in English*, third edition (Penguin, Harmondsworth, 1987).

8. 1 Enoch, in *The Old Testament Pseudepigrapha*, Volume I, Apocalypse Literature and Testaments, edited by James H. Charlesworth (Darton, Longman and Todd, London, 1983).

9. Amos Funkenstein, 'A Schedule for the End of the World, the Origins and Persistence of the Apocalyptic Mentality', in Saul Friedländer, Gerald Holton, Leo Marx and Eugene Skolnikoff, eds, *Visions of Apocalypse, End of Rebirth?* (Holmes and Meier, New York and London, 1985).

10. George Steiner, 'Through That Glass Darkly', in *No Passion Spent* (Faber and Faber, London, 1996).

3. Revelation Revisited

1. Northrop Frye, *Anatomy of Criticism* (Princeton University Press, New Jersey, 1957).

2. Jacobus de Voragine, *The Golden Legend* (Princeton University Press, New Jersey, 1993).

3. In reading Revelation I have relied on the following: Leonard L. Thompson, *The Book of Revelation, Apocalypse and Empire* (Oxford University Press, Oxford and New York, 1990); J. P. M. Sweet, *Revelation* (Westminster Press, Philadelphia, Pennsylvania, 1979); David L. Barr, 'The Apocalypse as a Symbolic Transformation of the World, a Literary Analysis', in *Interpretations*, Volume 38, 1984, pp. 39–50; Martha Himmelfarb, 'Revelation and Apocalypse, the Transformation of the Visionary in the Ascent Apocalypses', in J. J. Collins and J. H. Charlesworth, eds, *Mysteries and Revelations* (*Journal for the Study of Pseudepigrapha* Supplement, JSOT Press, Sheffield, 1991).

4. Bernard McGin, 'Revelation', in Frank Kermode and Robert Atler, eds, *The Literary Guide to the Bible* (Collins, London, 1987).

5. St Augustine, *City of God* (Penguin, Harmondsworth, 1972). Quotations from Book XV, Chapter 1, and Book XIV, Chapter 28.

6. Norman Cohn, *The Pursuit of the Millennium* (Pimlico, London,

Notes

1993). Christopher Hill, *A Nation of Change and Novelty, Radical Politics, Religion and Literature in Seventeenth-Century England* (Routledge, London, 1990); *Milton and the English Revolution* (Faber and Faber, London, 1997); *The Levellers and the English Revolution* (Cresset Press, London, 1961).

7. Eric Hobsbawm, *Primitive Rebels, Studies of Archaic Forms of Social Movement in the 19th and 20th Centuries* (Manchester University Press, Manchester, 1959).

8. Leon Festinger, Henry W. Riecken and Stanley Schachter, *When Prophecy Fails* (University of Minnesota Press, Minneapolis, 1956).

9. D. H. Lawrence, *Apocalypse* (Penguin, Harmondsworth, 1976).

10. See entries for Tany, Robins and Nayler in the *Dictionary of National Biography*.

11. Alexander Gordon, 'The Origins of the Muggletonians', in *Proceedings of the Literary and Philosophical Society of Liverpool*, Volume 23, 1869, and 'Ancient and Modern Muggletonians', Volume 24, 1870.

12. Joseph Train, *The Buchanites From First to Last* (William Blackwood and Sons, Edinburgh, 1846).

13. Herbert Wisbey, *Pioneer Prophetess, Jemima Wilkinson the Publick Universal Friend* (Cornell University Press, Ithaca, New York, 1964).

14. J. F. C. Harrison, *The Second Coming, Popular Millenarianism 1780–1850* (Routledge and Kegan Paul, London, 1979).

15. Roy Porter, 'The Prophetic Body, Lady Eleanor Davies and the Meaning of Madness', in G. Calvi, ed., *Baroco al femminale* (Laterza, Rome, 1993). *The Diary of Beatrice Webb*, edited by Norman and Jeanne Mackenzie (Virago, London, 1982).

4. Joanna Southcott's Box

1. MS letter from G. Hollingworth, dated September 1913, in the National Portrait Gallery Archive, Orange Street, London.

2. Joanna Southcott, *The Strange Effects of Faith* (Exeter, 1801), p. 59.

3. From a testimonial printed at the end of Joanna Southcott's *The Answer of the Lord to the Powers of Darkness* (London, 1802).

4. Quoted in E. P. Thompson, *The Making of the English Working Class* (Penguin, London, 1991).

5. William Howard, *A Letter to Joanna Southcott, the Pretended Prophetess* (London, 1811).

6. Quoted in A. W. Exell, *Joanna Southcott at Blockley and the Rock Cottage Relics* (Blockley Antiquarian Society, 1977). In her *Second Book of Visions* (London, 1803), Joanna confirmed that 'all who sign for Christ's Kingdom to be established, and Satan's to be destroyed, shall be sealed to the day of redemption, to inherit the Tree of Life', p. 64.

7. 'Hurt not the earth, neither the seas, nor the trees, till we shall have sealed the servants of our God', cries the angel in Revelation (7: 3) The figures for the sealed come from James K. Hopkins, *A Woman to Deliver Her People, Joanna Southcott and English Millenarianism in an Era of Revolution* (University of Texas Press, Austin, 1982). There is also a good account of sealing in J. F. C. Harrison, *The Second Coming*.

8. C. Mathews, letter of 14 August 1814 to the *Independent Whig*.

9. Joanna Southcott, *A Dispute Between the Woman and the Powers of Darkness* (London, 1802), passim.

10. Joanna Southcott, *The Third Book of Wonders Announcing* *the Coming of Shiloh With a Call to the Hebrews* (London, 1814), p. 4.

11. Joanna Southcott, *A Dispute*, p. 114. See also *The Life and Prophecies of Joanna Southcott* (London, 1814).

12. Anonymous, *The Life and Prophecies of Joanna Southcott, From Her Infancy to the Present Time* (London, 1814). Other estimates put the cost of the crib at £1000.

13. A detailed account of the events of 1814 can be found in Hopkins, *A Woman to Deliver Her People.*

14. Richard Reece, *A Correct Statement of the Last Illness and Death of Mrs Southcott* (London, 1815).

15. G. R. Balleine, *Past Finding Out, the Tragic Story of Joanna Southcott and her Successors* (London, SPCK, 1956), Jane Rogers, *Mr Wroe's Virgins* (Faber and Faber, London, 1992).

16. Quotations from, E. P. Thompson, *The Making of the English Working Class*; Joanna Southcott, *A Warning to the Whole World* (London, 1803), p. 52; *Strange Effects*, preface; Joanna Southcott, *Letters and Communications of Joanna Southcott, the Prophetess of Exeter* (London, 1804), p. 113.

17. See Exell, *Joanna Southcott at Blockley*, and Joanna Southcott, *Letters and Communications.*

5. Joseph Smith's Kingdom

1. Letter of Lucius Fenn, reprinted in *Among the Mormons, Historic Accounts by Contemporary Observers*, eds, William Mulder and A. Russell Mortensen (Alfred A. Knopf, New York, 1958)

2. From 'Testimony of the Prophet Joseph Smith', prefixed to all modern editions of the *Book of Mormon.*

3. Malise Ruthven, *The Divine Supermarket, Travels in Search of the Soul of America* (Chatto and Windus, London, 1989).

4. Edmund White, *States of Desire, Travels in Gay America* (Andre Deutsch, London, 1980).

5. For a thorough historical overview of the Church's attitude to women, suffrage and contemporary feminism see Marilyn Warenski, *Patriarchs and Politics* (McGraw Hill Book Company, New York, 1978).

6. Such is the allure of Mammon's Chosen People that a fair few non-Mormons buzz around the Church proper just to taste the nectar of success. These are the Sunshine Mormons, the religious equivalent of fair-weather friends.

7. Quincey's account of his visit is reprinted in Mulder and Mortensen, eds, *Among the Mormons.*

8. Quoted in Fawn Brodie, *No Man Knows My History, the Life of Joseph Smith the Mormon Prophet* (Alfred A. Knopf, New York, 1963).

9. Michael D. Quinn, 'The Council of Fifty and its Members 1844–1945', and Andrew F. Ehat, '"It Seems Like Heaven Began on Earth", Joseph Smith and the Constitution of the Kingdom of God', both in *Brigham Young University Studies*, Volume 20 (1980).

10. Quoted in Andrew F. Ehat, 'It Seems Like Heaven Began on Earth'.

11. Quoted in Andrew F. Ehat and Lyndon W. Cook, *The Words of Joseph Smith, the Contemporary Accounts of the Nauvoo Discourses of the Prophet Joseph* (Brigham Young University Press, Provo, Utah, 1980).

12. Douglas Davies, *Mormon Identities in Transition* (Cassell, London, 1996).

Notes

6. The Prophetic Clock

1. J. B. Priestley, *Man and Time* (Aldus Books, London, 1964).

2. The borrowing of Jewish and Christian historical schemes from earlier Near Eastern chronologies is described by Nicholas Campion in *The Great Year* (Penguin Arkana, London, 1994).

3. See Frank Manuel, *Shapes of Philosophical History* (George Allen and Unwin Ltd, London, 1965).

4. M. James Penton, *Apocalypse Delayed, the Story of the Jehovah's Witnesses* (University of Toronto Press, Toronto, 1985); Joseph F. Zygmunt, 'Prophetic Failure and Chiliastic Identity, the case of the Jehovah's Witnesses', in *American Journal of Sociology*, Volume 75 (1970), pp. 926–48.

5. Harold Bloom, *The American Religion, the Emergence of the Post-Christian Nation* (Simon & Schuster, New York, 1992). The war cry comes from *The Watchtower*, 15 May 1992.

6. Paul Boyer, *When Time Shall Be No More, Prophecy Belief in Modern American Culture* (Harvard University Press, Cambridge, Massachusetts, 1995).

7. Quoted in Bernard McGinn, 'Revelation', in Frank Kermode and Robert Alter, eds, *The Literary Guide to the Bible* (Collins, London, 1987).

8. Richard Bauckham, *Tudor Apocalypse, Sixteenth Century Apocalyptism, Millenarianism, and the English Reformation from John Bale to John Foxe and Thomas Brightman* (Sultan Courtney Press, Appleford, 1978).

9. Thomas Brightman, *The Revelation of St John* (London, 1616).

10. Joseph Mede, *Apostasy of the Latter Times* (1641), in *Works*, Volume 2 (London, 1663–64).

11. Paul Christianson, *Reformers and Babylon, English Apocalyptic Visions From the Reformation to the Eve of the Civil War* (Toronto University Press, Toronto and London, 1978).

12. See W. H. Oliver, *Prophets and Millennialists, the Uses of Biblical Prophecy in England From the 1790s to the 1840s* (Oxford University Press, Oxford, 1978).

13. Bernard McGinn, *The Calabrian Abbot, Joachim of Fiore in the History of Western Thought* (Macmillan, New York and London, 1985). Raoul Vaneigem, *The Movement of the Free Spirit* (Zone Books, New York, 1994).

14. Quoted in John Spurr, *The Restoration Church of England, 1646–1687* (Yale University Press, New Haven, 1991).

15. T. D. Kendrick, *The Lisbon Earthquake* (Methuen & Co. Ltd, London, 1956).

16. Adam Smith, 'The History of Astronomy', was written in the 1750s, though not published until 1795. It is reprinted in *Adam Smith Essays on Philosophical Subjects*, W. P. D. Wightman and J. C. Bryce, eds (Clarendon Press, Oxford, 1980).

17. Morton Edgar, *The Great Pyramid* (Maclure, MacDonald & Co., Glasgow, 1924).

18. Betty Jo Teeter Dobbs, *The Foundations of Newton's Alchemy, or the Hunting of the Greene Lyon* (Cambridge University Press, Cambridge, 1975).

19. Francis D. Nichol, *The Midnight Cry* (Review and Herald Publishing Association, Washington, 1944).

20. Ernest R. Sandeen, *The Roots of Fundamentalism, British and*

Notes

American Millenarianism 1800–1930 (University of Chicago Press, Chicago, 1970).

7. Beyond the End

1. C. S. Lewis, 'The World's Last Night' (1951), in *Fern-seed and Elephants and Other Essays on Christianity* (Fontana, London, 1975).

2. Gershom Sholem, *Kabbalah* (Dorset Press, New York, 1974).

3. A good background on the subject can be found in Frank Manuel's *Shapes of Philosophical History*.

4. Friedrich Nietzsche, *Thus Spake Zarathustra* (1885) (Penguin, London, 1978).

5. Quoted in Morton D. Paley's introduction to *The Last Man* (Oxford University Press, Oxford, 1994). Later quotations from the novel also use this edition.

6. Jean Baudrillard, *The Illusion of the End* (1992), translated by Chris Turner (Polity Press, Cambridge, 1994).

7. Zygmunt Bauman, *Mortality, Immortality and Other Life Strategies* (Polity Press, Cambridge, 1992).

8. The original exposé was Marc Cooper's 'Bursting the Biosphere Bubble', in *The Village Voice*, 2 April 1991, Volume XXXVI, No. 14. An alternative account of the mission can be found in *Life Under Glass, the Inside Story of Biosphere 2* (Biosphere Press, Oracle, Arizona, 1993), by crew members Abigail Alling and Mark Nelson.

9. John Allen and Mark Nelson, *Space Biospheres* (Synergetic Press, Oracle, Arizona, 1986).

10. Jean Gimpel, *The End of the Future, the Waning of the Hi-tech World* (Adamantine Press, London, 1995).

11. Quoted in Matei Calinescu's, 'The End of Man in Twentieth Century Thought, Reflections on a Philosophical Metaphor', in Saul Friedländer, Gerald Holton, Leo Marx and Eugene Skolnikoff, eds, *Visions of Apocalypse, End or Rebirth?* (Holmes and Meier, New York and London, 1985).

12. *Cryonics, Reaching For Tomorrow* (Alcor Life Extension Foundation, Arizona, 1993). Additional material has been garnered from various editions of *Cryonics*, Alcor's quarterly magazine.

13. The scholastic debates on resurrection from St Paul to Aquinas are recounted in wonderful detail in Caroline Walker Bynum's *The Resurrection of the Body in Western Christianity, 200–1336* (Columbia University Press, New York, 1995).

14. Robert Ettinger, *The Prospect of Immortality* (1964) (Sidgwick & Jackson Ltd, London, 1965).

15. Jonathan Swift, *Gulliver's Travels* (1726) (Penguin, London, 1985). See Part III, 'A Voyage to Laputa', Chapter 10.

16. Max More, 'On Becoming Posthuman' (more@usc.edu), HTML format. I used the modified version, 15 September 1994.

17. Francis Spufford, 'The Difference Engine and *The Difference Engine*', in Francis Spufford and Jenny Uglow, eds, *Cultural Babbage, Technology, Time and Invention* (Faber and Faber, London, 1996).

18. Frank Jo Tippler, *The Physics of Immortality, Modern Cosmology, God, and the Resurrection of the Dead* (Doubleday, New York, 1991).

BIBLIOGRAPHY

The whole point of this book has been to make connections; to link up millenarian thinking to various patterns of secular thinking, thereby affirming that the similarities between peoples and cultures, ancients and moderns, and the way that faith and reason comprehend the world are more fundamental than their differences.

Insofar as establishing this principle of mutuality is concerned, the combined effect of reading only three books will suffice. These are: Norman Cohn's *The Pursuit of the Millennium* (Pimlico, London, 1993), Frank Kermode's *The Sense of an Ending* (Oxford University Press, Oxford, 1966) and William James's *The Varieties of Religious Experience* (Harvard University Press, Cambridge, Massachusetts, 1985). Cohn's book is the most thorough introduction to millenarianism one could wish for. First published in 1957, it spawned a mini-industry of secondary literature on apocalyptic sectarianism and yet, remarkably, it remains peerless. Kermode's book too remains unique, but this is largely because no one has even tried to usurp it. James I recommend for different, more personal reasons: since it first appeared in 1917, we have grown sophisticated in our approaches to religious feeling. So refreshing therefore is James's early plea for sensitivity and tolerance in dealing with the most far-fetched of testimonies to spiritual experience. James was the first truly modern religious critic, arguing passionately for the primacy of comprehending such experiences in their broadest aspects over making value judgements about them.

Rather than provide a comprehensive bibliography on millenarianism, listing every recherché production on minor sects and now-forgotten messiahs, I have limited myself to two tasks – that of pointing to various areas where apocalyptic thinking has made its presence felt in thought and action, and that of citing the most useful works on millenarian history.

The relationship of the Millennium to ancient myths of paradise and to the utopian imagination has been extensively explored. In the former category are Mircae Eliade's *The Myth of Eternal Return, or Cosmos and History* (1949) (Arkana Press, London, 1989) and Richard Heinberg's *Memories and Visions of Paradise, Exploring the Universal Myth of a Lost Golden Age* (Jeremy P. Tarcher Inc., Los Angeles, 1989), while good analyses of the latter include Mark Holloway's *Heavens on Earth, Utopian Communities in America 1680–1880,* (Turnstile Press, London, 1951) and W. H. G. Armytage's *Heavens Below, Utopian Experiments in England, 1560–1960* (Routledge and Kegan Paul, London, 1961). Emphasising the history of utopian ideas over their *praxis* are Ernest Lee Tuveson's classic study *Utopias and the Millennium, a Study in the Background of the Idea of Progress* (University of California Press, California, 1949) and Krishnan Kumar and Stephen Bann, eds, *Utopias and the Millennium* (Reaktion Books, London, 1993). The link between millennialism and socialist political theory, meanwhile, has been made by, among others, Eric Voegelin in *The New Science of Politics* (University of Chicago Press, Chicago, 1952).

Bibliography

Various thinkers have sought to unravel the workings of apocalypse in secular historicism, thus providing a framework within which to understand the pessimistic impulse underpinning books like Oswald Spengler's *The Decline of the West* (1918) (George Allen and Unwin, London, 1980). From Karl Löwith in *Meaning in History* (Chicago University Press, Chicago, 1949) and Frank Manuel in *The Shapes of Philosophical History* (George Allen and Unwin Ltd, London, 1965) to Reinhart Koselleck in *Futures Past, on the Semantics of Historical Time* (1960) (MIT Press, Cambridge, Masachusetts, 1985), they have found that the need to periodise human activity is rooted in the myth of the End. The influence of their approaches can be felt in the excellent contemporary reflections on apocalypse by Nicholas Campion and Damian Thompson;- *The Great Year, Astrology, Millenarianism and History in the Western Tradition*, (Penguin, London, 1994) and *The End of Time: Faith and Fear in the Shadow of the Millennium* (Sinclair Stevenson, 1996). For illumination on the more specific, and at the same time more visceral, relationship between apocalypse and the ends of centuries, see Hillel Schwartz, *Century's End, a Cultural History of the Fin de Siècle from the 990s to the 1990s* (Doubleday, New York, 1990) and Asa Briggs and Daniel Snowman, eds, *Fin de Siècle, How Centuries End, 1400–2000* (Yale University Press, London, 1996).

Early anthropological investigations of apocalypse that inspired a whole sub-anthropological discipline include Peter Worsley's *The Trumpet Shall Sound, a Study of Cargo Cults in Melanesia* (1957) (Paladin, London, 1970) and Vittorio Lanternari's broad-ranging *The Religion of the Oppressed, a Study of Modern Messianic Cults* (Alfred A. Knopf, New York, 1965), which charts the apocalyptic beliefs of various African nativist movements, as well as numerous Native American tribes and South American new

278

religious movements. If comparative religious studies may be counted as anthropological, then Norman O. Brown's 'The Apocalypse in Islam', in Valerie Andrews, Robert Bosnak and Karen Walter Goodwin, eds, *Facing Apocalypse* (Spring Publications, Dallas, Texas, 1982), is relevant here. So too is Winston L. King's 'Eschatology, Christian and Buddhist', *Religion*, 16 (1986). The modern and secular nuclear apocalyptic is thoughtfully covered by Robert Jay Lifton in *The Broken Connection, on Death and the Continuity of Life* (Simon and Schuster, New York, 1979) and Gordon Kaufman in *Theology for a Nuclear Age* (Manchester University Press, Manchester, 1985). Apocalypse as literary narrative, meanwhile, forms the backbone of Saul Friedländer, Gerald Holton, Leo Marx and Eugene Skolnikoff, eds, *Visions of Apocalypse, End or Rebirth?* (Holmes and Meier, New York, 1985), and Stephen D. O'Leary, *Arguing Apocalypse, a Theory of Millennial Rhetoric* (Oxford University Press, Oxford, 1994). And as a revolutionary narrative it structures the musings of the contributors to Sylvia Thrupp, ed., *Millennial Dreams in Action, Studies in Revolutionary Religious Movements* (Schoken Books, New York, 1970), and Thomas J. Altizer in *History as Apocalypse* (State University of New York Press, New York, 1985). A bold but largely unconvincing attempt to uncover an apocalyptic urge underlying modern consumerism is made by Stephen Brown, Jim Bell and David Carson in *Eschatology, Escapology and the Illusion of the End* (Routledge, London, 1996).

Listed chronologically by the historical periods they cover, the best works on millenarian history include: Oscar Cullman, *Christ and Time, the Primitive Christian Conception of Time and History* (Westminster Press, Philadelphia, 1950); Richard Landes, 'Lest the Millennium be Fulfilled, Apocalyptic Expectations and the Pattern of Western Chronography 100–800 CE', in Werner Verbeke, Daniel Verhelst and Andries Werkenhuysen, eds, *The Uses and Abuses of Eschatology in the Middle Ages* (Leuven University Press, The Netherlands, 1988); Bernard McGinn, *Visions of the End, Apocalyptic Traditions in the Middle Ages* (Columbia University Press, New York, 1979); Marjorie Reeves, *The Influence of Prophecy in the Middle Ages* (Clarendon Press, Oxford, 1969); Richard Bauckham, *Tudor Apocalypse, Sixteenth Century Apocalyptism, Millenarianism and the English Reformation from John Bale to John Foxe and Thomas Brightman* (Sultan Courtney Press, Appleford, 1978); Paul Christianson, *Reformers and Babylon, English Apocalyptic Visions From the Reformation to the Eve of the Civil War* (Toronto University Press, Toronto and London, 1978); Bryan W. Ball, *A Great Expectation, Eschatological Thought in English Protestantism to 1660* (E. J. Brill, Leiden, 1975); Robin Bruce Barnes, *Prophecy and Gnosis, Apocalyptism in the Wake of the German Reformation* (Stanford University Press, California, 1988); Christopher Hill, *Antichrist in Seventeenth Century England* (Verso, London, 1990); J. F. C. Harrison, *The Second Coming, Popular Millenarianism 1780–1850* (Routledge and Kegan Paul, London, 1979); Clarke Garrett, *Respectable Folly, Millenarianism and the French Revolution in France and England* (Johns Hopkins University Press, Baltimore and London, 1975); W. H. Oliver, *Prophets and Millennialists, the Uses of Biblical Prophecy in England From the 1790s to the 1840s* (Oxford University Press, Oxford, 1978); Ernest R. Sandeen, *The Roots of Fundamentalism, British and American Millenarianism 1800–1930* (University of Chicago Press, Chicago, 1970); Edwin S. Gaustad, ed., *The Rise of Adventism, Religion and Society in Mid-nineteenth Century America* (Harper and Row, New York, 1974); James H. Moorhead, *American Apocalypse, Yankee Protestants and the Civil War 1860–1869* (Fortress Press, Minneapolis, 1989); Eric Hobsbawm, *Primitive Rebels, Studies in Archaic Forms of Social Movement in the 19th and 20th Centuries* (Manchester University Press, Manchester, 1959); Timothy Weber, *Living in the Shadow of the Second Coming, American Fundamentalism, 1800–1930* (University of Chicago Press, Chicago, 1970); Paul Boyer, *When Time Shall Be No More, Prophecy Belief in Modern American Culture* (Harvard University Press, Cambridge, Massachusetts, 1994); Michael Barkun, *Religion and the Racist Right, the Origin of the Christian Identity Movement* (University of North Carolina Press, Chapel Hill, London, 1994).